Politics and Linkage in a Democratic Society

Denise L. Baer
*1992–93 American Political Science
Association Congressional Fellow*

David A. Bositis
*The Joint Center for Political and
Economic Studies*

PRENTICE HALL, ENGLEWOOD CLIFFS, NEW JERSEY 07632

Library of Congress Cataloging-in-Publication Data

Baer, Denise L.
    Politics and linkage in a democratic society / Denise L. Baer,
David A. Bositis.
        p.   cm.
    Includes bibliographical references and index.
    ISBN 0-13-682402-1
    1. Political parties—United States. 2. Pressure groups—United States. 3. Elite (Social sciences)—United States. 4. Political participation—United States. 5. Social movements—United States. I. Bositis, David A. II. Title.
JK2261.B3 1993
324'.0973—dc20   92-42231
                                                                              CIP

Acquisitions editor: Julie Berrisford
Editorial/production supervision and
    interior design: Alison D. Gnerre
Cover design: Carol Ceraldi
Prepress buyer: Kelly Behr
Manufacturing buyer: Mary Ann Gloriande

© 1993 by Prentice-Hall, Inc.
A Simon & Schuster Company
Englewood Cliffs, New Jersey 07632

Printed in the United States of America
10 9 8 7 6 5 4 3 2 1

ISBN 0-13-682402-1

Prentice-Hall International (UK) Limited, *London*
Prentice-Hall of Australia Pty. Limited, *Sydney*
Prentice-Hall Canada Inc., *Toronto*
Prentice-Hall Hispanoamericana, S.A., *Mexico*
Prentice-Hall of India Private Limited, *New Delhi*
Prentice-Hall of Japan, Inc., *Tokyo*
Simon & Schuster Asia Pte. Ltd., *Singapore*
Editora Prentice-Hall do Brasil, Ltda., *Rio de Janeiro*

This book is dedicated to

Mary Lucille Morgan Baer
and
Ora James Baer
and
Gertrude Antoinette Bositis, née, Bigwood

Contents

Preface

From the start, our primary intention in writing this book has been to return to first principles. In particular, we have sought to re-orient teaching and thinking on political parties away from a disjointed party-in-the-electorate focus to a more coherent set of principles based upon traditional party and elite theory but also incorporating new and evolving theoretical material describing major social, political, and organizational change. This is an exciting time to be thinking and writing about parties. The post-reform American party system is revitalized, and it is time to consider how the raw material of interests and parties are remaking American democracy.

We also had a second motivation in writing this volume. Party government theorists have long been slighted in political science. First, pluralists, in their day, ignored party government theory because they have never sought to employ any theory of party in their work, preferring a direct relationship between interests and elected officials. Second, progressives, who dislike and distrust parties, have generally seen fit to ignore party government theory since a recognition of that theory would, of course, require a recognition of the critical role of political parties in representative government. Ironically, contemporary critics of American politics are blind to the symbiotic relationship between strong interests and strong parties as well as the importance of this relationship for democratic government.

This book was written for students—in the broadest sense of that term—of politics, political parties, interest groups, and democracy. Many of the explicanda that we have attempted to explain have come from inquiring students, puzzling over a political system at once familiar and bizarre. Most of the illustrations contained herein have been employed with some degree of success on captive students.

There are many individuals who we wish to thank for their help in producing this volume. At the head of that list is our good friend, Corneilius P. Cotter. Neil read and provided insightful, learned, and cogent comment at all stages of the writing of this book. More important, from first we met, Neil has encouraged us in our theoretical and empirical pursuits. He has encouraged us to look at organizations and institutions, leadership, culture, and how all these matters relate to one another, as well as their significance for democratic political rule. Several years ago, Neil observed that our consanguinity has skipped a generation of scholars. The generation following Neil reaped the harvest of voting behavior research. We have taken Neil's observation one step further in our critique of the textbook model of party.

We must also thank John S. Jackson, III, who commented on some of these chapters, and who has been a long-time collaborator (on The Party Elite Study), teacher, and friend. It was John who long ago secured David's appointment as Democratic precinct committeeman in Southern Illinois, and then Denise's as precinct committeewoman. We have both since attended many other Democratic and Republican party affairs at the local, state, and national level, but we continue to share a special fondness for the Jackson County Democratic Party.

We would also like to extend our thanks to some new friends. First, Ralph Goldman has been most generous in reading and commenting on some of this material, as well as providing us with information (and leads) on a variety of subjects, including the evolving study of political parties in the field of political science. We would also like to thank Paul David, who provided us with source material on the APSA Report on responsible parties and related matters. Likewise, we would like to thank Paul Herrnson, who previewed some of this material and offered many helpful suggestions. Finally, since we cannot claim to have taken all of their sound advice to heart, we must take final responsibility for any errors that follow.

Books, like babies, of which we've had two more since this project began, are both a labor of love as well as hard work and occasional pain. This book, like all our babies (of which we've had four), was born at home in the wee hours of the night. Unlike our babies, this book was not born at home by choice. Many of our colleagues have had the assistance of such analgesics as research grants, reduced teaching loads, sabbaticals, and research and secretarial assistance. Sorry to say, this book had no such midwife at the University of Akron.

Finally, David Bositis would like to extend his appreciation to The Joint Center for Political and Economic Studies, not for any direct contribution to this volume, but rather for providing such an amiable and intellectually stimulating place to work.

chapter 1

An Invitation to Politics[1]

> *Politics is not observations.*
> *Politics is what we create,*
> *by what we do,*
> *by what we hope for,*
> *by what we dare to imagine.*[2]

Senator Paul Wellstone (D-MN)

Politics is an interpersonal and social activity that is not easy to describe in words. A very common and useful definition of politics comes from political scientist Harold Lasswell's (1958) book entitled *Politics: Who Gets What, When, How.* While Lasswell very accurately captures several elements of *political conflict*, his pithy definition ignores the *social* dimension of politics. And it is the social aspect of politics as most people experience it that political scientists have the most difficulty describing. Political science as a discipline focuses on *observations*—observing the results or end-products of politics, such as why it is that one group gains government benefits, while others fail. Yet for many politically active citizens, politics is about remaking the future, not analyzing

[1]With apologies to Peter Berger, whose widely influential *Invitation to Sociology* (1963) invited many students to sample the intellectual adventure of sociology, we intend to invite students both to politics and to political science. Berger stresses that sociology is a distinct enterprise, which involves alienation from society. Politics for us is for the average citizen and not to be limited to those inculcated with the "high culture" of political science. Yet we find political science intensely intellectually engaging. Any intellectual enterprise is designed to answer questions because we are curious, not because we need to know. Thus, we invite students to two interrelated but distinct enterprises.

[2]Senator Wellstone proffered this definition of politics during the first convention of the Coalition of Democratic Values in Chantilly, Virginia, January 26, 1991.

what has already happened. Former political science professor[3] Paul Wellstone (D-MN) offers an action-based definition: "Politics is what we create." Notice that Senator Wellstone stresses that it is *we*—a group—who comprise politics, and that it refers to the future—*what we create*.

Politics is meant to be *inviting*—and this book is an invitation to politics. Politics is not just for the educated or the elite, but for real people with everyday concerns. Many students conceive of politics and political conflict as a rational debate over policy issues—as something only available for the educated and informed. One of our favorite definitions of politics comes from party scholar E. E. Schattschneider (1975), who stresses the *social* aspect of politics when he tells us that politics is not some dispassionate intellectual enterprise, but rather more akin to choosing who we would like to father our children:

> Political conflict is not like an intercollegiate debate in which the opponents agree in advance on a definition of the issues. As a matter of fact, *the definition of the alternatives is the supreme instrument of power*; the antagonists can rarely agree on what the issues are because power is involved in the definition. . . .

> The outcome [in the competition of conflicts] is not determined merely by what people want but by their priorities. . . . *All depends on what we want most.* . . . What they want more becomes the enemy of what they want less. *Politics is therefore something like choosing a wife, rather than shopping in a five-and-ten-cent store.* (p. 66, emphasis added)

One of the major struggles in politics is over the scope of conflict. Schattschneider contrasts the *socialization* of conflict with the *privatization* of conflict. By this, he means that conflict may be *limited* by keeping it private (out of the public domain of discussion and governmental influence) or by localizing it (thereby reducing the number of groups contesting the issue). Conflict is *expanded* when it is "socialized" by bringing government into play and by nationalizing the issue (thereby increasing the number of groups contesting the issue). More powerful interests work to privatize conflict, while repressed minorities and weaker interests work to socialize conflict. The competition over what conflicts become public ones occurs because of the interests involved, not because of the moral superiority on one side or the other. Philosophical ideals such as individualism, free enterprise, localism, privacy, and economy in government complement the privatization of conflict, while others, such as equality, consistency, equal protection of the law, justice, liberty, freedom of movement, freedom of speech and association, and civil rights, support the socialization of conflict. Rationalizations aside, however, "control of the scale of conflict has always been a prime instrument of political strategy, whatever the language of politics may have been" (Schattschneider, 1975, p. 8).

The contagiousness of conflict is key to democratic society—a free society "gives a high priority to the participation of the public in conflict"

---

[3]Wellstone was a professor of political science at Carleton College in Minnesota until his election to the U.S. Senate in 1990.

[Schattschneider, 1975, p. 5]. In this book, we will compare political interests and groups represented by political parties with those represented by interest groups and learn that parties are critical to democracy precisely *because* they tend to socialize and democratize conflict. Yet some groups—those embodying "the progressive temperament"—attack politics and conflict in politics. The Progressive movement as a political movement was most active and successful in the early twentieth century, but many contemporary groups like Common Cause and the League of Women Voters reflect the progressive temperament. This is of grave concern to a free society because attacks "on politics, politicians, and political parties and the praise of nonpartisanship" control and delimit the scope of conflict. In effect, these efforts are "designed to take important public business out of politics altogether" (Schattschneider, 1975, p. 12).

Politics is the stuff of everyday life—and in democratic societies political power should be available to everyone. Because it is not always so, however, the *study* of politics—as we have tried to illustrate here briefly through the work of Schattschneider—is essential to understanding the limits of political influence. Politics is not an intellectual enterprise, although the discipline of political science is. In this chapter, we look at politics from three perspectives: politics as an individual pastime, politics as a group endeavor, and the study of politics as a scholarly enterprise. While there are a number of insights to be gained from a scientific and theoretical study of politics, we will learn that political science as a discipline has been strongly shaped by the Progressive temperament. Because politics is not a science, values must be considered when discussing any theory of politics. Our own normative commitment here is to parties as unique and essential agents of democracy—a nonprogressive view.

POLITICS AS AN INDIVIDUAL PASTIME

The place that citizen participation occupies in a democratic society is central to any theory of democracy. Yet different theories of democracy offer different views of citizen participation. Many pluralist theorists who wrote shortly after World War II, such as Joseph Schumpeter (1943), Harry Eckstein (1966), Robert Dahl (1956), Giovanni Sartori (1962), and Bernard Berelson writing with Paul Lazarsfeld and William McPhee (1954), stressed the important need for stability and downplayed the value of citizen participation. Schumpeter, for example, defined democracy as an *institutional arrangement* whereby democracy existed if there were mechanisms for elections. For Schumpeter and others, the quality of participation was not of major importance so long as there were elections. Indeed, these post–World War II theorists stressed the *dangers* of participation and downplayed political parties as instruments of democracy. Voting might serve as a check on excesses of leadership, yet voting was the only form of approved widespread citizen participation. Indeed, many of these theorists approved of a low voter turnout rate as *contributing* to their understanding of democracy. Berelson et al. (1954) conclude their study of voting with a paradox:

> *Individual voters* today seem unable to satisfy the requirements for a democratic system of government outlined by political theorists. But the *system of democracy* does meet certain requirements for a going political organization. The individual members may not meet all the standards, but the whole nonetheless survives and grows. (p. 312)

Democracy was maintained not through widespread citizen participation, but rather through bargaining and compromise among interest group leaders. The major normative value offered by this theoretical perspective on democracy is *stability*. We term this theory, along with Carole Pateman (1970), the *contemporary* or *pluralist theory of democracy*.

The classical or *participatory theory of democracy* stresses the important effect that politics has on the development of character. It is only through politics, the participatory theory assumes, that one becomes transformed from a private citizen to a public citizen by an increased ability to take into account interests wider than one's own. Carole Pateman (1970), a contemporary political philosopher, has drawn from classic theorists of democracy such as Jean Jacques Rousseau (1712–1778) and John Stuart Mill (1806–1873) to argue that participation is more than a protective adjunct to a set of institutional arrangements. Drawing upon Rousseau, Pateman makes three key arguments. First, participation has a psychological effect on those who participate. By making decisions, citizens develop a sense of responsibility for individual, social, and political action. Citizens' sense of freedom increases as they have a real sense of control over their lives. Second, collective decisions (those made by the entire community *for* the entire community) are more easily accepted by the individual. Decisions in politics almost always involve some sacrifice on the part of an individual or group. If one understands the need for sacrifice for a common good, one is more likely to accept the personal costs as necessary. And third, participation increases the feeling of community and a sense of integration in that community—a sense of identity and group consciousness. Thus, the major function of participation for classical theorists is *educational*, not regime stability.

Pateman makes a critical point: these modern pluralist theorists of democracy have fundamentally revised and altered the normative significance of democracy. Revisionist theorists such as Schumpeter, Dahl, and others, Pateman argues, are really theorists of *representative government*, not of democracy. Democracy is universally valued because of its effect on the character of its people, yet the modern revisionists have misappropriated the normative value of democratic theory while denuding it of its significance.

These philosophical discussions about the meaning of democracy and politics are not merely pedantic scholarly controversies. Consider a recent controversy over a show of the late artist Robert Mapplethorpe's work sponsored by the National Endowment for the Arts. Many conservatives like Senator Jesse Helms (R-NC) were appalled at some of the explicit sexual and homosexual scenes depicted. Helms has led an effort to reduce funding for the NEA and to restrict its ability to fund works based solely on artistic criteria. Pulitzer Prize–winning author Larry McMurtry,[4] currently president of PEN American Center (an international writer's organization), has attacked these critics as only offering "blind criticism." McMurtry was incensed that political commentators such as Rowland Evans, Robert Novak, Patrick Buchanan, James J. Kilpatrick, and others saw fit to criticize the artworks under contention without even bothering to see them in person. McMurtry (1990) makes an even more important point about understanding art—and politics:

> Suppose I wrote a column describing the Mona Lisa as just a rather smoky picture of an overweight lady who needs to get her teeth fixed. Only those who have seen the painting itself would know how grossly reductive I had been. . . .
>
> A simple point needs to be reasserted here: *only art is art; all descriptions of it are reductive.* George Will writes very well about baseball (and he actually goes to games); still a ballgame is a lot more involving than a column about one. . . .
>
> I say, go look at it before you say it isn't art. You might be surprised by the object itself. Photographs won't do; descriptions in newspapers won't do either; you have to *look* at it, as you should at any art object. (p. A21, emphasis added)

The same simple truth can be said about politics: **only politics is politics; all descriptions of it are reductive.** If politics is social, it is an activity that is *intersubjective.* Put another way, words cannot describe a hug, nor can one person experience a hug alone. It is a social activity requiring interaction between two or more people. There are a number of important aspects to this basic insight. First, and perhaps most important, one cannot experience politics through the media—television and newspapers provide distorted and reductive images of politics. Those who have never attended a political gathering and worked with others to attain a political goal have not experienced politics. Second, voting by itself is *not* a form of politics. Voting is a solitary act that cannot have any formative effect on character: one registers alone and one votes alone in the secrecy of the voting booth. Voting is not a social act unless one works in a social context to persuade others to vote the same way. For this reason, we think politics is best construed as a *group endeavor.*

---

[4]McMurtry is the author of *Lonesome Dove* and *The Last Picture Show,* among other well-known novels.

POLITICS AS A GROUP ENDEAVOR

There are many different types of groups in politics. The concept of *group* as we use it here is both simple and intuitively obvious, yet it is a term with substantial political implications. As the Swedish sociologist Ralf Dahrendorf (1959) has defined the term, group refers to a collection of individuals who live their lives together and possess their own organizations (i.e., control their own organizations) where group socialization occurs and there is a group consciousness, where there are group leaders, and where there are intergroup channels of communications. Examples of groups include women, blacks, and business, agricultural, and labor organizations. Because individuals in groups choose to interact *as a group*, these groups are naturally occurring. This is critical to politics because the members of the group share ideals, values, and goals. As members of the group, individuals learn their respective roles— most importantly the role of group member—and the leaders of the group can mobilize members for collective political activity.

The significance of the term group can best be understood in contrast to similar but nongroup aggregations of individuals as defined by social scientists. We use the term *aggregation* to refer to the artificial grouping of individuals. By this we mean that they are grouped only in the mind of an analyst observing society, not because the individuals themselves choose to interact and form a group. *Stratum* and *statistical aggregation* both refer to aggregations of individuals with certain similar characteristics such as an income between $10,000 and $15,000 and residing in urban areas. Because these are artificial groupings, these similarities usually have little or no political significance—unless, of course, the individuals comprise a group (i.e., possessing an organization, a group consciousness, and group communication). For example, an elderly couple may have an income of only $15,000 and yet be relatively well-off because they have few expenses, are fully insured, and own their own home, while a young family with two children may be impoverished at this income level due to the expenses of renting and the costs of raising dependents. These two types of couples would not have much in common politically, yet they could be aggregated together by a statistical commonality of income and area of residence.

Some examples of commonly used statistical aggregations include the *underclass, baby boomers, yuppies,* and *new collar voters*. Generally, census or polling data is used to construct these aggregations. The underclass, for example, is statistically defined according to certain, mostly economic, criteria. Many observers naively wonder why the poor do not mobilize to remedy their status, as if the mobilization of people involves nothing other than spontaneous outbursts of anger and revolt. However, members of the underclass have no systematic group-based socialization and control no organizations or channels of communications. Underclass members do not associate with one another to pursue political—or any other—objectives. As we shall see in later chap-

ters, the major movements in the United States with any claim to representing those who are impoverished—the labor and the civil rights movements—drew upon existing groups and group identities that had nothing
to do with the artificial concept of underclass. The term underclass, may, of
course, be useful as a theoretical concept. But it is important not to confuse
artifice (something man-made, not naturally occurring) with real political
groups. Theories are only models to help us understand complex reality, not
to replace it.

Scholars are usually careful to distinguish between groups and aggregations. Public opinion pollsters often use the same methods as scholarly
researchers; however, they are frequently less careful about making this distinction in the course of their business. Pollsters, after all, ply their wares by
convincing clients that they can appeal to "public opinion" outside of established groups and group leaders. For example, many political consultants
have made a career out of the baby boom generation—a statistical aggregation
of all those born between 1946 and 1964 (when the birth rate dramatically
increased after World War II)—as if it represented a concrete political or
social group. Baby boomers do not live together or control organizations
devoted to baby boomers, nor are they socialized to baby boomer political
and social norms. The calculations of the statistician cannot substitute for the
collective social experiences of group members. In particular, one great divide
in the baby boom generation is the Vietnam war: those born after 1955 were
not subject to the draft, while those born before 1955 either served in the
war, demonstrated against it, or had close friends and peers who served. Yet
other consultants have sought to slice up the baby boom generation into those
who are more well-off (yuppies) and those who are less well-off (new collar
voters). These two statistical aggregations likewise represent no existing,
concrete group. Real people do not identify with the statistical matrices of
pollsters.

A further important insight into the concept of group can be gained
from understanding the concept of *mass*—an important scholarly concept. As
indicated above, critical to concept of group is the notion of differentiation;
group members are alike, but, equally important, they are *different* from nongroup members. The concept of mass—as in mass media—refers to *undifferentiated*; members of a mass are defined to be alike, even if they do not
interact on a face-to-face basis (thereby developing group norms). The mass
media is directed at an audience assumed to be alike in certain particulars
(relevant to those in broadcasting). Most channels of communication are not
so directed; for every network like NBC or CBS, there are dozens of CBNs,
Jet Magazines, Gay Community News, and Catholic Free Presses—specialized
group channels of communication. This is important in understanding why
group members are relatively impervious to communications from outside
their group, including from the mass media. In matters of politics that are
critical to groups, whether labor or African-Americans, or the religious right,

voices from the mass media are *not* voices spoken with the dialect and cadence of the group, and therefore, these voices fail to influence and persuade those group members.

The concept of group is increasingly more important politically because of the new racial and ethnic mosaic emerging in the United States, alongside changing residential patterns. America is extremely mobile: about one in five Americans changes his or her residence each year. These changing residential patterns directly affect political power. Each decade since 1920 (when the number of seats in the U.S. House of Representatives was fixed at 435), the census is used to reapportion the 435 seats in Congress among the states and within state and local legislative bodies based upon shifting population densities. In the past 20 years, there has been a tremendous population shift from the *Frostbelt* (the states in the Northeast and Middle West) to the *Sunbelt* (the states in the South and West). Only 8 to 10 seats were reallocated among the states for each census from 1930 to 1970. After the 1980 census, however, 17 seats moved from the Frostbelt to the Sunbelt. With the 1990 census, 15 more seats are shifting from the Frostbelt to the Sunbelt. And it is expected that about 11 seats will shift to the Sunbelt after the next census.

Changing residential patterns are important because the increasing power of the Sunbelt states also means the increasing influence of minority groups. More than half of blacks (53%) and Asians (60%) and three-quarters of Hispanics (76%) live in these states. In particular, two-thirds of Hispanics live in just three states—Florida, Texas and California—states expected by the year 2001 to have 42% of the electoral college votes[5] needed to elect the U.S. president. Minority populations are increasing in size as well. In only 10 years, about one-third of school-age children will be from minority populations—i.e., black, Asian, or hispanic. In 1980, only one in five Americans was a member of minority group. By 2030, one in three will be from a minority population. This dramatic change is taking place because of new immigration patterns and the fact that some minority groups have higher birth rates.

During the 1950s, only about 300,000 immigrants, the vast majority of whom were of white European stock, entered the United States yearly. Now about twice that number enter the United States each year, only about 11% of which are European. Today, about 8 out of 10 legal immigrants are either from Asia (40%) or from Latin America (38%). Blacks currently are the largest minority group in the United States (60% of the minority population). The high birth rate among Hispanics, combined with high levels of immigration, means that the size of the Hispanic population is increasing rapidly. It is expected that by the year 2030, Hispanics will comprise about 18% of the total population, blacks will comprise 15%, and Asians 5%. If these trends

[5]The electoral college is the institution which provides for the election of the president. There are 538 electoral college votes (435 apportioned among the states based on congressional representation, plus 2 for each state based upon the Senate, plus 3 additional votes allocated to the District of Columbia). A majority or 270 votes are needed to elect the president.

hold, by 2030, non-Hispanic whites will be the minority in large western states like California and Texas.

These changing group dynamics mean protracted conflicts between groups as some see increased needs and others feel their interests threatened. Conflict is contagious (see Box 1-1), and conflict over race has been one of the most fundamental conflicts in American politics. In the 1990 midterm elections, race became a prominent issue in several hotly contested races. Louisiana state representative Republican David Duke, a former Klu Klux Klan leader, won 60% of the white vote in the state's October nonpartisan primary in his unsuccessful attempt to unseat Senator Bennett Johnson (D-LA)[6] by making racial quotas a key issue in his campaign. One of the more effective campaign ads was one used by Sen. Jesse Helms (R-NC) in his close race with black Democrat and former Charlotte mayor Harvey Gantt. Shortly before the election, Helms aired an ad showing a chest shot of a white man crumpling a job rejection letter, with a voice-over stating, "You needed that job, and you were the best qualified. But they had to give it to a minority because of a racial quota. Is that really fair?" In addition to airing in North Carolina to potential Helms supporters, the ad was aired and discussed on national news programs. It offended many because it so blatantly appeared to exacerbate racial antagonisms, but Senator Helms narrowly won the election with 52% of the vote. For many, Helms was legitimately able to use this controversial ad because shortly before the election President George Bush had vetoed the Civil Rights Bill pushed by the Democratic leadership, claiming that it established quotas in hiring. The Democratic and Republican Parties have taken opposing positions on this issue. This use of the controversy over racial quotas in campaigns is likely to increase as the size of the minority population increases.

Conflict in politics is *maximized* in free societies. In a brilliant analysis, political scientist E. E. Schattschneider stresses that "what happens in politics *depends on the way in which people are divided* into factions, parties, groups, classes, etc." (Schattschneider, 1975, p. 60). Not all *potential* conflicts become politically significant, however.

> There are billions of potential conflicts in any modern society, but *only a few become politically significant*. The reduction of the number of conflicts is an essential part of politics. Politics deals with the domination and subordination of conflicts. A democratic society is only able to survive because it manages conflict by establishing priorities among a multitude of potential conflicts. . . .
>
> In the competition of conflicts there is nothing sacred about our preference for big or little conflicts. *All depends on what we want most.* The outcome is not determined merely by what people want but by their priorities. What they

[6]Johnson won in the primary by winning a majority (53.9%) of the primary vote, thereby avoiding a runoff election between the top two vote-getters. David Duke won 43% of the vote. Louisiana is 29.6% black, a voting bloc that votes overwhelmingly Democratic.

BOX 1-1
The Contagiousness of Conflict

On a hot afternoon in August, 1943, in the Harlem section of New York City, a Negro soldier and a white policeman got into a fight in the lobby of a hotel. News of the fight spread rapidly throughout the area. In a few minutes angry crowds gathered in front of the hotel, at the police station and at the hospital where the injured policeman was taken. Before order could be restored about four hundred people were injured and millions of dollars' worth of property was destroyed.

This was not a race riot. Most of the shops looted and the property destroyed by the Negro mob belonged to Negroes. As a matter of fact neither the white policeman nor the Negro soldier had anything to do with the riot they had set off; they did not participate in it, did not control it and knew nothing about it.

Fortunately, for the survival of American civilization conflict rarely erupts as violently as it did in the 1943 Harlem riot, but all conflict has about it some elements that go into the making of a riot. Nothing is so contagious. Parliamentary debates, jury trials, town meetings, political campaigns, strikes, hearings, all have about them some of the exciting qualities of a fight; all produce dramatic spectacles that are almost irresistibly fascinating to people. At the root of all politics is the universal language of conflict.

The central political fact in a free society is the tremendous contagiousness of conflict.

Every fight consists of two parts: (1) the few individuals who are actively engaged at the center and (2) the audience that is irresistibly attracted to the scene. The spectators are an integral part of the situation, for, as likely as not, the *audience* determines the outcome of the fight. The crowd is loaded with portentousness because it is apt to be a hundred times as large as the fighting minority, and the relations of the audience and the combatants are highly unstable. Like any other chain reaction, a fight is difficult to contain . . . the audience is overwhelming; it is never really neutral; the excitement of the conflict communicates itself to the crowd. *This is the basic pattern of politics.*

The first proposition is that the outcome of every conflict is determined by the *extent* to which the audience becomes involved in it. That is, the outcome of all conflict is determined by the scope of its contagion. . . . The moral of this is: If a fight starts watch the crowd, because the crowd plays the decisive role. . . .

The second proposition is a consequence of the first. The most important strategy of politics is concerned with the scope of conflict.

Source: Schattschneider, 1960, pp. 1–3.

want more becomes the enemy of what they want less. (Schattschneider, 1975, pp. 64, 66)

A major issue in political conflict is whose game do we play? This is a question that the study of politics should help us answer.

POLITICS AS A SCHOLARLY ENTERPRISE

Political science developed quite late as a scholarly discipline among the social sciences. The American Political Science Association was organized in 1903. By contrast, psychology and sociology were organized much earlier[7] and, much earlier than political science, sought to establish their disciplines as empirical studies of human behavior. Each new social science discipline sought to distinguish itself by separating its approach from other, earlier organized disciplines. Psychology organized first, drawing in large part from the work of Sigmund Freud (1856–1939) on the internal states of the mind. Russian physiologist and experimental psychologist Ivan Petrovich Pavlov (1849–1936), whose research established the theory of conditioned learning, and John Watson (1878–1958), the founder of the behaviorist school in psychology, laid the basis for the *scientific* study of human learning and behavior.

The founders of modern sociology include Emile Durkheim (1858–1917) and Max Weber (1864–1920). Weber greatly influenced sociological theory through his introduction of the concept of *ideal types*. Durkheim's *Rules of Sociological Method* (first published in 1895) stresses that sociology is not interested in the psychological states of individuals (which would have made it only a subfield of psychology), but rather in the effect of social institutions on groups—the collective social mind. Durkheim's analysis of suicide among Jews, Protestants, and Catholics applied the methods of natural science (empirical methods and statistics) to the study of social institutions and human behavior. According to Durkheim, Protestants were more likely to experience what he called *anomie* (a lack of social norms) than were Jews and Catholics and therefore had higher suicide rates. Note that Durkheim stressed the role of social institutions (religious denominations)—not individual psyches—upon individual behavior. This emphasis was necessary to establish sociology as a distinct and separate social science discipline.

Political science has no one whom it can claim as a founding father—

---

[7]The organization of the American Political Science Association followed on the heels of a "whole family of new professional associations. There were founded, in quick order, The American Historical Association, 1884; the American Economic Association, 1885; the American Statistical Association, 1888; the American Academy of Political and Social Science, 1889; the American Sociological Society in 1903; and the American Political Science Association in 1903" (Somit and Tannenhaus, 1982, pp. 22–23). Our point here is not simply the development of an organized professional society, but, rather, the development of an academic discipline, which occurred much earlier for psychology and sociology, based on the seminal works of theorists such as Max Weber, Emile Durkheim, and Sigmund Freud.

an individual or set of individuals (like Durkheim for sociology) whose work laid the theoretical basis or justification for political science as a separate discipline. Instead, political science evolved in the early twentieth century as departments of government and politics began appearing in the early 1900s, peopled with "intellectual refugees" from departments of history, law, diplomacy, and philosophy. "Political science at the time of the creation of the APSA was less a distinct discipline than a holding company for a variety of endeavors that were in various ways related, but no longer easily resided in other disciplines" (Gunnell, 1983, p. 16). In the early years of the discipline (1903–1921), academicians comprised a minority of the membership of the American Political Science Association.[8] Except for a common interest in politics and government, those early professors of government and politics had no common intellectual discipline or method. Instead, the work of early political scientists was strongly shaped by the methods of their former disciplines—historical analysis of the evolution of political institutions (from history), philosophical and legal analysis of the constitution as interpreted by the Supreme Court (from philosophy and law), and a strong emphasis on the institutions and leaders of government (from diplomacy). Because of this untheoretical origin, some observers feel that political science ought to be reabsorbed by the other social sciences. For example, journalist George F. Will (who holds a doctorate in political science from Princeton) has suggested that

> we should take all the political philosophers and send them off to the philosophy departments, send the political sociologists to sociology, the political historians to history, and so on. Then turn the abandoned political science offices into squash courts. (Nelson, 1977, p. 20)

This early lack of common theoretical focus was particularly unfortunate, because in the absence of an overarching set of theoretical concerns, early political science became strongly influenced by the dominant political movement of the era—*progressivism*. Progressivism, a political reform movement, first emerged around 1890 and exerted a dominant influence in politics until about 1920. Other social and political groups—women, labor, and farmers— were important during this era, but progressives provided the dominant characterization of the era. Progressives were reformers whose ethic was based upon "indigenous Yankee-Protestant political traditions, and upon middle class life" (Hofstadter, 1961, p. 9). Progressives attacked interests in politics. We think this is unfortunate for several reasons. First, progressivism underestimated the significance of groups to the formation of values. Second, the

---

[8]Somit and Tannenhaus (1982) note that "in 1912, one of the few years for which detailed statistics are available, 20 per cent were 'professors and teachers,' 31 per cent were 'lawyers and businessmen,' 37 per cent could not be classified, and the remaining 12 per cent represented library and institutional affiliations" (p. 55).

progressive temperament which places such great stress on voting—and voting only—has thrown away the benefits of true participation. Third, and perhaps most important, the progressives were hostile to political party organizations. In their preference for "a more direct connection between voters and candidates for public office," progressives sought to institutionalize parties as a "public utility" (Epstein, 1986, p. 171).

Progressivism was distinct from earlier reform movements in American politics in that it viewed *government* as a major ally in its reform cause. Progressives viewed law as something that ought to be shaped to achieve their ends. Progressivism sought to regulate business, political interests, and parties to serve the "common good." According to historian Richard Hofstadter (1961), progressivism

> demanded the constant, disinterested activity of the citizen in public affairs, argued that political life ought to be run, to a greater degree than it was, in accordance with general principles and abstract laws apart from and superior to personal needs, and expressed a common feeling that government should be in good part an effort to moralize the lives of individuals while economic life should be intimately related to the stimulation and development of individual character. (p. 9)

Progressives viewed the Constitution as a flawed document. Rex Tugwell, a prominent progressive (and close friend to Herbert Croly of *The New Republic*) was best known for his desire to entirely rewrite the Constitution. This is hardly surprising: the Constitution does not accord the voter much of a role in the system of republican governance. The progressives would prefer it otherwise.

Progressivism was opposed by a different ethic—that of new immigrants to the United States, who understood politics for the individual as arising out of family needs and placed personal loyalties and obligations above abstract codes of moral behavior. These values were the basis of the political machine and the party boss, which progressives opposed. One of the major reforms proposed by the progressives was the introduction of nonpartisan elections—a reform that struck at the heart of the immigrant culture:

> Nonpartisanship is a characteristic expression of . . . the middle-class Anglo-Saxon Protestant political ethos. The principle of nonpartisanship is consistent with, and indeed logically implies, the view that politics, rather than being a struggle between practical and private interests, is (or at any rate ought to be) a disinterested effort to discover what is best for the community "as a whole." (Banfield and Wilson, 1963, p. 154)

Progressives also celebrated "public opinion"—a new and progressive concept of independent opinion developed outside the communication channels of the party and interest group. Progressives feared the "corruption, inefficiency, and unthinking partisanship which they believed characterized governments dependent on the votes of Negroes in the South and non-Anglo-Saxon immigrants in the North" (Kousser, 1974, p. 252). In earlier years, newspapers were partisan. During the progressive era, nonpartisan newspapers and journals grew and helped to form attitudes independent of the party. A new form of journalism developed—muckraking[9]—in which reporters sought to expose corruption in government and politics. Progressives were great believers in progress and reform of public opinion and behavior. The formation of public opinion, however, was "weighted toward those who were sufficiently wealthy and organized to articulate and propagate their beliefs" (Link and McCormick, 1983, pp. 57–58).

The hallmark of progressivism was the attempt to mold attitudes and opinion toward those of Yankee Protestant political values. One political movement during the progressive era that was *not* progressive in impulse was the settlement house movement. Inspired by the example of Toynbee Hall in London, established by Oxford University students in 1884, educated young people—most commonly young women[10]—went to live and work among the poor in slum neighborhoods. In addition to providing a whole range of social and educational services, the settlement house workers sponsored "lectures, art exhibits, pageants, and festivals" to "awaken poor immigrants to their own cultural heritage" (Link and McCormick, 1983, p. 73). Instead of importing alien Yankee values, settlement workers like Jane Addams of Hull House in Chicago and Lillian Wald of Henry Street Settlement in New York sought to develop pride among the immigrants in their own unique ethnic heritage and to strengthen their family units.[11]

The progressive Yankee, however, worried about the "Irish Conquest of Our Cities" (Hofstadter, 1961, p. 177). The Irish were among the more well-established immigrant groups. In many cities, for example, Boston, Chicago, Cleveland, New York, Philadelphia, Pittsburgh, and St. Louis, the native-born were then outnumbered by the immigrants and their children. Among the many innovations advocated by the progressives and widely implemented during this era were restrictions on voter registration and suffrage designed to limit the voting power of immigrants as well as blacks in the South. Pro-

---

[9]The term muckraking originated from a 1906 speech by President Theodore Roosevelt (who supported progressive aims—he was the first "progressive" president) in which he attacked the methods of the "muckrakers" as sensational and irresponsible.

[10]The settlement house movement attracted many young, educated women because it allowed women to move beyond the traditional women's sphere dominated by the constraints of husbands and families. The number of women graduating from college quadrupled between 1890 and 1900 (from 2,500 to 8,500), yet employment opportunities remained extremely limited. In their settlement house work, however, these women were able to confront all aspects of human existence without limitations.

[11]Settlement house workers initiated a whole series of social and educational programs: they "taught classes in homemaking, cooking, sewing, and carpentry; they established nurseries, kindergartens, and employment agencies; and they built playgrounds and founded clubs for groups of every age and sex" (Link and McCormick, 1983, p. 73).

gressives believed that the vote should be limited to educated people, so the introduction of the secret ballot (heretofore, voters arrived at the poll with a ballot printed by the political party of their choice) required literacy. And the requirement that voters must register in advance of voting greatly reduced the turnout of the immigrant classes. Ironically, the progressives stressed voting as the duty of all good citizens, but simultaneously limited voting to those who voted for "good government" ends as understood by the Yankee Anglo-Saxon ethic.

The conflict between these two ethics held by opposing social groups was spawned by many social changes, including the rising tide of immigration and the development of a new urban, native-born middle class, along with the rapid expansion of the professions—education, journalism, medicine, and the law. Long-established organizations (e.g., American Medical Association, American Bar Association, National Education Association) grew rapidly, while many new professional associations organized, from the American Association of Advertising Agencies (1917), to the U.S. Chamber of Commerce (1912), the American Association of University Professors (1915), and the Farm Bureau Federation (1919). Professionals who sought to apply their developing expertise to politics and government were a core component of the progressive reformers.

All of the social science and natural science disciplines were affected by the progressive reform temperament. Yet political science was affected in different ways than other disciplines. Other social science disciplines remained relatively impervious to the progressive emphasis on reform and proper behavior. Peter Berger, in his widely reprinted *Invitation to Sociology*, warns prospective sociologists that "people who are interested in human beings only if they can change, convert or reform them should also be warned, for they will find sociology much less useful than they hoped" (Berger, 1963, p. 24).

Political science as a new discipline was relatively undeveloped at the turn of the century. This made political science more open to the ideas of the progressive movement than the other social sciences. Ironically, the first major difference was that political science provided none of the major intellectual leaders of progressivism. These included economists such as Richard T. Ely and Thorstein Veblen, historians such as Mary Ritter Beard and her husband Charles A. Beard,[12] philosophers William James and John Dewey, journalists Herbert Croly and Lincoln Steffens, and legal scholar Oliver Wendell Holmes, Jr. The reason that *other* academic disciplines provided intellectual leadership was that these progressive intellectuals were reacting against the dominant theoretical perspective of their own discipline. Without an over-

---

[12]Beard is commonly viewed as an historian. His major thesis was that history (particularly in the realm of economics and politics) encompasses all aspects of civilization. He taught at Columbia University and helped to found the New School for Social Research there. However, Beard did serve as a president of the American Political Science Association in the mid-1920s, and some of his work was published in the *American Political Science Review*.

arching theoretical perspective, political scientists had nothing to react against to produce a new—progressive—way of thought.

Second, political science as a profession trained and produced many of the leaders of the progressive movement—those reformers who sought to restructure government to limit the dangers of popular participation. A major beacon of academic progressivism was found at Johns Hopkins University in the late 1880s and 1890s. Johns Hopkins had one of the earliest graduate programs in an American university. Progressivism at Johns Hopkins centered around political scientists such as James Bryce,[13] who served as the tenth president of the American Political Science Association, and Woodrow Wilson, the Johns Hopkins University president. Bryce and Wilson greatly influenced urban municipal reformers like Frederic Howe, a charter member of the National Progressive Republican League, formed in 1911.

> When Howe went to Johns Hopkins University for graduate study, he was well prepared to respond to the passionate preachings of an academic Mugwump[14] like Woodrow Wilson, who spoke out against the indifference and loss of responsibility among the public, and to the high-minded addresses of Lord Bryce, who lamented the spoils system, corruption, the failure of democracy, and [in Howe's own words] the "decay of responsibility among the kind of people whom I knew. That was what impressed me most: the kind of people I knew had neglected their duties." (Hofstadter, 1961, p. 205)

The professions not only trained many of the progressive reformers, but also added their skills to the growth of government. Think tanks, more than a thousand of which exist today (with about one hundred in Washington, DC alone), trace their origins to the rise of the social sciences and the progressive impulse toward reliance on policy experts.

Third, political science absorbed the popular progressive temperament in lieu of the theoretical development of the discipline. Many early political scientists, such as Andrew White, John Burgess, Charles Adams, Herbert Adams, and Thomas Reed, argued that political science assumed the obligation to train future leaders and citizens. Albert Somit and Joseph Tannenhaus stress that

[13]Viscount James Bryce was a British statesman and historian who was a popular ambassador to the United States (1907–1913). Bryce, the author of the widely read *The American Commonwealth* (1888), was a prominent critic of American political parties and machines, referring to city bosses as "vulgar figures with good coats."

[14]The Mugwumps, nicknamed after a renegade Algonquin Indian Chief, were Republicans who had bolted the Republican Party to protest against James G. Blaine as their presidential candidate in 1884. Blaine, a gifted orator and one of the initial founders of the Republican Party, had been tarnished by scandals from his 1876 senatorial campaign when letters he had written appeared to offer political favors in exchange for railroad stock. The Mugwumps had supported the Pendelton Civil Service Act, passed in 1883 after a disgruntled jobseeker had assassinated President James A. Garfield. In general, the Mugwumps were well-educated men from eastern and midwestern cities who were alarmed by the alleged corruption of party politics.

while all academic disciplines tend to have common characteristics, in one respect American political science is unique—it has assumed responsibility for transmitting to the nation's youth the knowledge and patriotic sentiments deemed essential for the successful functioning of our democratic system. (1982, p. 45)

The growing progressive distrust in universal suffrage that had been the theory and practice in the United States since 1860 was mirrored in the new discipline of political science. By 1918, two Yale historians concluded that "the theory that every man has a natural right to vote no longer commands the support of students of political science" (Kousser, 1974, p. 253). The American Political Science Association, organized around the study of government and politics, proved complementary to the emphasis of progressives on the positive use of government. A major early party scholar, Charles Merriam, who believed parties to be necessary for democracy,[15] nonetheless was an active progressive reformer. One early contribution was the work of political scientists who studied pressure groups and concluded that governmental policy often reflected group interests. However, consistent with the progressive emphasis on the "common good," pressure groups were seen as evil—opposed to the public interest. As David Truman (1951) summarized the early progressive political science treatment of interest groups:

> The "lobby" and the "pressure group" are familiar to many, but they are accepted in the way that the typhoid bacillus is, as an organism that is a feature of civilized existence but that must be eradicated if society is to develop and prosper.... Since the publication in 1908 of A. F. Bentley's pioneering book, *The Process of Government*, academicians have given increasing attention to political groups.[16] *As often as not, however, the assumptions implicit in such treatments have been close to those popularly held.* (p. 46, emphasis added)

The adoption of progressive values on the positive use of government alongside the distrust of the average citizen and voter probably hindered the development of political science theory. Those who wish to reform society often fail to see the world the way it really is, and the ability to look at things empirically is a prerequisite for any serious study of politics.

The first comprehensive empirical political science theory—pluralism—did not develop until after World War II. Pluralism and a new stress on empirical political science developed alongside a phenomenal growth in the profession. In 1946, the American Political Science Association had only 4,000

[15]Merriam believed that the political party "is one of the great agencies through which social interests express and execute themselves" (Merriam, 1922, p. 391).

[16]Truman refers here to: Peter H. Odegard, *Pressure Politics: The Story of the Anti-Saloon League* (1928); E. Pendleton Herring, *Group Representation Before Congress* (1929) and *Public Administration and the Public Interest* (1936); Harwood L. Childs, *Labor and Capital in National Politics* (1930); E. E. Schattschneider, *Politics, Pressures and the Tariff* (1935); Belle Zeller, *Pressure Politics in New York* (1937); Dayton D. McKean, *Pressures on the Legislature of New Jersey* (1938); and Oliver Garceau, *The Political Life of the American Medical Association* (1941).

members; "in two decades membership soared to 14,000" (Somit and Tannenhaus, 1982, p. 145). David Truman, quoted above, was an early major theorist of pluralism. Pluralism developed as a result of the introduction of distinctive political science methods—known as behavioralism—stressing the empirical study of politics. Behavioralists argued that political scientists should stress pure research, and avoid discussion of values like democracy, whose truth or falsity could not be established scientifically. Increasingly, the emphasis was on treating politics as a system, susceptible to a general theory consisting of a "deductive system of thought so that a limited number of postulates, as assumptions and axioms, a whole body of empirically valid generalizations might be deduced in descending order of specificity" (Easton, 1965, p. 9). However, "whatever the impact of behavioralism on other aspects of the discipline, the idea that political scientists should attend strictly to scientific inquiry made slow headway" (Somit and Tannenhaus, 1982, p. 195). Behavioralism was blind to its own value-biases in its effort to look at "what is" rather than "what ought to be." Pluralism developed as a hybrid of the progressive stress on democracy and the behavioralist emphasis on science. John Gunnell (1983) refers to this hybrid as "liberal pluralism":

> Although behavioralism, mainstream political science, and advocates of pluralist democracy were not entirely congruent categories, they often coincided in the work of individuals such as V. O. Key, Jr., David Easton, Robert Dahl, Gabriel Almond, and David Truman. (p. 21)

Pluralism provided a distinct counterpoise to the progressive temperament—pluralists stressed the critical and *necessary* importance of interest groups to democracy. Far from attacking interests in politics, as did the progressives, pluralists celebrated interest groups as essential to a free society, while downplaying the importance of voting and widespread citizen participation. In contrast to the progressives who advocated a *direct* relationship between voters and candidates, the pluralists stressed the crucial role that interest groups played as *intermediaries*. Group leaders acted as intermediaries representing the views of group members to candidates and public officials and the views of government and other group leaders to their own group members.

For pluralists, parties also performed an intermediary role, albeit one that worked primarily through the activities of interest groups. Parties were decentralized and lacked any principled program. Moreover, pluralists believed that the American party system and particularly the machine party "had produced good results precisely because of its alleged defects" (Banfield, 1980a, p. 20). Pluralist theorists included David Truman, Robert Dahl, Nelson Polsby, Edward Banfield, and Aaron Wildavsky, whose work stressed the important contribution of interest group leaders to democracy. Pluralists have been extremely critical of the progressive belief in reform. Edward Banfield provided probably the strongest statement of this when he asserted that "a political system is an accident, and that to meddle with one that works well is the greatest foolishness of which men are capable" (1980a, p. 20). Further, Banfield stresses that "reforms" may make matters worse even if well intended, like those of the progressives.

> I put the word "reform" in quotation marks to call attention to its misuse by those who think any change that aims at improvement is a reform even if it makes matters worse. Properly speaking, a change is a reform only if it makes matters better in the manner intended. As Burke[17] said in his *Letter to a Noble Lord*, "to innovate is not to reform." (p. 20)

Despite the powerful theoretical model offered by pluralism, it would be a mistake to assume, however, that the opposition to political interests found in the progressive temperament had disappeared from political science. In fact, one scholar of interest groups recently concluded that most political scientists are antipluralist (Berry, 1989a). Consider this plaint from Michael Nelson, a political scientist, about "what's wrong with political science" (see Box 1-2). Nelson attacks the behavioral revolution in political science, which produced pluralism and studies of mass politics. Instead, Nelson expresses a strong interest in political science as training for democratic citizenship, with political scientists hanging out shingles as "experts" in government. Nelson argues that instead of imitating our sister sciences or—as George Will suggests—disappearing into the other social sciences, we go back into our pre-behavioral days when the progressive temperament was dominant "to bury our mistakes, and take the fork in the road we bypassed then." Political science should produce, in the words of early progressive political scientist Thomas Reed, "better minds for better government" (Nelson, 1977, p. 20). Of course, pluralism remains a widely accepted viewpoint among some of the most respected scholars in American politics, including Nelson Polsby, Edward Banfield, Aaron Wildavsky, Robert Dahl, and others.

We began this section with the question "Whose game do we play?" We have reviewed two major opposing paradigms or models in political science—the progressive temperament and pluralism—only to learn that values do indeed affect how we answer this question. The progressives extolled democracy but acted to exclude groups and interests from politics in their search for purity in the representation of the "public interest."

The pluralists extolled interest in politics but viewed the party only as an arena for competing interests and their leaders while they believed that mass participation in politics should be limited in order to preserve democracy. Despite these differences, neither progressivism or pluralism has provided an adequate explanation of important changes in parties and interest groups in

---

[17]Edmond Burke (1729–1797), a British statesman and philosopher, provided one of the earliest defenses of political parties. His most famous work, *Reflections on the Revolution in France* (1790), criticizes the French Revolution and argues for the slow evolution of society.

BOX 1-2
What's Wrong with Political Science

I don't know how many times I've had this conversation.

"I'm a grad student in political science," I'd tell people foolish enough to ask.

"Oh, mm-hmm. That must be very interesting. What does one do with a degree in, uh, political science?"

"I plan to hang out a shingle. You know: Michael Nelson. Political Scientist. By Appointment Only."

"Hang out a —? Oh, I get it, very funny. No, really, what does one do with a —?"

"One teaches."

That is about the extent of what a political scientist can do with all his years of advanced and specialized training: teach undergraduates who are, I suppose, hoping to learn how to read the newspaper a bit more intelligently, and teach the graduate students who will someday take his place. The "real world" places almost no value, financial or aesthetic, on the training we political scientists receive. . . .

Maybe I'm crazy, but this bothers me. You would think, wouldn't you, that newspapers (which report on government), businesses (which are vitally affected by what government does to and for them), and the government itself would have some interest in the services of highly educated people who study government for a living. You would think, to be crassly material, that the market would be willing to pay such people for their services.

After all, other social sciences are valued in the marketplace. Nearly half of America's psychologists and economists actually practice their professions. A psychologist can hang out a shingle and reasonably expect that people will come knocking at his door. *Psychology Today* sells half a million copies every month. . . . The bearer of a PhD in economics may not get on the Council of Economic Advisors or *Time*'s Board of Economists, but he can take some comfort in knowing that these things exist as he chooses from a range of high paying careers in business and govern-

the past two decades. As we shall see in later chapters, there has been an explosion of interest group activity, and new groups have been brought into politics. Both progressives and pluralists have viewed these changes with alarm—the same changes we and other party scholars view as democratizing and strengthening the party system. While the stress of empirical political scientists

ment. . . . I won't belabor the comparison. Suffice it to say that there is no *Political Science Today* magazine, no Council of Political Science Advisors. . . .

Perhaps nothing illustrates the barrenness of the behavioral movement—its sacrifice of concern for learning how the system really works for the sake of intricate statistical models—better than the University of Michigan's Center for Political Studies. . . . Michigan's flagship has been its election studies series. Back in the dark, pre-behavioral days, students of politics used to approach elections primitively, by exploring questions like these: What is their role in a democracy? What effects do they have on what the government does? Are elections a good or a bad thing? The first contribution of the Michigan people was to take the most trivial of all these questions—How do people decide who to vote for?—and study the hell out of it. . . .

One is impressed, in reading the collected works of three decades of Michigan and other behavioral researchers, with both the dullness of their questions and the poverty of their answers. . . . the problem seems clear enough: over the years we have spent most of our energy rushing to imitate our sister social sciences' methods of finding answers, conveniently fooling ourselves into forgetting that they have something we lack—a rich legacy of provocative questions born of long years of purposeful thinking. . . . we still have our best option left . . . it requires us to go back several decades to the pre-behavioral days, bury our mistakes, and take the fork in the road we bypassed then.

That fork, of course, leads to a political science dedicated to education for democratic citizenship, to "better minds for better government" in Thomas Reed's phrase. . . . The pollyanna-like civics training most people got in school, which probably did not even mention bureaucracy, political parties, pressure groups, mass media and other components of real-world politics, left them no better informed. . . . In short, we can hang out shingles. There is a market for political scientists, a set of ears willing to listen.

Source: Nelson, 1977, pp. 13–20.

on the facts does allow some comparison of theories, values do matter. The study of politics is also an engaging intellectual enterprise. We hope that we have invited you not only to politics, but also to political science. We turn in the following chapters to the contribution of interest groups, political parties, and elites to democracy. As E. E. Schattschneider said, "politics is a collaboration of ignorant people and experts."

chapter 2

Interest Groups and Democracy

Whenever at the head of some new undertaking you see government in France, or a man of rank in England, in the United States you will be sure to find an association.

Alexis de Toqueville, after touring America in 1831–32

There is a interesting paradox about interest groups in America: on the one hand, interest groups are regarded as essential to American democracy— indeed a distinguishing feature of the oldest democracy in the world; on the other hand, interest groups are considered to be a serious threat to democracy. Many commentators concerned about recent changes in American politics have said that we have too many interest groups. In this chapter we will review major theories of democracy and interest groups and unravel this paradox. We examine first the preservation of liberties that allow for unlimited representation of interests, and then the problems raised by representation. This is known as the *Madisonian dilemma.*

JAMES MADISON AND THE PRESERVATION OF LIBERTY

Interest groups are guaranteed rights in the U.S. Constitution through the Bill of Rights. The First Amendment provides that "Congress shall make no laws respecting an establishment of religion, or prohibiting the free exercise thereof; or abridging the freedom of speech, or of the press; or the right of the people peaceably to assemble, and to petition the Government for a redress of grievances." The First Amendment was adopted in large part because of reservations from the crucial large states of New York and Virginia. As the price of a free and open society, the First Amendment permits people to express their political views, to organize on behalf of causes, and to lobby the government. James Madison, a delegate from Virginia, an author, and probably the principal architect of the Constitution, was keenly aware of the dangers to the republic posed by unbridled self-interest.

Madison, our fourth president (1808–1816), is widely regarded as a foremost American political philosopher. His views are expounded brilliantly in the *Federalist Papers*, a series of 85 widely publicized letters to the public written by James Madison, Alexander Hamilton, and John Jay under the nom de plum of Publius to persuade reluctant delegates to ratifying conventions to support the proposed Constitution. Perhaps the most famous *Federalist Paper* is Number 10 (see Box 2-1), written by Madison. Madison was concerned, after the conflicts of the Confederation made government unworkable,[1] primarily about governmental stability and the problems posed by what he termed "the violence and mischiefs of faction." Here he doubtless had in mind the groups involved in the debtor and propertyless groups such as Shay's Rebellion in 1786 against sheriff's auctions of seized property in Massachusetts. Factions are dangerous, Madison believed, because they encourage selfish interests, inflame the passions, and excite mutual animosities, which undermine the common good. But to remove the causes of factions "by destroying the liberty which is essential to its existence," Madison claimed, is "worse than the disease." This is the Madisonian dilemma. Madison concludes that one cannot control the *causes* of factions, but one can design a government that can control its *effects*. By this, Madison refers to the *republican principle* through which government is delegated to representatives (who presumably have cooler heads) as opposed to direct democracy in small city-states. Note in the excerpt in Box 2-1 that Madison also uses the terms "party" and "faction" interchangeably. Also, the larger size of republican government and its division into states limits the spread of factions. More modern writers might have said that Madison's republican principle was "to divide and conquer," meaning that with interests scattered in different governmental jurisdictions, effective national organization was impossible. The importance of *Federalist Paper No. 10* is its exposition of both the liberty of interests and concerns about their deleterious effects should they become too powerful.

---

[1]The Articles of Confederation, in effect from 1776 to 1787, established "a league of friendship and perpetual union" among the 13 original colonies. Each former colony or state was considered sovereign. Because they feared a strong national authority, the national government consisted only of a legislature—the Continental Congress—with no president or court system. The Continental Congress had no power to tax or to regulate commerce and had no power to raise an army. The national government therefore was entirely dependent on the largess of the states for money and for protection.

BOX 2-1
Excerpts from *Federalist Paper No. 10*

By a faction I understand a number of citizens, whether amounting to a majority or minority of the whole, who are united and actuated by some common impulse of passion, or of interest, adverse to the rights of other citizens, or to the permanent and aggregate interests of the community.

There are two methods of controlling the mischiefs of faction: the one, by removing its causes, the other, by controlling its effects.

There are again two methods of removing the causes of faction: the one, by destroying the liberty which is essential to its existence; the other by giving to every citizen the same opinions, the same passions, and the same interests.

It could never be more truly said than of the first remedy that it was worse than the disease. Liberty is to faction what air is to fire, an ailment without which it instantly expires. But it could not be a less folly to abolish liberty, which is essential to political life, because it nourishes faction than it would be to wish the annihilation of air, which is essential to animal life, because it imparts to fire its destructive agency.

The second expedient is as impracticable as the first would be unwise. As long as the reason of man continues fallible, and he is at liberty to exercise it, different opinions will be formed. . . .

Concurrent Majorities and the Road Not Taken

Not all constitutionally based interpretations were hostile to interest groups. A theory of *concurrent majorities* was developed by American statesman John C. Calhoun in the 1840s in the increasing debate over states' rights and slavery. Calhoun's theory, published as a pair of disquisitions after Calhoun's death in 1850, treated factions not as inherently bad, but rather viewed varying group interests as vital to the nation. According to Calhoun, each of the interests in society should be granted a veto power over any major policy proposal that affected them. Only a concurrent majority of all interest groups would permit a national policy affecting the entire nation to be developed. This represents an interesting perspective on the notion of a broad community interest. Calhoun's theory was different from Madison's: he assumed that interests would be concentrated in different regions and states, while Madison assumed that interests would be scattered. With federalism, minority interests in the nation could nonetheless be a majority in their own state (see Box 2-2). In fact, historian Paul Kleppner (1991) notes that groups are heavily concentrated in specific localities:

The latent causes of faction are thus sown in the nature of man; and we see them everywhere brought into different degrees of activity, according to the different circumstances of civil society. A zeal for different opinions concerning religion, concerning government, and many other points, as well of speculation as of practice; an attachment to different leaders ambitiously contending for pre-eminence and power; or to persons of other descriptions whose fortunes have been interesting to the human passions, have, in turn, divided mankind into parties, inflamed them with mutual animosity, and rendered them much more disposed to vex and oppress each other than to co-operate for their common good. . . . But the most common and durable source of factions has been the various and unequal distribution of property. Those who hold and those who are without property have ever formed distinct interests in society. Those who are creditors, and those who are debtors, fall under a like discrimination. A landed interest, a manufacturing interest, a mercantile interest, a moneyed interest, with many lesser interests, grow up of necessity in civilized nations, and divide them into different classes, actuated by different sentiments and views. The regulation of these various and interfering interests forms the principal task of modern legislation and involves the spirit of party and faction in the necessary and ordinary operations of government.

. . . A republic, by which I mean a government in which the scheme of representation takes place, opens a different prospect and promises the cure for which we are seeking.

By 1890 foreign-born Germans and their native-born children made up only 15 percent of the nation's electorate, but they were nearly half of the voting population in Wisconsin, nearly a third in Minnesota, and about a fifth of the voters in New York, Ohio, Illinois, and Iowa. French Canadian immigrants made up less than one percent of the nation's voting age population, but over 20 percent in New Hampshire and Vermont. . . . By 1890 Catholics were on the verge of majority status in Rhode Island, and they made up nearly a third of the voting age population of seven other eastern and midwestern states. But they were less than 20 percent of Indiana's electorate, less than 10 percent of Oregon's, and no more than five percent of the voters in any southern state (except Louisiana). (pp. 13–14)

Calhoun thus turned Madison's system of factional checks and balances on its head, while agreeing with Madison that interests were essential and endemic to society and sharing his fear of the tyranny of the majority. For Calhoun, the various interests in society *were* the community and their views should be protected by a veto power over the national government. Calhoun's theory was evident in his early conflict with Andrew Jackson over the tariff. While

BOX 2-2
The Geographic Basis of Leadership Selection

Consider the following highly simplified political system: (1) there are five election districts of equal population each electing a single representative; (2) there are one hundred voters of which forty are farmers, forty are merchants; twenty remaining are professionals, mechanics, actors and other types; and (3) each occupation votes along occupational lines for their distinct interests. It is entirely possible that due to a variety of circumstances the actual distribution of citizens is as shown [below].

	Election District					
	1	2	3	4	5	TOTAL
Farmers	11	11	11	4	3	40
Merchants	6	6	6	10	12	40
Others	3	3	3	6	5	20
TOTAL	20	20	20	20	20	100

[The table] clearly shows that either by chance or conscious design the partitioning of the electorate into separate districts can lead to distortions of preferences. Observe that while farmers represent only 40 percent of population, their physical distribution allows them to control three of five election districts, while merchants, who are equal in number to farmers, clearly dominate only one district (number 5). Thus, full citizen participation coupled with strict observance of majority preferences will invariably lead to farmers winning on each issue. Of course, these hypothetical figures can be manipulated any number of ways, e.g. farmers could be given eight votes per district and hence be a minority in every district, but the point to be emphasized is that since it is extremely unlikely that *each* election district will mirror the entire population, it is almost certain that distortions of the above type will occur.

Source: Weissberg, 1976, pp. 61–62.

serving as Jackson's vice president, he authored anonymously the widely circulated *South Carolina Exposition and Protest*, in which he argued that the tariff of 1828 was unconstitutional and that aggrieved states had the constitutional right to nullify or override the law within their borders. During his later years in the U.S. Senate, he eloquently defended the right of southern states to secede from the Union.

Few American leaders have had Calhoun's vast experience in elective and appointive office,[2] yet his intriguing theory became identified with the increasingly divisive debate over slavery. Calhoun stressed that to be constitutional, federal laws should benefit all *equally*. This was evident in a symbolic confrontation with Andrew Jackson in 1830, when Calhoun responded to a toast by Jackson to "Our Union: It must be preserved" by saying "The Union next to Liberty the most dear. May we always remember that it can only be preserved by distributing equally the benefits and burdens of the Union." With the advent of the Civil War and the victory of the North and the eradication of slavery, Calhoun's theory became a matter for philosophical debate rather than a constitutional issue.

The Madisonian Heritage

Madison's linking of factions and parties as necessary evils reflected his times; indeed the widespread distrust of political parties by early American leaders greatly hindered their development for some 40 years in the United States after the ratification of the Constitution. Yet, as we shall see, Madison's fear of the "mischiefs of faction" have remained of concern to many throughout American history from the early progressive attacks on "pressure groups" to the present-day concern about "hyperpluralism" and the "balkanization of America" with too many "single issue groups."[3] In the 1950s, however, a newly empirical political science developed a theoretical justification for how interest groups contribute to democracy—a theory known as *pluralism*, which we will examine in detail.

[2]John C. Calhoun (1782–1850) served in the House of Representatives (1811–1817), as secretary of war (1817–1825), as vice president (1825–1832) under both John Quincy Adams and Andrew Jackson, as secretary of state (1844–1845) under President Tyler, and in the U.S. Senate (1832–1843, 1845–1850).

[3]The term *hyperpluralism* comes from a column by *Washington Post* reporter David Broder published in 1979. (Broder himself refers to an observation made by British journalist and political scientist Anthony King that the then contemporary American parties were "only coalitions of sand.") In 1978, Kevin Phillips, a former aide to President Richard Nixon, author, and political commentator, spoke of the "balkanization of America." Both terms have been used by political scientists. Hyperpluralism, defined as "too many groups getting too much of what they want," has been adopted by many political scientists. It is found, for example, in a popular introductory text, *Government in America*, co-authored by Robert Lineberry, George C. Edwards, and Martin P. Wattenberg (1991). As we shall see, what Broder has popularly identified as a decline in pluralism is really a version of an old theory—mass society theory.

PLURALISM AND THE GROUP THEORY
OF POLITICS

Pluralism as a theory is based upon a *group theory* of politics. It describes how
leaders and citizens are linked in modern societies. The theory was developed
in the aftermath of World War II, when many social science scholars were
concerned with the seeming instability of some electoral democracies during
periods of rapid electoral change. One social scientist described this intellectual
concern as follows:

> the experience of two world wars, the revolutions in Russia and Germany thirty
> years ago, the rise and fall of Mussolini and Hitler, the Civil War in China, the
> expansion of the Soviet sphere of influence into the very heart of Europe and
> the ensuing tensions between the partisans of capitalism, socialism and com-
> munism have aroused an intensified interest in the study of those forces which
> have contributed to the present crisis of Western society. (Heberle, 1949, p. 347)

Interest groups were viewed as essential to regime stability. Ironically, social
scientists in this era[4] viewed both interest groups and their demise as distinctly
modern phenomena. We now turn to a review of the evolution of pluralist
societies.

The Evolution of Pluralism as a Type of Society

In Figure 2-1, we categorize four different types of societies: communal,
pluralist, totalitarian, and mass societies. These are ideal types—no real society
exhibits all of one set of characteristics and none of the others. Each type is
differentiated from the others by the availability of nonelites (the "masses")
for political mobilization and the responsiveness of elites to nonelites. The
availability of nonelites for mobilization depends upon the degree to which
they are absorbed by "primitive" groups. Primitive groups involve face-to-
face interaction, as opposed to "secondary" groups, which represent a statistical category or aggregation, not naturally occurring groups. The responsiveness of elites requires competition among elites for nonelite allegiance and
approval (in terms of votes or dollars), thus guaranteeing "both multiple
choices and open channels of communication" (Kornhauser, 1959, p. 55).

COMMUNAL SOCIETY.   Early societies evolved first from communal society
characterized by primitive groups. Primitive groups, including primary groups
based solely upon face-to-face interactions, are strong and pervasive. Groups
in primitive societies are entirely family and extended kinship groups. Leadership is inherited, as is one's status in the tribe or clan. All relationships are

[4]Theorists of pluralism and mass society came from many social sciences—psychology,
sociology, and political science. Major theorists included Hannah Arendt (1954), Erich Fromm
(1945), Karl Mannheim (1940), Robert Nisbet (1953), and Phillip Selznick (1952). A summary
of their theories is found in William Kornhauser (1959).

Figure 2-1   Groups and Linkages of Elites and Masses

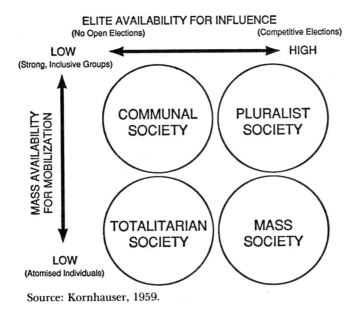

ELITE AVAILABILITY FOR INFLUENCE
(No Open Elections)   (Competitive Elections)

Source: Kornhauser, 1959.

personal, and everyone with whom one interacts is a member of the same group. Relationships are reciprocal and unique—such as mother and daughter. Examples of communal societies include tribal groups and the medieval world. Kornhauser (1959) points out that

> Such a population is very difficult to mobilize unless powerful forces have eroded communal ties, as happened in the Late Middle Ages, when the incipient processes of urbanization and industrialization began their destruction of the medieval community, thereby unloosing portions of the population for participation in the various millennial movements that flourished during this period. (p. 40)

PLURALISTIC SOCIETY.   As society evolves, structural differentiation and specialization results in new associations based on other than family associations. Universal relationships develop, such as store clerk and customer or employer and employee, that apply to a class of persons, rather than a unique individual. Individuals interact in an increasingly wider range of groups. Instead of relationships circumscribed totally by multigenerational kinship groups, new types of groups arise characterized by interest or age (such as peer groups found in schools and among teenagers). Yet not everyone one meets is a member of one's group—he or she may be a stranger. Finally, in complex, modern pluralistic societies, large voluntary associations appear, which have no relation to one's family but are still crucial in their formation of social identity and values. Examples of such large voluntary associations would be community and ethnic groups, labor organizations, and churches. In both communal and pluralistic societies, groups remain a strong and pervasive part of one's existence.

Groups perform a critical role in society: they intermediate between the individual and the larger polity. Groups provide a context for two-way communication[5]—between leaders and followers. In both societies, the role of the group is to absorb the emotional lives of the group members. These groups are formed on a nonpolitical basis and minimize the interest of individuals in politics. Leaders of groups, however, will be interested in politics. Groups, thus, in the modern pluralistic society provide a medium of communication between group members, their group leaders, and the governmental or political leaders. These two societies differ in the responsiveness of leaders to the views of group members (see Box 2-3). In the communal society, leadership is determined solely by accident of birth. In the pluralistic society, leadership is dependent on popular support—usually by elections. Indeed, in pluralistic societies, political participation is primarily determined by voting and participation in naturally occurring local community groups, but not in overtly political groups. Nonelites are unavailable for mobilization because the

> people possess multiple commitments to diverse and autonomous groups. The mobilization of a population bound by multiple commitments would require the breaking up of large numbers of independent organizations, as totalitarian movements have sought to do. (Kornhauser, 1974, p. 41)

Recall that pluralist theorists assume that people are *not* naturally interested in politics—politics is a remote and abstract phenomenon to the average individual. Thus, pluralists make a strong distinction between local nonpolitical groups and national or political groups.

TOTALITARIAN AND MASS SOCIETIES.   There are two other undesirable societies, which social science writers of this era were concerned about: the *totalitarian* and the *mass society*. In both of these societies, groups have declined in importance to the point of disappearance. In lieu of face-to-face groups based upon some social or economic identity, individuals are socially isolated and atomized from their family and community of birth. Further, their face-to-face interaction with a group of similar individuals is quite limited. They do not get their information or identity from group norms, but from the mass media. The two societies differ in terms of the responsiveness of their leaders: in the totalitarian society the leaders are unresponsive to the mass, whereas in the mass society leaders are multiple and competitive and overly responsive to mass movements. "Totalitarian movements are highly organized by an elite

---

[5]The concept of the two-step flow of communication was originally developed by Bernard Berelson and Paul Lazarsfeld and their research colleagues (Lazarsfeld, Berelson, and Gaudet, 1944; Berelson, Lazarsfeld, and McPhee, 1954).

bent on total power, whereas mass movements tend to be amorphous collectivities, often without any stable leadership" (Kornhauser, 1974, p. 47). Totalitarian leaders control the mass media and use it exclusively for propaganda—one-way communication from the leaders to the undifferentiated masses. In mass society, no one faction of leaders has such dominant control—leaders seeking influence make demagogic emotional appeals to vulnerable isolated individuals, saying whatever they believe the masses wish to hear. Through such unscrupulous leadership, a mass society has the potential to degenerate into a totalitarian society.

The Political Theory of Pluralism

Like Madison's dilemma, these social scientists theorized that a stable society was protected when groups were strong and insulated individuals from demagogic appeals. Pluralist theorists, however, went one step further and asserted that the pluralist society was not only stable, but also a democracy. James Madison, on the other hand, denied that America was a democracy—for him, it was a more truly a republic. Carole Pateman (1970), a contemporary philosopher, has been sharply critical of pluralist theorizing. She argues that the pluralists have usurped the normative edge of democratic theory—with stress on the educational benefits of participation—without providing for *real* participation in a pluralist society. "In the contemporary theory of democracy it is the participation of the minority elite that is crucial and the non-participation of the apathetic, ordinary man lacking in the feeling of political efficacy, that is regarded as the main bulwark against instability" (p. 104). Like Madison's farsighted *Federalist Paper No. 10*, Pateman charges that pluralists are theorists of representative government, not of democracy. A representative government is not a bad government—Madison indeed thought it *preferable* to democracy. The point here is that the normative value of representative government (stability) is not the same as that of classical or participatory democracy (educational).

The earliest work in group theory was that of Arthur Bentley, a sociologist by training. His major work, *The Process of Government* (1949), was first published in 1908, yet ignored for decades. However, it served as a catalyst for later work, and many referred back to Bentley's scorn of the concept of "the public interest." For Bentley, society was "nothing other than the complex of the groups that compose it" (1949, p. 455). The empirical theory of pluralism, apart from its widespread acceptance in the 1950s as a political theory, was even more firmly grounded as a true, empirical description of politics with the groundbreaking work of such behavioralists as David Truman (1971) (originally published in 1951), who described American politics and government as a complex set of interactions and bargaining among a panoply of diverse interest groups. Truman's group theory of politics was strongly based in social psychology and anthropology (see Box 2-3). Truman asserts that

BOX 2-3
Excerpts from David Truman's *The Governmental Process*

In all societies of any degree of complexity the individual is less affected directly by the society as a whole than differentially through various of its subdivisions, or groups. In the first place, even in the simplest society, it is literally impossible for any one individual to function in all the groups of which the society is made. Just as he can become highly skilled in only one or a few techniques, so he can participate in only a limited number of the groups that are formed about such specializations. In a society in which locality groupings are important, an individual never "belongs" to more than a few and rarely to more than one. In the second place, the positions occupied by the individual in his society limit the effects upon him of society as a whole. The technical term usually applied to these positions is *statuses*. He may not participate in those groups confined to persons of the opposite sex or of a differing age level. Ordinarily he belongs to only one "extended" family, one church, one economic institution, and one political unit at a given level, such as the nation. At any point in time and frequently over his entire life span he cannot belong to more than one class or caste grouping.

To the extent that the range and type of behavior in these groupings vary from one to another . . . the patterns of action and attitude among individuals will differ from one another in large measure according to the clusters of group affiliations that the individuals have. . . . It is simpler and more realistic to say with James Madison that the tendencies toward such groupings are "sown in the nature of man." . . .

In recent years the social psychologists and cultural anthropologists have done much to explain the manner and extent of group influences upon our behavior. The most important of these influences from the standpoint of molding the individual's personality and adjusting him to his surroundings are those that operate during infancy and childhood— the family, neighborhood, school, and friendship groups, commonly known as primary groups. In the process of growing up, the child receives from face-to-face groups, especially those that include adults, and from the opportunities that they afford, the means whereby he defines his self in relation to the world about him. He learns what to do and what to avoid, and in what terms various objects and behaviors are to be understood if he is to be an accepted and approved member of the unit involved. These terms vary considerably among groups, depending on their circumstances. Such groups almost without design select those aspects of the culture with which the child becomes acquainted and determine the values which he shall attach to them. . . . *Although no two human organisms will develop identically in any one of the environments mentioned; the limitations, aspirations, and values that each holds will have developed in relation to the groups with which each has been early associated. . . .*

Psychologists distinguish various mechanisms whereby the group places its imprint upon the personality of a participant. . . . In general terms, every individual, from infancy onward, tries to make himself an accepted participant in a group, or more properly, a set of groups, that makes up his social environment. . . . Most individuals in any cultural setting find it intolerably painful not to be accepted by the groups in which they move or in which they hope to move. A measure of conformity is the price of acceptance.

The psychological pressure on the individual from his group affiliations does not decrease in intensity or effectiveness as the individual matures. When the full set of attitudes toward "me," "I," and "mine," which make up what the psychologist calls the ego, are formed—though their exact content is not static—the individual feels even more strongly the need to be accepted in his "own" group and to avoid being left out. . . . Sherif has performed a series of laboratory experiments that bear closely on [these group influences]. . . . Newcomb's study of attitude changes in a highly self-contained college community is also significant at this point. . . . Other examples of these group influences could be drawn from a number of sources. Justly famous is the study made in the Hawthorne works of the Western Electric company. . . .

It appears, then, that the group experiences and affiliations of an individual are the primary, though not the exclusive, means by which the individual knows, interprets, and reacts to the society in which he exists.

Source: Truman, 1971, pp. 15–21, emphasis added.

"Man is a social animal. . . . Man becomes characteristically human only in association with other men" (1951, pp. 14–15).

Truman's theory of groups considered *organized* groups as only one stage of the group process. Potential interests or "latent groups" *could* organize when faced with a challenge. One of the strongest elements of Truman's theory was his survey of the history of when groups formed. When established patterns of interactions are disturbed, new groups may be formed. Groups tended to form in waves (such as happened during the 1890s) during historical eras of rapid change in specialization in modern societies and "the continual frustration of established expectations. So closely do these developments follow, in fact, that the rate of association formation may serve as an index of the stability of a society, and their number may be used as an index of its complexity" (Truman, 1951, p. 57).

The strength of Truman's work lies in his empirical grounding of pluralism in psychological and anthropological research. Truman also believed that groups supported democracy. He argued that groups were governed by a "democratic mold" in the United States. By this, he meant that groups were organized internally by democratic ideas. In making this argument, Truman was responding to the work of an earlier scholar, Roberto Michels, first published in 1915. Michels had studied European socialist parties at the turn of the century. Michels (1962) introduced *the iron law of oligarchy:* "Who says organization says oligarchy." Oligarchy means rule by a few, and Michels' widely read work was interpreted to mean that in any organization, the leadership dominated while the members deferred. Truman argued that this was not true for groups in the United States because of the democratic mold. Thus, for Truman, not only were new groups free to form, but they were governed internally by democracy.

The Challenge from Sociology

Arriving half a century after the discipline of political science was formally organized in 1903, pluralist theory provided the first empirical and scientific theoretical grounding for political science. Further, pluralism allowed political scientists to consider America democratic. Sociologists provided a quite different approach to understanding power and democracy, dating from Robert and Helen Lynd's study of "Middletown" (a pseudonym for Muncie, Indiana) in the 1920s and 1930s. The Lynds employed the "positional approach" to community power: this method of determining who has power meant identifying the most important institutions and the top officials of the community. The Lynds found that a small business elite dominated Muncie and that this elite was dominated by a single family. This was known as *elite theory*, which we will consider more fully in Chapter 4.

By the 1950s, when political scientists were developing the pluralist definition of democracy, the study of community power was well established in sociology. Floyd Hunter's study of Atlanta in 1953 introduced the "reputational approach" in order to discover hidden power holders (apart from their institutional positions). His new method relied on the judgment of informed individuals in the community. Hunter discovered a power network dominated by leaders of the business community, stressing that "organizational leaders are prone to get the publicity; the upper echelon economic leaders the power" (1953, pp. 86–87). The study of community power became extremely popular, with more than 300 journal articles and books published by the 1970s (Domhoff, 1978). Based primarily on Floyd Hunter's new method of studying community power, sociologists outlined a power structure in which private power dominated by economic leaders ruled America, with political and civic leaders only exercising administrative power.

The Political Science Rebuttal

Because Hunter's work attacked the fundamental assertion of pluralism that power was open in the United States, his work was subjected to considerable criticism by political scientists. Nelson Polsby stressed that a major flaw in Hunter's approach was that he asked "Who runs this community?" without first asking "Does anyone at all run this community?" (1960, p. 478). The most influential critique was provided by Robert Dahl in his study of power in New Haven, Connecticut, in *Who Governs?* (1963). Dahl employed the "decision-making approach," arguing that Hunter's focus on *hidden* power holders could never be disproved. Instead, Dahl argued that the major criterion should be participation in key community decisions—the powerful would not be those *reputed* to be powerful, but those who actually participated most effectively in community decisions. Dahl found political leaders preeminent in major community decisions in New Haven and largely independent of business leaders. Business leaders participated only in those decisions of direct concern to them. Influence varied from policy area to policy area— power was not *cumulative* as assumed by Hunter, but *dispersed* among a range of political interests (see Box 2-4).

Pluralism became widely accepted in political science, as behavioral studies found considerable support for pluralist assumptions. Mass studies of the electorate, including the widely cited *The American Voter* (Campbell et al., 1960), found voters to be largely inattentive and ill-informed about politics, with their political behavior conditioned by their group and party identities. A study entitled *The Washington Lobbyists* (Milbrath, 1963) found that interest groups did not have the overwhelming influence to "control the selection of officials or to affect the likelihood that an official can keep or enhance his position" attributed to them by the early progressive scholarship. Instead, "the influence of groups is derived from the fact that members of groups are citizens and the political system is designed to respond to the influence of

BOX 2-4
Assumptions of Pluralism

1. **Leaders Interact:** Although citizens do not directly participate in decision making, their many leaders do make decisions through a process of bargaining, accommodation, and compromise.

2. **Groups Competitive:** There is competition among leadership groups that helps to protect the interests of individuals. Countervailing centers of power—for example, competition among business leaders, labor leaders, and government leaders—can check each other and keep each interest from abusing its power and oppressing the individual.

3. **Elections and Parties:** Individuals can influence public policy by choosing among competing elites in elections. Elections and parties allow individuals to hold leaders accountable for their actions.

4. **Interest Groups:** Although individuals do not participate directly in decision making, they can join organized groups and exert influence by participating in them.

5. **Access Open:** Leadership groups are not closed; new groups can be formed and gain access to the political system.

6. **Power Dispersed:** Although political influence in society is unequally distributed, power is widely dispersed. Access to decision making is often determined by how much interest people have in a particular decision; and because leadership is fluid and mobile, power depends on one's interest in public democratic processes, and skill in organization and public relations.

7. **Multiple Leaders:** There are multiple leadership groups within society. Those who exercise power in one kind of decision do not necessarily exercise power in others. No single elite dominates decision making in all issues areas.

8. **Equilibrium:** Public policy is not necessarily majority preference, but it is an equilibrium of interest interaction—that is, competing interest group influences are more or less balanced and the resultant policy is a reasonable approximation of society's preferences.

Source: Dye and Ziegler, 1984.

their votes" (Milbrath, 1963, p. 342). In addition to Robert Dahl,[6] who stressed that power was exercised pluralistically by multiple elites, Charles Lindblom (Braybrook and Lindblom, 1963) concluded that policies emerging from de-centralized bargaining (of interest groups) were probably more effective and representative than those arising from hierarchical governmental direction. Other scholars extended the pluralist view to Congress (Polsby, 1964), urban politics (Banfield, 1961), and the federal budget process (Wildavsky, 1964). Yet pluralism, so widely grounded in empirical political science 30 years ago, came under attack in the 1960s and was largely discredited by the 1970s. Because no other single theory of interest groups has achieved the widespread acceptance that pluralism attained, interest groups are now criticized as special interests who *undermine* democracy. We now turn to the major critics of plu-ralism and examine the primary weaknesses of pluralism.

THE PLURALIST CRITIQUE

Many political scientists were critical of the basic assumption of pluralism that in an open society like the United States all groups could organize and be heard. The antipluralist position derives from the work of many scholars who operate from different theoretical perspectives. Major theories we will discuss in this section include participatory democracy, party government, false-consciousness, structuralist, nondecision, community power, and rational choice (see Table 2-1).

Participatory Democracy

The earliest critiques of pluralism came from theorists of traditional democratic thought with its emphasis on the creation of a democratic com-munity. Pluralism, many early critics charged, is "elitist" and "apolitical" be-cause it places emphasis on democratic values *only* among leaders and not all citizens (McCoy and Playford, 1967). These critiques were normative ones, based upon the pluralist notion that pluralism, like behavioralism, was thought to be value-free. According to Jack Walker, one of the more prominent early critics, the "principal orienting values" of classic democratic theory aimed to provide a vision "of the ideal polity which men should strive to create," while pluralism, with its focus on realism, confuses apathy with democratic consent. Carole Pateman (1970), discussed earlier, bases her emphasis on participatory democracy on the normative assumption that all should participate, while in pluralism only the group leaders directly participate. Walker argues that plu-ralism ignores other "outlets for individual distress and frustration" like crime

---

[6]Recently, Robert Dahl has substantially revised his expectations for pluralism in his *Eco-nomic Theory of Democracy* (1985). Dahl argues that economic concentration limits participation.

TABLE 2-1
The Anti-Pluralist Critiques

Theory	Theorist	Assumption	Critique
Participatory Democracy	Jack Walker (1966) Carole Pateman (1970)	One learns to participate *by* participating	Only minority participates Pluralism masks hidden conservative agenda
Party Government	E. E. Schattschneider (1942, 1960) Sarah McCally Morehouse (1981)	Parties are unique custodians of democracy	Interest groups are inadequate to represent majority
Structuralist	Charles Lindblom (1977)	Government depends on business to produce wealth and jobs	Business groups are privileged
False Consciousness	William Connolly (1974) Steven Lukes (1974)	Thought and practice are linked; dominant interests control how interests are conceptualized	Business class avoids challenge by creating a "false consciousness"
Non-Decisions	Peter Bachrach and Morton Baratz (1962) Matthew Crenson (1971)	Dominant groups prevent issues from being considered	Pluralism only studies "one face of power"
Interest Group Liberalism	Theodore Lowi (1979)	Bargaining with interest groups creates resistance to change	Subgovernments dominate discrete policy areas
Community Power	Dennis Judd (1984)	Economic and social elites use voluntary associations to augment their power	Private decisions are not decided pluralistically
Rational Choice	Mancur Olson (1965)	Individuals are rational	Individuals will not support group goals over individual goals

and suicide as well as nontraditional forms of participation like social movements and the activities of elites to suppress conflict. For this reason, the pluralist model has conservative implications. The danger in ignoring strong evidence of mass discontent, Walker concludes, is that (pluralist) political scientists may "become sophisticated apologists for the existing political order" even when there is no true democratic consensus or real opportunities for participation (pp. 289–91).

Party Government

E. E. Schattschneider proffered one of the earliest critiques of pluralism in his seminal works *Party Government* (1942) and *The Semisovereign People* (1960). Schattschneider argued that pluralism excluded most of the population from representation. "The flaw in the pluralist heaven is that the heavenly chorus sings with a strong upper-class accent. Probably about 90 percent of the people cannot get into the pressure group system" (1960, p. 35). It is only the political party that seeks to represent the collective interests of society "because organization is the mobilization of bias" (1960, p. 71). Parties and pressure groups operate under different organizational strategies. Even those groups that represent nonbusiness interests, Schattschneider stresses, "reflect an upper-class tendency" (1960, p. 33) because it is the more well-off who join associations. Pressure groups cannot ensure democracy because the scope of the pressure system is limited, and it is biased toward one class in society.

Schattschneider did not oppose pressure groups. For him, they were the "raw material of politics" protected by the "greatest rights in the decalogue of American civil liberties: the right of free association, the right of petition, the right of freedom of speech and agitation," which resulted in political parties as well as interest groups (1942, p. 202). What Schattschneider took issue with was the pluralist notion that parties were mere aggregators of interests: "The majorities formed by the parties are never mere aggregates of special interests, i.e., the parties and pressure groups consist of two different kinds of syntheses of interests" (1942, p. 31). Political parties seek to control government by winning elections. To do this, they "must appeal to general interests and promote accommodations and compromises among many interests, special and general" (1942, p. 198). Pressure groups do not seek to win elections as do parties, but more importantly, they do "not attempt to persuade a majority." In his famous study of *Politics, Pressures and the Tariff* (1935), Schattschneider observed that groups achieved influence through campaign contributions and personal "insider" connections. Wealthier corporate groups that were able to afford experienced Washington lobbyists had an advantage over less wealthy but larger groups. This bias distorts the process of representation. Techniques of lobbying and pressure politics are methods "of short-circuiting the majority" (1942, p. 189).

Schattschneider identifies a number of differences between parties and interest groups evident in stable two-party systems like the United States.[7] First, parties mobilize majorities, while interest groups mobilize minorities. Second, parties are responsible, while interest groups are irresponsible. By this, Schattschneider means that parties are the "custodians of the right to mobilize majorities." Interest groups do not claim to represent the majority. Third, membership in an interest group is more demanding than membership in a political party. Pressure groups assume "that all members have a special (i.e., intense) interest," which allow them to lobby government on narrow (intensely held) issues. Interest groups represent intense minority interests. Fourth, "parties are mutually exclusive, while interest groups are not." By this, Schattschneider means that the parties oppose each other—one cannot be loyal to *both* the Democratic and Republican parties. Interest groups, by contrast, are characterized by overlapping memberships. For example, one may be both a feminist (usually associated with liberal ideology) and a member of the National Rifle Association (usually associated with conservative ideology). Fifth, interest groups are private associations, while party internal organization and recruitment have been heavily regulated by the states since the progressive era. Parties compete within the federal two-party system, while interest groups are not limited by "Calculations, numbers and politics, majorities, geographic representation, and the simplification of the alternatives. . . ." And sixth, "pressure groups, unlike parties, are not subjected to a compulsory periodic public test of their strength in an election" (1942, pp. 198–99). Because of these distinctions, Schattschneider argues that democracy cannot be protected solely by interest groups, so pluralism is greatly flawed as a theory of politics.

Schattschneider's critique of pluralism was theoretical. His themes are echoed in Sarah McCally Morehouse's (1981) survey of pressure groups in the states (see Boxes 2-5 to 2-7). Morehouse found 22 states in which pressure groups were quite strong, 18 in which pressure groups were moderately strong, and 10 in which pressure groups were weak. Interest groups are most powerful in those states dominated by a single large company, corporation or interest group, and in rural, sparsely populated states. Interest groups are weaker in those states with large diversified economies and many different groups and organizations.

> Typical of the weak party states are parties that are nothing but holding companies for the diverse groups that contest under the party label. Politics in those states tend to be a politics of personalities, not issues. The party as an issue-oriented organization does not exist; party labels are meaningless. (Morehouse, 1981, p. 118)

With multiple interest groups, government leaders can play one group off

---

[7]In multiparty systems, parties begin to resemble interest groups in the mobilization of a minority.

BOX 2-5
**States in Which Pressure Groups Are
Strong (22)**

Alabama	Farm Bureau Federation, utilities, highway interests, Associated Industries of Alabama
Alaska	Oil, salmon, mining, contracting, labor unions, Chamber of Commerce
Arkansas	Transport, agriculture, utilities, natural resource (oil, timber, bauxite), insurance, local government (County Judges Association, Arkansas Municipal League), labor, Chamber of Commerce, Arkansas Free Enterprise Association
Florida	Associated Industries, utilities (Florida Power Corporation, Florida Power and Light), Farm Bureau, bankers, liquor interests, chain stores, race tracks, Phosphate Council
Georgia	Atlanta business group, Citizens and Southern Bank, Coca-Cola, Fuqua Industries, Delta Airlines, Trust Company of Georgia, Woodruff Foundation, education lobby, Georgia Municipal Association
Hawaii	Big Five Companies: C. Brewer and Co., Ltd. (sugar, molasses, insurance ranching); Thro. H. Davis and Co. (sugar, merchandising, foreign investment); Amfac, Inc. (sugar and merchandising); Castle and Coke, Inc. (sugar, pineapple, bananas, seafood, coffee, macadamia nuts, discount stores, steamship agent in Hawaii, land development, and property management); Alexander and Baldwin, Inc. (docks and warehouses, sugar, pineapples, merchandising); Dillingham Corporation (construction)
Iowa	Farm Bureau Federation, truckers
Kentucky	Coal companies, Jockey Club, liquor interests, tobacco interests, Kentucky Education Association, rural electric cooperatives.
Louisiana	Oil companies (Exxon, Chevron, Texaco, Gulf, Shell, Mobile, Mid-Continental Oil and Gas Association), gas pipeline interests, Louisiana Chemical Association, forest industry, rice industry, Louisiana Manufacturers Association, Farm Bureau, AFL-CIO

BOX 2-5 (*continued*)

Mississippi	Mississippi Economic Council, Farm Bureau, manufacturers association, medical association, public school teachers, association of local officials (county supervisors, mayors, sheriffs, etc.), segregationist groups (Citizens' Council, John Birch Society, Association for Preservation of the White Race, Women for Constitutional Government)
Montana	Anaconda Copper Company, Montana Power Company, State Chamber of Commerce, Northern Pacific Railroad, Great Northern Railroad
Nebraska	Farm Bureau, Omaha National Bank, Northern Natural Gas Company, Union Pacific Railroad, Northwest Bell Telephone, education lobby
New Hampshire	Public utilities, paper manufacturing, lumber, race track lobby
New Mexico	Oil and gas, school teachers, liquor dealers, banks, truckers, cattlemen, business groups
North Carolina	Textile, tobacco, furniture, utilities, banks, teachers
Oklahoma	Phillips Petroleum, Kerr-McGee, other oil companies (Texaco, Mobile, Humble, Atlantic-Sinclair, Sunray, DX Division, Hess Oil), transportation companies, power companies, local public officials
Oregon	Utilities (Pacific Power and Light, Portland General Electric), lumber companies, public school (Oregon Education Association), railroads and truckers, organized labor (AFL-CIO, Teamsters, Longshoremen), Farm Bureau, Agricultural Association, insurance lobby
South Carolina	Planters, textiles (DuPont, Stevens, Deering-Milliken, Fiberglass, Textron Chemstrand, Lowenstein, Burlington, Bowaters), Electric and Gas Company, banks
Tennessee	Manufacturers association, County Services Association, Farm Bureau, Municipal League, Education Association, liquor lobby
Texas	Chemical Council, Mid-Continent Oil and Gas Association, Independent Producers and Royalty Owners, State Teachers' Association, Manufacturers' Association, medical association, Motor Transport Association, insurance organizations

Washington	Boeing Aircraft, Teamsters, government employees, school teachers, AFL-CIO, highway interests (oil, asphalt, contractors, car builders), timber, banking, commercial fishing, pinballs, public and private power, gravel, wine and beer, Grange
West Virginia	Union Carbide, Bethlehem Steel, Occidental Petroleum, Georgia, Baltimore and Ohio Railroad, Norfolk and Western Railway Company, Chesapeake and Ohio Railway Company, United Mine Workers

Adapted from *State Politics, Parties and Policy* by Sarah M. Morehouse, 1981, Holt, Rinehart and Winston. Used with permission of the author.

against another. Further, Morehouse concludes, "strong parties can control the entry of pressures into the government" (1981, p. 118). Note that Morehouse's research suggests that the phenomenon of *hyperpluralism* so feared by pluralist mass society theorists actually leads to stronger party organizations.

Structuralist Critique

Conservative Charles Lindblom (an early contributor to pluralist theory) provides the *structuralist critique*. In is book *Politics and Markets* (1977) Lindblom points out that even without a "pressure system," the market economy places limitations on what government can do. In a capitalist economy, it is private business that creates wealth, jobs, and high employment—not the government. Since businessmen are entrusted with these responsibilities, government must provide an environment that will encourage businessmen to have confidence and invest in the economy. Thus, the government will defer to business without pressure. It is business that must be encouraged, not government.

False Consciousness Critique

False consciousness is a concept used to explain how individuals might be apathetic, or uninvolved in politics even when they have real problems or grievances. The notion of false consciousness, while initially derived from the writings of Karl Marx, is used widely even among non-marxists as well as marxists.[8] Non-marxist political philosopher William Connolly (1974) criticizes

[8]Theoretical grounding for the notion of false consciousness is also derived from linguistic philosophy, and in the Freudian model of interpretation, in which truths must be accepted by the patient for them to be valid explanations. This has given rise to two alternative social science models apart from behavioralism: interpretive and critical (Fay, 1975).

BOX 2-6
States in Which Pressure Groups Are Moderately Strong (18)

Arizona	Copper companies (Phelps Dodge), oil companies, farm groups, Arizona Power Company, "school lobby," liquor lobby
California	Pacific Gas and Electric, Standard Oil of California, Bank of America, California Teachers Association, Lockheed Aircraft, Transamerica, Kern County Land Company, Bankers Association of America, California Real Estate Association, California Growers Association, University of California, AFL-CIO
Delaware	DuPont Chemical Company, insurance lobby
Idaho	Idaho Power Company, Idaho Farm Bureau, stockmen, mining and forest industries, railroads, county courthouses, Mormon Church, Idaho Education Association, AFL-CIO
Illinois	Illinois Manufacturers Association, Illinois Chamber of Commerce, coal operators, insurance companies (State Farm and Allstate), Illinois Education Association, Illinois Medical Society, AFL-CIO unions (Steelworkers), retail merchants, race tracks, Farm Bureau, Chicago Tribune
Indiana	AFL-CIO, Farm Bureau, Indiana State Teachers' Association, Chamber of Commerce
Kansas	Banks, power companies, timber, pipeline companies, railroads, Farm Bureau
Maine	Big three: electric power, timber, textile and shoe manufacturing; Farm Bureau; Grange; liquor and beer lobby; horse-racing lobby; conservation groups

pluralism because of the critical link between thought and political action. Connolly stresses that the "language of politics is not a neutral medium that conveys ideas independently formed; it is an institutionalized structure of meanings that channels political thought and action in certain directions" (p. 1). The problem, Connolly argues, centers around the interpretation of the "unexpressed and latent preferences of the underclass in American society" (1974, p. 52). Pluralists like Nelson Polsby assume that "people partic-

Maryland	Bankers, industrialists, AFL-CIO, liquor lobby
Missouri	Missouri Farmers Association, AFL-CIO, Missouri Bus and Truck Association, Teamsters, Missouri State Teachers Association, brewers
Nevada	Gambling, utilities, banks, mining, livestock, insurance, railroads
Ohio	Insurance, banking, utilities, savings and loan associations, Chamber of Commerce
Pennsylvania	Steel companies (U.S. Steel, Republic, Jones and Laughlin, Bethlehem); oil companies (Standard, Gulf, Sun, Atlantic); public utilities; service industries; Pennsylvania State Teachers Association; Welfare Rights Organization; AFL-CIO
South Dakota	Farmers Union, rural co-ops and rural electrification interests, Farm Bureau, Chamber of Commerce, banks, South Dakota Wheat Growers Association, South Dakota Stockgrowers Association, Northern States Power, Homestake Mine, liquor lobby
Utah	Utah Mining Association, Utah Manufacturers Association, Utah Industrial Council, Utah Farm Bureau Federation, Salt Lake City Chamber of Commerce, Utah Education Association, AFL-CIO, Farmers Union
Vermont	Farm Bureau, Associated Industries of Vermont
Virginia	Virginia Electric Power, Virginia Manufacturers Association, Chamber of Commerce, railroads
Wyoming	Wyoming Stock Growers Association, Rocky Mountain Oil and Gas Association, Farm Bureau Federation, Wyoming Education Association, Wyoming Association of Municipalities, Union Pacific Railroad, truckers

Adapted from *State Politics, Parties and Policy* by Sarah M. Morehouse, 1981, Holt, Rinehart and Winston. Used with permission of the author.

ipate in those areas *they care about the most*" (1959, p. 235), with the result that the underclass is not considered to *have* any preferences unless they participate. In doing so, Steven Lukes (1974) argues pluralism has defined away a central facet of political life: certain groups are able to protect their interests by shaping and controlling how opposing groups define their interests. For example, if American workers agree with Dwight Eisenhower's Secretary of

BOX 2-7
**States in Which Pressure Groups Are
Weak (10)**

Colorado	Colorado Cattlemen's Association, Denver financial interests, oilmen, Chamber of Commerce billboard interests, Colorado Education Association, Colorado Municipal League, AFL-CIO, Colorado Farmers Union, League of Women Voters
Connecticut	Connecticut Manufacturers Association, insurance lobby, Farm Bureau Federation, Grange, AFL-CIO
Massachusetts	Labor, Roman Catholic Church, public utility interests, real estate lobby, Associated Industries of Massachusetts, Chamber of Commerce, insurance companies, Massachusetts Federation of Taxpayer's Association, racetrack interests, state employees, liquor interests
Michigan	General Motors, Ford, Chrysler, American Motors, United Automobile Workers, AFL-CIO
Minnesota	Railroad Association, 3M, Dayton Hudson Corporation, Northern States Power Company, Honeywell, Northwestern Bell Telephone, banking, beer, iron mining, liquor, Minnesota Education Association, Teamsters, Minnesota Association of Commerce and Industry, AFL-CIO, Farm Bureau, Farm Union, League of Women Voters

Defense, Charles E. Wilson that "what is good for General Motors is good for America," then workers will not defend their own interests as valid ones.

Nondecisions Critique

One of the more devastating critiques of pluralism (also from the left) is that of *nondecisions*. Peter Bachrach and Morton S. Baratz (1962) provided the theoretical critique in their elucidation of the "two faces of power." Pluralism, they contend, only studies one face of power—decisions "on the table," or those already in the public arena. What is *not* studied are those decisions that are forcibly kept "off the table"—the ones that are never publicly considered. This can happen through political socialization, which prevents individuals from recognizing their needs as legitimate (similar to Lukes' false consciousness), anticipatory actions taken by subordinates or public officials to avoid bringing an issue to the attention of elected officials, and direct action to keep an issue "off the table." What differentiates Bachrach and Baratz from

New Jersey	Johnson and Johnson, Warner-Lambert Pharmaceuticals, Prudential Insurance, Campbell's Soup, Becton Dickinson, First National State Bank in Newark, New Jersey Manufacturers Association, Hess Oil, Garden State Race Track, New Jersey Farm Bureau, New Jersey Education Association, Chamber of Commerce, AFL-CIO
New York	Education lobby (Board of Regents, N.Y. State Teachers' Association, N.Y. Federation of Teachers), Associated Industries of New York, Empire State Chamber of Commerce, Bankers Association, AFL-CIO, Teamsters, state medical association, Roman Catholic Church, New York City Lobby
North Dakota	Education lobby (North Dakota Education Association, PTA, School Boards, Department of Public Instruction), Farmers Unions, Farm Bureau, North Dakota Stockmen's Association, Association of Rural Cooperatives
Rhode Island	AFL-CIO, Associated Industries of Rhode Island, insurance companies, public utilities, banks, racetrack associations
Wisconsin	AFL-CIO, United Auto Workers, business interests, Farmers' Union, liquor lobby, local public officials

Adapted from *State Politics, Parties and Policy* by Sarah M. Morehouse, 1981, Holt, Rinehart and Winston. Used with permission of the author.

Lukes is that they assume that groups may seek to push their interests, but it is the actions of the dominant groups which keep important issues *off* the table. Matthew Crenson provided one of the more interesting empirical analyses of nondecisions in his study *The Un-Politics of Air Pollution* (1971). Crenson compared the different policies toward air pollution in Chicago, Illinois, and Gary, Indiana, two adjoining communities with similar air pollution problems. Crenson found that while Chicago dealt with air pollution as a political issue, Gary did not, primarily because of the power of private elites.

Community Power Critique

The concept of community power as dominated by an economic elite remains an attractive theory, despite the early rebuttal by pluralists. Many potentially governmental functions remain in the private sphere. Those who study urban and state government stress the critical role of private power in the cities. While municipal reformers of the progressive era sought to limit the local party machine and the scope of politics in city government, economic and social elites shifted their activity from the public sphere—government—to the private sphere—voluntary groups.

> The function of status allocation and recognition once had been fulfilled by public officeholding, in the "golden age" when patricians dominated city affairs. In the industrial city, new ways of fulfilling those functions had to be devised. Beginning about the turn of the century, there was a proliferation of private institutions that served to enhance the influence of the upper class. (Judd, 1984, p. 111)

Social welfare (e.g., the American Red Cross, family welfare, and charity) and cultural functions (symphony, museums, and libraries) were all the purview of local community groups. Research on a number of large cities, according to Dennis Judd, indicates that these groups served as social-screening devices for those with proper credentials, including race, "wealth, occupational status, family and religion" (1984, p. 112).

Interest Group Liberalism Critique

Yet another attack came from those who argued that interest groups had become too powerful—in particular Theodore Lowi's charge of "interest group liberalism." The major difficulty with pluralism is that it does not recognize the difficulties new interests have in gaining entry into the policy process. When lobbying groups arise to defend their interests and government begins bargaining with these groups, these groups gain privileged access, which limits the entry of new groups. For Lowi and others like Jack Walker (1966), pluralism justifies the status quo. A concept which captures many of these points is the *subgovernment model*. The subgovernment model appeared as early as 1939 when Ernest Griffith critiqued "policy whirlpools" in his *Impasse of Democracy*. While "whirlpools" did not prove a popular term, the concept did, surviving under many different names: *iron triangles, triple alliances, cozy little triangles*, and *subgovernments*. The concept of subgovernment (or iron triangle) is commonly presented in most introductory textbooks as characteristic of policymaking. Subgovernments consist of a cozy consensual and mutually supportive arrangement between a congressional subcommittee, a government bureau or agency, and an interest group that dominates policymaking in a narrow policy area. Each tripod of the triangle agrees on supporting the policy in question (such as price support for sugar production) with little or no conflict or opposition from opposing groups. Subgovernments represent a monopoly over the policy process with little interference by either the president, political parties, or Congress as a whole. Each element in the subgovernment offers key resources (funding, information, or favorable rules of laws) necessary to the others. Policy is made independently or even in contradiction of other policies (made by other subgovernments). An example of a subgovernment would be the tobacco lobby, the tobacco subcommittee in the Agricultural Committee, and the tobacco desk in the Department of Agriculture. The cooperative nature of policymaking within each subgovernment means a biased policy in favor of the political interest—in this case, the continuance of tobacco subsidies. Congress as a whole and the president cannot influence this process, which occurs at the subgovernment level, particularly as the congressional subcommittee members, the bureaucrats, and the lobbyists are permanent fixtures in Washington, while presidents come and go. In particular, partisan conflict is absent as both Democrats and Republicans agree on support for their narrow policy area. The concept of subgovernment means that party government is impossible when interest groups are powerful. Subgovernments are noteworthy because they attack the pluralist stress of issues "on the table"—those brought to government for resolution.

Logic of Collective Action Critique

The foremost challenge to pluralism, however, came from economist Mancur Olson. In 1965, Olson's *The Logic of Collective Action* was published. Olson's theory assumed that humans were rational, unlike Truman, who viewed humans as social and psychological beings. Olson attacked the very attractiveness of pluralism. He argued that it was not the empirical theory that Truman (and others) presented it as. Instead, it was only a political theory— one closely tied to political philosophy—despite the attempt to be more scientific. Olson was particularly critical of the assumption that potential or latent groups will organize whenever there is reason to do so. The pluralists mistakenly disparaged organization over potential or latent interests. What is critical is *actual groups*. Olson distinguished between selective and collective types of incentives. Collective incentives give rise to the famous *free rider* problem. *Collective goods* or goals are changes in public policy that are indivisible and available to anyone regardless of whether they worked for the goal or not. Examples of collective goods include clean air, affirmative action, and maternity leave. Collective goals are often understood ideologically because they involve reliance on the government. *Selective incentives* are only available to those who participate in a group. Selective incentives can be social (the friendship of associating with like-minded people) or material (an economic incentive that can be measured in dollars). Many organizations provide social benefits to their members. In addition, many provide economic incentives by offering professional benefits (subscription to a journal, information about the profession, job opportunities, etc.) or services at a reduced cost (cheaper car insurance, lower rates on credit cards, etc.). What is particularly undemocratic is that one may join a group for selective benefits, but the organization may use the strength of their numbers to support collective or ideological goals.

Michael Best and William Connolly (1987) provide a good example of the free rider problem by considering the purchase of a pollution control abatement device (see Figure 2-2). If the individual buys a pollution control abatement device for his car but no one else buys it, then the air pollution problem will remain serious and the individual will have paid the cost without obtaining the benefit. That is the worst possible circumstance. On the other hand, if the individual does not buy the device but everyone else does, then the individual has obtained the benefit (clean air) without paying the cost. This is the best possible circumstance.

Based upon rational choice theory, Olson argues that the bigger the group, the more the free rider problem applies. This is *Olson's law of large groups*. Based on this law, Olson pointed out three illogical assumptions made by pluralism.

> **Pluralist Illogic No. 1:** *Participation in groups is universal and individuals will join groups to further their interests.* Olson argues that if individuals are interested in their own welfare, they will not make any sacrifices to help a group attain political (i.e., public or collective) goals.
>
> **Pluralist Illogic No. 2:** *Small and large groups are similar—they attract members for the same reasons.* Olson argues that small groups are better than large groups. Small, privileged and intermediate groups attract members for different reasons than large, latent groups due to the free rider problem. For large latent groups, an individual's support is not decisive, and they will get the benefit anyway. Purely political organizations cannot induce members to work for collective goals. Lobbying, for Olson, is only a by-product of the capacity to coerce or persuade individuals to join *for other selective incentives that give an individual benefit.* Therefore, groups purporting to represent large latent interests do not in fact do so because their members have joined not in support of group or collective goals,

Figure 2-2   Individual Versus Collective Rationality In the Purchase of Pollution Abatement Devices

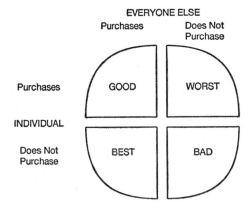

Source: Best and Connolly, 1987, p. 82.

but because of some individual benefit unrelated to the public good sought by the group.

Pluralist Illogic No. 3: *Groups will counterorganize and attain an balance.* Olson argues that the equilibrium of groups is fallacious—outcomes are *not* symmetrical. Smaller groups are better organized and defeat larger groups. Three factors greatly limit the size of a group: (1) The larger the group, the smaller the fraction of the group that will benefit. (2) The larger the group, the smaller the share of each. This raises the problem of getting enough of a reward to "reimburse" each member for the individual costs of their joining the group. (3) The larger the group, the greater the organizational costs. There are special costs attached to organizing a large group: the costs of communicating with members, bargaining with members to attain a consensus, and creating, staffing, and maintaining an organization.

Olson predicts that no large group will be ideological. This applies to potential conservative as well as liberal groups. For example, Olson predicts that the national Chamber of Commerce will never become an effective lobbying force, just as he would predict the same for liberal groups. Interestingly, Olson and the pluralists were describing the same political system of the 1950s—nonideological parties and nonideological interest groups. Both Olson's rational choice theory and pluralist theory predicted low levels of party and interest group conflict. But Olson's theory was empirical, and provided little solace that the United States pressure group system provided for democracy.

Assessing the Antipluralist Critique

Pluralism has been attacked by theorists of all ideological persuasions and from a variety of different theoretical perspectives. Even Charles Lindblom and Robert Dahl, two early pluralists, have recanted key pluralist assumptions. Yet pluralism remains attractive to some of the most respected scholars in American politics—Edward Banfield, Austin Ranney, Nelson Polsby, and others. To make sense of pluralism and the antipluralist position, it is important to separate the *empirical* theory of pluralism from the *political* or *normative* theory of pluralism. Normative theories state what ought to be, while empirical theories state what is.

EMPIRICAL THEORY OF PLURALISM RECONSIDERED. None of the antipluralists have attacked any of the basic assumptions of how values and attitudes are formed. The central role of the group in the early socialization process of the young child and in the daily life of the adult is unassailed. And as we shall see in Chapter 5, the concept of group remains vitally useful in understanding the development of the contemporary social movement. Many of the antipluralist writers have been found to agree with James Madison that interests are necessary to liberty and ought not to be banned. Thus, while the early work of the Robert Dahl (the political theory of pluralism) has been attacked, the work of David Truman (the empirical theory of pluralism) stands as a fundamental statement of how interests develop and change.

Olson's rational choice theory did, however, attack the pluralist notion that potential group members will form or join an actual (i.e., organized) group to pursue group goals. For most political scientists, Olson's theory was completely persuasive. But events have proved his theory lacking. For the civil rights movement, which began in the 1950s, and the women's rights movement of the 1960s *did* organize for collective goals—events we will discuss more thoroughly in Chapter 5. And the national Chamber of Commerce has become more active, cohesive, and effective in pursuing collective ideological goals on behalf of business. Jack Walker (1983), a noted political scientist, has concluded that none of the major interest group theorists

> offer convincing explanations of the changing composition of the group struc-ture in the United States. The political system is beset by a swarm of organi-zational bumblebees that are busily flying about in spite of the fact that political scientists cannot explain how they manage it. (p. 397)

Just as science cannot explain how bumblebees fly given their poor aerody-namic physique, political scientists relying on pluralist or rational choice the-ories have been found wanting in their ability to explain how purposive groups have organized in the past three decades.

POLITICAL THEORY OF PLURALISM RECONSIDERED. The antipluralists have leveled devastating critiques on the contribution of interest groups to de-mocracy. In particular, the antipluralists have convincingly demonstrated that interest groups are inadequate as mobilizers of majorities, and that the con-stellation of established interest groups limits access by new groups. Ironically, these criticisms carry considerably less weight in the context of recent changes in American politics.

A number of dramatic changes have taken place in the national con-stellation of interest groups over the past three decades. Interest group schol-ars have identified an explosion in the interest group advocacy system. First, older groups have become more active and more professionalized in lobbying government. Business has always been active in lobbying government. In the past, very few firms had offices in Washington. Studies of business found that over half (63%) of the corporate public affairs departments had upgraded their offices and increased their staffs between 1975 and 1980, while among 400 firms with offices in Washington, about half had started those offices between 1970 and 1980 (Berry, 1984, p. 21). Further, the number of Wash-ington lawyers (whose practice is primarily lobbying) increased dramatically over the same period.

Second, new groups have formed with increasing frequency. Jack Walker's (1983) survey of 564 lobbying organizations indicates that about one-third of them originated between 1960 and 1980. Another study by Kay Schlozman and John Tierney (1986) found that about 40% of lobbying groups organized after 1960 and 25% after 1970. Jeffrey Berry's (1977) study of 83 citizen's or public interest groups found that about half (47%) had formed just in the 5 years between 1968 and 1972. Of course, these figures are somewhat over-stated because they do not include groups that had ceased to exist by the time of the survey, but by every measure the past three decades have resulted in a vast increase in the activities and numbers of interest groups.

There are a number of critical changes in the pressure groups system as a consequence. First, open conflict is increased among interest groups. A major study by Robert Salisbury and colleagues (1987) found that a survey of agricultural, health, labor, and energy policymaking showed that about 75% of interest group lobbyists cited other lobbies as their adversaries. Second, recent research has found that partisan change does affect access to policy-makers. Mark Peterson and Jack Walker (1986) found that the replacement of Democratic President Jimmy Carter by Republican President Ronald Reagan in 1980 resulted in a dramatic reversal of access for groups. Instead of contacts established in "politically isolated subgovernments . . . [persisting] no matter what the outcome of the election," interest groups found that it "was difficult to build such safe enclaves around a group's favorite programs in the 1980s" (p. 172).

Pluralists like Nelson Polsby (1983a) have been critical of the new con-stellation of interest groups. Because the new groups do not fit neatly into the pluralist paradigm, pluralist theorists have chosen to interpret the increase in citizens groups as an increase in single-issue groups. This interpretation allows these groups to be explained via mass society theory. Single-issue groups, based as they are on issues, rather than traditional communal or ethnic iden-tifications, derive from erratic emotional concerns of socially atomized indi-viduals. Therefore, for pluralist theorists, the new citizens' groups do not have to be understood as a new phenomenon. Insofar as individuals at the mass level are not thought capable of informed issue judgments, the new activism and the "organizational bumblebees" can be understood as a degeneration of pluralism. These groups are then criticized as undermining political leader-ship. Instead of applauding these new groups as proving the pluralist concept of potential groups organizing for group goals, pluralist theorists have at-tacked them as dangerous extremist groups which make pragmatic compro-mise impossible.

Understanding contemporary changes in interest groups has also proved difficult for critics of pluralism. Jeffrey Berry, a scholar specializing in interest groups, is highly critical of the subgovernment model as no longer descriptive of most policymaking. In contrast to the hyperpluralist position, Berry (1989a) stresses that the rapid increase in the number of interest groups does not result in hyperpluralism because

more interest groups do not simply mean bigger subgovernments. Bargaining becomes more complex, control and coordination by key actors becomes more difficult, boundaries become harder to define, and the likelihood of conflict between competing coalitions increases. (p. 239, emphasis added)

As Berry notes, a number of scholars specializing in the study of interest groups have been questioning the utility of the subgovernment model since Hugh Heclo proposed an alternative model in 1978. Heclo suggested that a better conceptualization is that of the "issue network." Issue networks are more competitive, work in the open, and involve large coalitions of shifting interests, which involve strong partisan competition. Why has the outdated model of subgovernments proved so popular despite the fact that it no longer describes comtemporary politics? Berry concludes that "political scientists have had difficulty abandoning subgovernments because they fit so well within a dominant paradigm of interest group politics" (1989a, p. 240). This dominant paradigm is antipluralist. "Since the publication of *Who Governs?* considerable effort has been devoted to disproving its pluralist argument that democratic ends are reached through the bargaining and compromise of affected interests in an open political system (Berry, 1989a, p. 256). Berry is concerned about the dominance of the antipluralist values in political science because the values of these political scientists make them *misunderstand the nature of interest group conflict over public policy.* While Berry does not use the term "progressive," he is critical of the view that private interests dominate policymaking—a view that characterizes progressivism as well as the concept of subgovernment he is criticizing.

DO INTEREST GROUPS CONTRIBUTE
TO DEMOCRACY?

It is commonplace to learn in textbooks that we are suffering from *hyper-pluralism*—pluralism "gone sour" with too many interests in politics—and that American political parties are declining as a result. The textbook model of parties that we will introduce in Chapter 3 views the relationship between parties and interests as a competitive one: if interest groups are too strong, then parties are weak. This is a overly simplistic notion. Just as air is a necessary condition to make a fire (oxygen is essential), but not a sufficient condition *by itself* for a burning fire to appear, interest groups appear to be necessary but not sufficient for democracy. What is unfortunate about this assumed conflict—as Morehouse's work demonstrates—is that the strength of political parties *precisely* depends upon the diversity of groups and the quality of group participation in politics.

The increased partisanship and open conflict of major interest groups brings considerable optimism to discussions over the prospects for democracy. However, what the prospects for democracy involve do not change the laws of interest group behavior (such as the tendency toward oligarchy), nor do they make interest groups better equipped to represent majorities. The tactics of interest groups remain the same—they still seek to circumvent majorities by appealing to elected officials over the heads of the public. However, the increase in the number of interest groups and the increase in the openness of their conflict provides greater scope for the political party—the "custodian" of the right to mobilize majorities. Thus, while the antipluralists are misplaced in their pessimism, the stress on political parties as critical and unique to democracy remains an important insight. Interestingly, as we shall see in detail later, the pluralist defenders have not viewed the changing interest group structure as positive. Instead, pluralists view the increased conflict and participation with alarm as indicative of the breakdown of American politics into a mass society. The key problem for pluralists is that they had predicted that groups would moderate political views, and they therefore had no theoretical handle with which to understand interest groups that were ideological and competitive, and in particular, they were incapable of distinguishing traditional insider interest groups from the new social movements. But that is another story for another chapter.

chapter 3

Political Parties and Democracy

[P]olitical parties created democracy . . . modern democracy is unthinkable except in terms of parties.

E. E. Schattschneider

In this chapter we discuss the contribution of political parties, voting, and party competition to democracy. The notion that voting *is* democracy is widely held in the United States. To party theorists, this notion is misleading because it is mechanistic and ignores the crucial role of the party *organization* in forming and defining public opinion, recruiting leaders, and offering choices on important public issues. Voting is perhaps a minimum necessary condition for democratic government. More important, the denial of voting rights to persons because of group-level characteristics (e.g., gender, race, or other outgroup status) is unquestionably undemocratic. For party theorists, however, what is most important for democratic governance is *genuine party competition*. The critical theoretical question thus becomes how party competition guarantees democracy, an issue on which diverse theorists have disagreed.

Political party theorists are in agreement that party competition is essential to democracy. Because parties are central to democracy, theorists whose primary study is not political parties—pluralists and others—have also discussed the relationship of parties to democracy. Because pluralist and progressive writers draw upon different theoretical perspectives and base their work on opposing definitions of democracy, it is important to consider how party theorists argue that democracy is served by party government. In particular, why is it that genuine party competition develops in some areas and not others? Key issues dividing theorists include (1) the role of the public and the place of voting in a democracy, (2) the role of third parties in party competition, (3) interpretations of the progressive era, (4) whether responsible parties are appropriate to the American context, and (5) the strength of contemporary political parties. Before considering alternative views, we will first consider the views of those scholars who specialize in political parties. In particular, we will focus on the work of V. O. Key and E. E. Schattschneider in some depth. Both Key and Schattschneider favored party government and were critics of progressivism, yet neither was a pluralist.

PARTY COMPETITION AND DEMOCRACY

Party competition has varied across the United States by region. Generally, parties have been considered strongest in the East and Middle West and quite weak in the South and the West. As we shall consider later in this chapter, party government failed in the South after the Civil War and particularly with the development of the one-party South in the late 1800s. By contrast, true parties with a genuine mass base never developed in the West. Of course, most states in the West entered the Union after the Civil War ended and therefore were not engaged in the same conflicts as the North and the South. Put another way, the new states of the West did not divide on national issues.

The West differed in important ways from both the South and the North. It was more agricultural and less industrially developed, it experienced rapid population shifts and a more migratory and unstable population, and it was more sparsely settled, with smaller differences between the cities and the countryside. Compared to the East, the West was also less in need of the simplification of the party machine: school attendance and literacy were much higher, and there were more professionals than east of the Mississippi. Further, the West was never as pivotal as the South in American politics. Parties with an electoral base never developed in the West. The early "parties"—particularly in California—were dominated by the railroad and mining interests. In California, the Central Pacific Railroad sought to control public officials to further their economic interests—an economic goal, not a political one. The Central Pacific Railroad focused on the convention system, not electoral and mass politics, and worked through controlling officials via the existing party labels. Ironically, this not only made parties weak, but also rendered the political system all the more vulnerable to the progressive reform impulse in the late 1800s (Gimpel, 1991).

The West raises an interesting issue—when is a party not a true "party"? "If," as William Nisbet Chambers (1967) reminds us, "the beginning of wisdom is to call things by their right names, [then] some attention is due to what we mean by a political party and by a party system" (p. 5) and it is crucial to begin with some basic definitions.

What Is a Political Party?

Party government theorists like Key and Schattschneider have viewed parties as very distinctive social formations. Chambers provides the most concise definition of a political party based upon the views of traditional political party theorists (see Box 3-1). *Party systems* are made up of political parties. What makes them systems is that they are comprised of relatively durable patterns of interactions between two or more political parties. Because of its durability, each party must consider the other party in its bid for political power. This results in a stability in the pattern of competition between the two (or more) political parties. A *political party* is a group or social formation characterized by linkage, symbols of identification, and in-group perspectives. In other words, parties reflect a political culture with distinct world views. Parties link leaders and followers in the public. Parties are unique as organizations because they seek power in government. Political parties are to be distinguished from *factions*—shifting groups of competing elites who are *not* linked to popular followings. Factions often compete on the basis of personal ties and personalities, not because of differences in philosophies of government or differences in political culture.

The Significance of Party Government

Both Key and Schattschneider were in considerable agreement over what party government entailed. Party government was based on competitive parties. According to Schattschneider, "democracy is a competitive political system

---

BOX 3-1

PARTY SYSTEMS

- Are based in durable patterns of interactions and conflict between social groups
- Include *at least* two political parties as units which
  Compete against each other in electoral and governing institutions and result in predictable consequences and behavior among party leaders

THE POLITICAL PARTY

- Exhibits a structure or organization
- Links leaders to a popular following
- Generates in-group perspectives and symbols of party identification among leaders and followers
- Contests elections
- Seeks offices and power in government

Source: Adapted from Chambers, 1967, pp. 6–7.

BOX 3-2
E. E. Schattschneider (1892–1971)

E. E. Schattschneider was described by his colleagues at Wesleyan University as a "seminal writer on American politics, compelling teacher, irrepressible raconteur, guiding force in professional associations, and political activist" (Greenstein and Vose, 1971). His major works included *Politics, Pressures and the Tariff* (1935), *Party Government* (1942), and *Semisovereign People* (1960). Schattschneider consistently criticized interest groups as insufficient for democracy; they not only circumvent majoritarian processes, which are the hallmark of parties, but they have a pro-business and upper-class bias. He combined this with a great respect for the average citizen, believing that only parties provided for democracy — a "collaboration of ignorant people and experts" (1960, p. 137). Schattschneider stressed the role of conflict and power in his work, arguing that parties fail democracy when they are characterized by sectionalism and localism. As Chair of the Committee on Political Parties of the American Political Science Association in 1950, Schattschneider endorsed the reform of American political parties to make them more issue-oriented, national, and responsible. In assessing his own work, Schattschneider concluded that "I suppose the most important thing I have done in my field is that I have talked longer, harder and more persistently and enthusiastically about political parties than anyone else alive" (Adamany, 1975, p. xviii). Schattschneider, while a distinguished political scientist who served as president of the American Political Science Association (1956–57), chose to devote himself to undergraduate teaching at Wesleyan College for the bulk of his career.

in which competing leaders and organizations define the alternatives of public policy in such a way that the public can participate in the decision-making process" (1960, p. 141). When competition did not exist — either in nonpartisan elections, or in one-party states — democracy suffered. For Schattschneider, American democracy was founded on the separation of economic and political power. Political power represents a countervailing power to vested economic interests. Schattschneider asserts that the problem with one-party politics is that it "tends strongly to vest political power in the hands of people who already have economic power" (1975, p. 78).

Key's work offers similar themes, although it is somewhat more difficult to draw the same type of theoretical generalizations. As Walter D. Burnham concludes, "His theorizing, his genius more generally, had a strikingly *intuitive* character" (1988, p. 4). Key considered parties "a basic element of democratic institutional apparatus," which perform the essential functions of managing succession to power and obtaining public consent—or if necessary, attracting or organizing "discontent and dissatisfaction sufficient to oust the government" (1964, p. 9). In his monumental study of southern politics, Key found that business interests can unite more effectively in one-party factional systems.

> The grand objective of the haves is obstruction. . . . Organization is not always necessary to obstruct; it is essential, however, for the promotion of a sustained program in behalf of the have-nots. . . . over the long run the have-nots lose in a disorganized politics. (1949, p. 307)

Moreover, without the resources, support, and protection of an organized party, individual legislators can more easily be "bought" by established interests.

Schattschneider stressed the differences between pressure groups, which seek to mobilize minorities, and parties, which seek to mobilize majorities and therefore had a special role as makers of government (see Box 3-3). There are important similarities between fluid factions in a one-party system and interest groups. The parties will be more accountable because, if nothing else,

---

BOX 3-3
Schattschneider's Party Theory: Differences Between Interest Groups and Political Parties

Interest Groups	*Political Parties*
Mobilize minorities	Mobilize majorities
Seek only to influence government on narrow issues	Makers of government a bid for power
Irresponsible—lobbying and pressure tactics circumvent popular majorities	Responsible—power depends on persuading a majority of voters
Members share a strong narrow interest, pay dues	Voters have no obligations, only rights in the party—not true "members"
Memberships overlap many other interest groups	Parties are mutually exclusive—cannot be loyal to both parties
Private associations—records are secret	Parties are regulated—finance and votes public
No public test of strength— leaders may exaggerate group membership/support	Periodic public test of strength in elections

BOX 3-4
V. O. Key (1908–1963)

V. O. Key has had far-reaching influence on the discipline of political science. Serving as president of the American Political Science Association from 1956–57, Key encouraged the new behavioral research. As a faculty member at Johns Hopkins and Harvard Universities, he trained many distinguished political scientists, including Walter Dean Burnham and David Mayhew. His major publications include *Politics, Parties and Pressure Groups* (1942), *Southern Politics* (1949), *American State Politics* (1956), and *The Responsible Electorate* (published posthumously in 1966). Key's overriding theme in all his works was the role of party government—or more precisely the lack of it. Key, originally from Texas, wrote the seminal work on the limitations of one-party government in *Southern Politics*. In particular, Key found in *Southern Politics* that it was the have-nots who suffered when party government was lacking. Another major theme in Key's work was his antiprogressivism—in particular, Key criticized the institution of the direct primary as limiting party government. Key is the source of many important concepts in the study of parties and elections: "friends and neighbors" voting, attentive publics, the tripartite system of understanding parties, critical elections and realignment, secular realignment, and the distinction between faction and party. Many voting behavior scholars trace their work on realignment to Key, a great proponent of empirical research. His influence in obtaining funding for the Michigan election studies helped launch the University of Michigan Survey Research Center. While neither a narrow voting behavior specialist nor a pluralist, Key himself preferred inductive logic, and therefore provided little in the way of overarching theory. His disappointment in the inability of the public to play the role intended for it was manifest in his work on public opinion. However, in *The Responsible Electorate*, Key asserted that "voters are not fools." Key was married to Dr. Luella Gettys, an early political scientist and author of several scholarly books. It was the practice in those days for married women to lose their teaching posts upon marriage. Following their marriage, Gettys assisted Key in his work.

they will provide a competition between the "ins" and the "outs"—two stable competing leadership teams. Voting in one-party or nonpartisan elections tends to be of the parochial "friends and neighbors" variety in which people vote mostly for people they know or who come from their local neighborhood. Key stresses that a "powerful localism" in voting results in "low voter interest in public issues and a susceptibility to control by the irrelevant appeal to support the home-town boy" (1949, p. 37). Political personalities, temporary alliances, and floating factions lack a consistent and effective opposition to the "ins." Politics in a competitive system offers more than a simple switching of leadership teams. More important, and to repeat Key's and Schattschneider's dictum, it is the *have-nots* who suffer when parties are not competitive. The fundamental issues in politics are economic ones, such as those that divide the national parties. As David Mayhew puts it, for Key, "class-related economic issues or cleavages . . . had a favored ontological status as 'genuine,' 'fundamental,' or 'rational' " (1988, p. 25). Schattschneider is well known for favoring the "socialization of conflict" whereby the conflict is based on national issues serving the interests of the have-nots. It is the powerful, private economic interests who favor the "privatization of conflict." For Schattschneider, the parties socialize conflict because they seek to mobilize majorities; thus parties are uniquely democratic institutions.

Localism and sectionalism—prevalent in machine politics and in one-party factional states—discourage the definition of issues along fundamental lines. Where the parties are competitive, national issues become more prominent and local issues are suppressed. Competitive parties also offer a better policy choice for the voters. This is true because the parties represent different socioeconomic groups. The durability of these groupings or coalitions means that the issues upon which the party stands are well known to their party followers, while the opposing party's stands will be more sharply differentiated. Competitive parties also encourage participation in two important ways. Not only does voter interest and turnout increase in competitive systems, but parties will seek to reduce the cost of participation (e.g., by registering voters in their homes and offering rides to the polls) when there is a competitive advantage to do so. Competitive parties thus play a critical role in extending suffrage and expanding the electorate.

A significant issue for party government theorists is the relationship of the party organizational structure to the party system. This question was first posed by Roberto Michels in his analysis of the German Social Democratic Party (first published in 1915). Michels' answer to the question was to conclude that "power is always conservative." With the development of the party organization, "the struggle for great principles becomes impossible" (1962, p. 366). This happens because the party gradually develops a durable leadership group as the organization increases in size. This leadership becomes increasingly professional and specialized and thus increasingly separated and distant from the average citizens whom the party represents. This growing gap between the leaders and the followers eventually culminates in the development of a cohesive elite whose primary incentive is to stay in power. They evolve into a self-perpetuating elite because as the organizational leaders they control (1) the information available to the followers about the organization and its successes or failures, (2) the organs of communication to their followers, and (3) the recruitment and socialization of new leaders. Aspiring leaders who do not threaten the interests of the established elite cadre are absorbed and co-opted. This is, briefly, the reasoning behind Michels' famous *Iron Law of Oligarchy*—"Who says organization says oligarchy" (1962, p. 32)— one of the most widely quoted laws in the study of bureaucracies. If equally applicable to parties and bureaucracies as Michels argues, the Iron Law of Oligarchy provides little optimism for democracy. Party theorists since Michels have reacted to the seemingly conspiratorial aspect of the oligarchical elite by emphasizing the unique historical development of parties.

The French political scientist Maurice Duverger (1954) took issue with Michels' Iron Law of Oligarchy by proposing a distinction between the *cadre* and the *mass-party* structures. The cadre party consists of a set of leaders or notables active only at election time, while the mass party is comprised of leaders and party members or adherents interacting in an ongoing organization in pursuit of common ends. While American parties were characterized as cadre, the socialist mass member parties represented the modern party of the future. Duverger acknowledged that the parties were indeed run by elites. However, the socialist party elites were different in that they had "sprung from the masses." The mass party leaders and their adherents had reciprocal roles and responsibilities in the party. Duverger concluded that in the mass party, the relationship was not one of the elites exploiting the masses as Michels had concluded. Parties, according to Duverger, do organize to achieve a competitive advantage. Parties first began as the cadre style—as legislative factions based in caucuses of elected officials. Organization of mass followings linked to elected officials—the linkage function—came later. The parties on the left—or the have-nots—organized a mass following first. After all, their only possible political influence lay in numbers, not in their friends in high places— the resource of the haves. Hence, the incentive for the parties of the haves on the right to develop a mass membership party came after the organization of the socialist parties in Europe. It occurred as a competitive response to the opposing party. Duverger terms this the "contagion from the left."

Samuel Eldersveld's 1962 study of Detroit area precinct committeepersons provided another important correction of Michels' theory, particularly as it applied to the United States. Eldersveld attacked the concept of the oligarchic elite on two grounds. First, the organizational structure of American parties is not hierarchical as Michels proposed. It is, instead, a *stratarchy*. A stratarchy is not top-down in terms of power, but is instead based on a "reciprocal deference structure" in which leaders at all levels act independently but also defer to each other. The basis for leadership is rapport, not the expertise Michels stressed. Eldersveld found that it was the local party organizations that were the strongest, not the national party organizations. The national organizational party leaders engage in "downward deference" to local interests, political culture, and inertia. Contrary to the authoritarian or bureaucratic models of organization, which place power at the top, the "critical action locus of the party structure is at the base" (1964, p. 9). Eldersveld studied local parties. A study of the national party committees during this era came to the same conclusion: Cornelius Cotter and Bernard Hennessy stress that the national committees are unlike other organizations in that they have responsibility without power, and are "non-things" with "little identifiable and definable being" (1964, p. 11).

Second, Eldersveld found that the party is comprised of *diverse elites* with diverse motives and different career patterns, not a single unified elite cadre oriented solely toward power as such as Michels found in Europe. This diversity among elites derives from the quixotic nature of political authority and the high level of turnover among party personnel. Further, competition between subcoalitions of the parties may result in upward recruitment for some (promotion) and in a loss of position for others (demotion) (1964, p. 144). Cotter and Hennessy (1964) concurred with Eldersveld: the position of state party chair, in particular, appears to suffer extremely high turnover due to the "factional fights which rack so many state parties every two or four years" (p. 59). Eldersveld stresses that parties are incohesive because some party elites are primarily oriented toward the party, and not by a desire to wield power. "For many of these the party means 'status,' not 'power,' and the continuity of their commitment to party tasks contributes to stability in the face of constant flux and potential disequilibrium" (1964, pp. 11–12). A party is thus a stable "social group" uniting "an agglomeration of people with a rich variety of motivations, drives and needs" (1964, p. 303). This is an important point—parties are a group, not an artificial or tactical alliance.

The stability of the leadership cadres in durable, competitive parties means that the party is more likely to recruit and socialize a better quality of leaders than is true of floating factions. In addition, in V. O. Key's felicitous phrase, parties are likely to act as a "solvent of separation of powers." By this, Key means that parties encourage joint executive-legislative responsibility. At the national level, unified and productive government is particularly notable when Congress and the president are effectively controlled by the same party, for example, during the first 2 years of Ronald Reagan's (1981–1982) and Lyndon Johnson's (1964–1965) presidencies, Franklin Roosevelt's first term (1933–1936), and the first 2 years of Woodrow Wilson's administration (1913–1914).

The hallmarks of a competitive party system are stable social groups comprising opposing "social formations," regularized conflict, accountability to the public for decisions made, responsibility and discipline across divided government, stable well-trained leaders, well-defined issues based on fundamental cleavages, a simplification of the policy choices, a limitation of the power of vested economic interests, and increased participation and turnout at the polls. For these reasons, parties in a competitive party system serve democracy.

Why a Two Party-System?

The American political system is characterized by a *two-party system*. This means that no minor or third party can seriously compete for political power. Since the Civil War, the two major parties have been the Democratic Party and the Republican Party. However, a large number of third and minor parties have made their brief appearance in American politics from time to time. A *third party* is one that can realistically elect a small number of public officials because it draws a significant level of electoral support. Third parties can challenge the monopoly of power of the two major parties. By contrast, a *minor party* will persist even though it poses no electoral threat to the major parties. Because minor parties do not bid for power, they do not need to conciliate diverse interests. The adherence to principles divorced from a bid for power in government—very much like an interest group—typifies a minor party. Contemporary examples of a minor party would be the Liberal, Conservative, and Right-to-Life Parties in New York State. All three parties endorse candidates, but these candidates are often either the Democratic or Republican Party nominee who is closest to them. Thus, in many ways, these minor parties operate more akin to an interest group or minority faction than they do as a political party whose function is to mobilize majorities and to make a government. Typically, *a significant third party challenge will result in the major parties adopting at least some of the third party's programs* as their own in order to attract their followers. This tactic systematically undercuts the support of the third party, and the members of its coalition are eventually absorbed by one of the two major parties.

Many party scholars have viewed this as a good thing because a two-party system automatically produces majorities that have the power to govern and the provision of only two choices for the voter reduces the information cost of participation. Some scholars, in particular V. O. Key, believe that the two-party system arises from a traditional duopoly of interests in the United States, originally coalescing around the personalities of Hamilton and Jefferson. For Key, this duopoly of interests, while resting on a consensus on fundamentals that avoids extremism, is a "moving consensus" on issues, not a static separation of interests. Others—most notably E. E. Schattschneider and Douglas Rae (1967)—stress the way the election system (single-member districts, plurality election rules) is structured to grant a monopoly of power only to the two major parties. Still others—in particular pluralist theorists—have gone further and explained the persistence of the two-party system as due to a basic consensus in both parties resulting in an issueless politics. Certainly, socialism has never been a major force in American politics as it has been in Europe. The historian Louis Hartz (1955) has stressed that the United States, lacking an indigenous feudal heritage, also lacked an indigenous revolutionary or socialist heritage, which would legitimize a socialist party. It is important to determine which of these three positions is most accurate because third parties have all but disappeared in the twentieth century, a factor that may diminish party competition and, therefore, democracy. To examine this further, we turn first to a discussion of responsible parties, then to a comparison of alternative conceptions of voting in a democracy, and finally to an analysis of the decline of third parties in American politics.

Party Theory, the Doctrine of Responsible Parties, and Party Reform

As we have seen, all party theorists have stressed the crucial role of party responsibility as the key to party government. However, most political scientists have come to associate the doctrine of responsible party government with a single document: a set of recommendations issued by the Committee on Political Parties of the American Political Science Association (APSA) in 1950, entitled *Toward a More Responsible Two-Party System*. Although this committee was chaired by E. E. Schattschneider, he did not draft the document, nor did he concur in all its recommendations. The document itself was primarily drafted by Paul David, Bertram Gross, and Fritz Marx (David, 1979). Of the 17-member committee,[1] only Schattschneider was renowned as a party theorist. The report generated much controversy and received considerable criticism at the time (Goodman, 1951; Ranney, 1951; Stedman and Sonthoff, 1951; Sonthoff, 1951). As a result of the controversy, its recommendations, rather than the more genuinely theoretical work of major party scholars like Key and Schattschneider, became identified with the theory of party government and party responsibility. Ironically, many of its recommendations have been implemented in recent years, with the result that critics of contemporary reforms of the party system have used *Toward a More Responsible Two-Party System* as a theoretical guide to understanding contemporary parties. While it is improbable that the efforts of a group of academics and party theorists are solely responsible for the recent transformation of the American party system, their prescription for a more responsible system is remarkably like one that developed almost 20 years after their academic musings first appeared in print. We will first consider the recommendations of the report, then turn to a discussion of the early and contemporary controversy over the document.

---

[1]The members of the Committee included: Thomas S. Barclay, Stanford University; Clarence A. Berdahl, University of Illinois; Hugh A. Bone, University of Washington; Franklin L. Burdette, University of Maryland; Paul T. David, Brookings Institution; Merle Fainsod, Harvard University; Bertram M. Gross, Council of Economic Advisors; E. Allen Helms, Ohio State University; E. M. Kirkpatrick, Department of State; John W. Lederle, University of Michigan; Fritz Morstein Marx, American University; Louise Overacker, Wellesley College; Howard Penniman, Department of State; Kirk H. Porter, State University of Iowa; J. B. Shannon, University of Kentucky; and E. E. Schattschneider, Wesleyan University, as chairman.

RECOMMENDED REVISIONS.   The Committee recommended a large-scale revision of the American party system. Enamored of the British parliamentary system, the Committee called for the transformation of the American party system of that era into one that was more effective, responsible, and democratic. The essential elements of the responsible party doctrine included specific recommendations on (1) how electoral majorities are to be mobilized, (2) how they are to be linked to the government, and (3) how the government is to translate the popular majorities into public policy. Responsible parties link the parties' supporters in the electorate, the various party organizations, and the party-in-government in order to provide coherent policy alternatives. Party discipline is required as well as a coherent program upon which elections are contested.

The Committee's report suggested a number of very specific changes (see Appendix) to nationalize and rationalize party politics from the top down. It recommended that the parties create a centralized and integrated party organization (the "party council") at the national level, which would determine membership criteria for participation in party affairs (for example, qualifications for primary voters and seating of delegates at national conventions). Further, this national organization would institute sanctions against state and local party violations of national party rules. They would participate in the recruitment, nomination, and election of congressional candidates, and they would institute sanctions against members of Congress who do not support party positions. Finally, intraparty unity and democracy were to be encouraged through the use of primaries. The report also proposed reforms of the congressional parties, their leadership, and the election system and encouraged academics to become more involved in the parties.

EARLY CRITICISMS.   A major criticism voiced against the report was that it promoted a political system that was thought to be foreign and out of sync with the American experience. Leon Epstein (1983), in a review of how political science has treated the relationship of parties to democracy, divides political scientists into two camps: *responsible party theorists* and *indigenous party theorists*.[2] Those who defend the indigenous American parties against the criticisms of the APSA report and assorted reformers do not offer a neat document that summarizes their position because they are defending an existing system that they believe to be, on the whole, a good one. For the most part, their arguments are in the form of a critique of the responsible parties doctrine as expressed in the APSA report. The American constitutional struc-

---

[2]Epstein reluctantly places V. O. Key within the indigenous parties camp, while admitting that Key might require a category of his own. We think that Epstein too strongly considers the APSA document as the core of the party responsibility position and ignores important similarities between Key and Schattschneider and other theorists. Further, Key was not a pluralist, and pluralism represents the major theoretical position of the indigenous party supporters.

tures—in particular the separation of powers and checks and balances system in the national government—they argue, are major structural impediments to the realization of some of the basic requirements of the responsible parties model. The federalized and fragmented nature of our elections for the Congress and the presidency are important political obstacles to attaining the centralized party unity required in a responsible party system.

Edward Banfield (1980b), in an essay published in 1961, provided a positive construction of indigenous American institutions. Party factions, according to Banfield, increase the options of party leaders. Rather than being incomplete parties like European parties, American political parties allow for stable government and continuity between administrations of different parties by allowing for leaders to choose pragmatically between "interests" (e.g., the "profit-minded," the "sectional-minded," and the "nationality-minded") and "principles." The party leader (or president) "could afford to offend some elements of the party on any particular question because there would be enough other elements unaffected, or even gratified, to assure his position. The more fragmented his party, the less attention he would have to pay to any one fragment of it." Both parties would be "fundamentally in agreement" because of the "countless compromises within the parties" (1980, pp. 140–41). Each party would of necessity have to attract middle-of-the-road support. The type of party system desired by those who advocate the indigenous party model is one where pragmatism takes precedence over principle and where parties are more alike than different.

CONTEMPORARY REFORMS. Democratic Party reform was initiated following the contentious 1968 Democratic convention. The first reform commission, the McGovern-Fraser Commission, named after its two chairs, Senator George McGovern and Representative Don Fraser, was authorized by that convention. Following the McGovern-Fraser Commission, a series of reform commissions were authorized by each successive nominating convention until 1988 (see also Chapters 5 and 6). The first commission, the McGovern-Fraser Commission, published a report detailing the abuses of the state parties, *Mandate for Reform* (1970). The McGovern-Fraser Commission also issued new national party rules for the selection of nominating convention delegates in 1972. Concomitant with the reforms of the Democratic presidential nominating process, other unrelated reforms of the political process (e.g., passage of the Federal Election Campaign Act with the public funding of presidential elections, numerous congressional reforms, shortening of residency requirements for registration) were enacted, and many changes have taken place in American politics. Most noted among these changes have been an increase in the use of state primaries for the selection of nominating convention delegates, and a decline in party identification.

While the party system of today cannot truly be said to be a responsible one, it is much closer to that ideal than before. *Many of the changes advocated in the APSA report have been instituted in one form or another.* Due to the efforts of various reform commissions, the national Democratic Party exercises substantial control over the conduct of the national party conventions. Rules governing the selection and composition of state delegations to the national conventions are firmly in place. The use of primaries in the nomination process in both parties for all offices has increased substantially since 1950. The four congressional party campaign committees (the Democratic and Republican Senatorial Campaign Committees, the Democratic Congressional Campaign Committee, and the National Republican Congressional Committee) recruit candidates and provide funds and services to their respective nominees. Finally, the 1980s have seen substantial evidence of party voting in the U.S. Congress (presently around 80%).

CONTEMPORARY CRITICISMS AND THE DECLINE OF PARTY THESIS. Pluralists have been sharply critical of the contemporary reforms of the Democratic Party, which have expanded participation in the party system. They have argued that parties have declined as a consequence of the reforms—the "reform thesis." Nelson Polsby (1980) believes that reforms caused "the gate keeping functions of party leaders and party organizations . . . to atrophy" (p. 55). Byron Shafer (1983) concludes that "at bottom, the result of all these reforms was the diminution, the constriction, at times the elimination, of the regular party in the politics of presidential selection (p. 527). Other major proponents of the "reform thesis" include Edward Banfield (1980a,b); James Ceaser (1982), Jeane Kirkpatrick (1976, 1979), Everett Carll Ladd, Jr. (1977, 1981), Nelson Polsby (1980, 1983a,b), and Austin Ranney (1975, 1978). Ironically, they have compared them to the Progressive era reforms, which limited participation. For example, Banfield (1980a) argues that the recent reforms were the culmination of "more than a century of effort" (p. 30). With a similar grand sweep of history, Ceasar (1982) lumps the reformers of the Progressive era, the intellectual positions staked out by the APSA Committee on Political Parties, and the contemporary "proponents of an open presidential election process" (p. 97) together as indicators of the same phenomenon despite their differences.

ASSESSING THE DECLINE OF PARTY THESIS. Pluralist criticism of party reforms and their predictions about its effects are inconsistent with contemporary party scholarship. There have indeed been declines in party identification, but unless one considers voters as members of parties, it is hard to view parties as declining.

> Despite the growing number of Americans who claim to be "independents," the vast majority of these voters will cast ballots for the major-party nominees. That was true when Maurice Duverger conducted his voting studies [in the 1940s and 1950s], and that remains the case today. (Bode and Casey, 1980, p. 5)

Indeed, Joseph Schlesinger (1985) points out that a decline in party identification actually leads to increased party competition and stronger parties. The reflexive party identification is no longer true, but organizational strength is not a function of inherited psychological ties. Studies of the national party organizations have found them developing permanence, stability, and regular roles in the party system (Herrnson, 1988, 1990). And a major study of state and local party organizations has found that they are stronger, not weaker (Cotter, et al., 1984). Thus, the emergent national party organizations in the postreform era have not resulted in weaker state and local parties. The pluralist critics of contemporary party reform have ignored the fact that the reforms were instituted from *within* the party system by individuals and groups who cared about parties as effective actors representing them.

The groups seeking party reform did not develop a definition of the public interest or seek to advance some common good. Nor did they write a new philosophy of government and democracy, as did the progressives. In fact, *no* document elaborating their philosophy exists. Instead, they sought specific redress for the pervasive discrimination they experience when trying to work within the party system. William Crotty (1980), a noted student of party reform, concludes that "party theory played no discernible role in party reform" (p. 45). Kenneth Bode, research director of the McGovern-Fraser Commission and a member of the Mikulski and Winograd Commissions, and Carol Casey, a staff assistant on the McGovern-Fraser Commission and research director for the Mikulski Commission, note that far from being a philosophical attack on the party, the reforms were a pragmatic response to practical problems.

> These guidelines were developed in response to very real and serious flaws exposed in the tumultuous political arena of 1968. . . . Viewed within the context of the time, the eighteen guidelines adopted by the McGovern-Fraser Commission were a moderate response to very real problems within the Democratic party's nominating process. (1980, pp. 5–6, 11).

Moreover, the reforms of the party system (the "reform thesis") did not occur in a vacuum, but were rather a result of successive formal efforts to establish the existence of a central as opposed to a confederate authority structure within the party, as well as demands for greater accountability of public officials generally and a broadening of political participation. The reforms in Congress (see Appendix A) paralleled party reform but were in no way caused by any academic theory or the APSA report. Leroy Rieselbach, who has studied congressional reform extensively, concluded (1986) that the reformers' goals and motives were "mixed" and that the congressional reforms themselves were "political, pragmatic, and more-or-less spontaneous reactions to seemingly irresistible forces. They have been piecemeal, not wholesale; individually modest, not radical; ad hoc, not the products of comprehensive planning" (p. 42). In addition, during this same era, the states underwent extensive reforms, stimulated in large part by the reapportionment revolution requiring implementation of the principle "one man, one vote" (required by the land-mark Supreme Court decisions in *Baker* v. *Carr* [1962] and *Reynolds* v. *Sims* [1965]). These changes included the proportional representation of urban constituencies for the first time in state legislatures, rewriting of the state constitutions in the 1970s, and considerable augmentation of the powers and prestige of governors. One scholar has termed this revolution "Goodbye to Goodtime Charlie" (Sabato, 1978). In short, the 1970s was an era of reform in all spheres of American politics with no academic blueprint guiding the process.

This fundamental point has been ignored by pluralist critics of party reform, who treat party reforms as occurring in a political vacuum and as some natural extended consequence of the Progressive era, which ended some 50 years earlier. Pluralist critics argued that the party reforms were unnec-essary and led to party decline. The new groups included were not grass-roots based, the pluralists argued, and thus raised fears of degeneration into a mass society. This was an interesting twist for pluralists—pluralist theorist David Truman thought all groups were legitimate,[3] but the political pluralists made distinctions between groups. Reform critics such as Nelson Polsby (1983a) argued that the new groups, "those speaking for interests widely perceived as historically disadvantaged such as black, Hispanic-American, and militant women's groups," were "creatures of the mass media" rather than organizing "around the economic or status needs of their clientele" (p. 133). We will discuss these points in further detail in a later chapter, but it is important to note that the nonideological parties the pluralists preferred stemmed from the Progressive era and were artificially created. With the rise of social move-ments, which we shall cover in Chapter 5, new forces were active in American politics. The pluralist and party government theorists differ greatly in their conception of the place of citizens and voting in party politics, to which we now turn.

THE PLACE OF VOTING IN A DEMOCRACY

Since the notion of *democracy as voting* is so broadly and almost obsessively held in the United States, many ideas that follow from it are likewise generally accepted. These include the ideas that voting is a civic duty, that each person's opinions matter, and that the "people" as individual citizens are supreme—*vox populi, vox dei*. Certainly, it is difficult to imagine the American system without some form of regularized voting. However, individual, in contrast to

[3]Truman (1958) notes that while the most common groups were economic ones, "so common have these groups become and so involved has government activity been with economic policy, that many writers have fallen into the error of treating economic groups as the only important interest groups" (p. 61).

group-based, voting (as well as its associated activities—broadcast journalism, polling, and political advertising) has never guaranteed individual liberties or access to the ranks of the political elite. Another problem with this interpretation is that the imagery that voting and democracy are equivalent often serves to disguise the most undemocratic of political systems. The intellectual historian H. Stuart Hughes (1964) observed of fascist and authoritarian political systems that "fascism became unnecessary when populations began to behave in a politically apathetic and disciplined fashion under regimes which remained *democratic in form*" (p. 9, emphasis added). "Democratic in form" refers to voting, or at least the imagery of the ballot box. This may be a more efficient means of maintaining an undemocratic government than others, because voting without other ways of participating can lead to demagogery.

Many factors have contributed to the belief that democracy *is* voting. It represents, in part, early American egalitarianism—an idea chiefly associated with Thomas Jefferson. Ideals from the Progressive era (1890–1920), which favored a direct relationship between citizens and candidates, placed voting (by educated citizens) at the core of democracy. Finally, the twentieth-century European experience with fascism and the political concerns that World War II European émigrés brought with them to the United States stressed voting as a limited and occasional form of widespread participation. These latter concerns are subsumed under the pluralist fears of "mass society." Three views on voting—the constitutional, the progressive and the pluralist or mass society theories—will be examined and then compared with the views of party government theorists.

Thomas Jefferson, James Madison, and the Constitutional Theory of Voting

Voting was only marginally important in colonial America, at least with regard to the federal system. Of course, since the Federalists were so obvious in their distrust of the "commoners," the developing Democrat-Republican faction seemed almost Jacobin[4] in their advocacy of suffrage rights. The reason that the Democrat-Republican era and Jeffersonian "egalitarianism" were not democratic in the modern sense was not related to policy. In fact, policy questions and changes can be debated and enacted in the most closed and undemocratic political systems.

The prerevolutionary era, the Federalist dominion, and the Democratic-Republican era were all part of a seamless web. The commoners in the early republic, including the Dutch in New York and the Scotch-Irish concentrated

---

[4]The Jacobins were a political club, named after the monastery where they met in Paris, of the French Revolution. The Jacobins instituted the "reign of terror" under the direction of Maximilien Robespierre which was used against not only the counter-revolutionaries, but also against their former allies. In the early conflict between leadership factions, a major division was between those who were sympathetic to the French Revolution and those who were not.

south and west of Pennsylvania, were all part of a people subordinated to the English or Yankee gentry. The noted cultural, political, and literary observer Van Wyck Brooks (1944) writes:

> The Revolution had been fought under the guidance of the gentry, who possessed most of the learning, talent and wealth, and the people still thought they were safer in the hands of these tried leaders, who had been trained for public life. Even the election of Jefferson meant a change of policy only, not a change of personnel, and the upper classes retained their dominant role; for the country was still English, and social distinctions were undisputed, and the masses had only a dim perception of their rights. (p. 29)

This is very significant. Jeffersonian egalitarianism was not accompanied by a permeable leadership class. As Josiah Quincy observed, "the glittering generalizations of the Declaration [of Independence] were never meant to be taken seriously. Gentlemen were the natural rulers of America after all" (Ostragorski, 1902, p. 18, note 1). So here were the democratic sentiments of the Jeffersonian era. Voting rights were accorded to the commoners. *However, the commoners had only acquired the right to vote for their superiors.* That is, of course, voting, but we think *not* democracy.

While Jefferson was responsible for advocating broader suffrage rights, the politics of the Democrat-Republican era were clearly of an aristocratic sort. Jefferson himself hardly qualifies as a representative of the people. He was a Virginian, an aristocrat, and a slaveholder who was prominent and influential for almost all of his adult life. His estate, Monticello, is in many respects an American version of Versailles,[5] translated of course to the materials and culture of the Virginia countryside. Among the founding fathers, Jefferson and Madison are the most important for our understanding of American politics. Jefferson is probably viewed as the more distinguished figure of the two, and he did, and for that matter still does, cast a rather long shadow (although we admit to some difficulty in distinguishing within the constitutional realm where Jefferson's ideas begin and John Locke's leave off; see Box 3-5). Madison was a follower of Jefferson in the political domain. He was Jefferson's secretary of state, which in the Democrat-Republican era was the position occupied by the heir apparent to the presidency. Madison was a strong advocate of the Bill of Rights, and he followed Jefferson's lead in authoring the Virginia Resolution (in opposition to the Alien and Sedition Acts), where he argued that the national government could not exercise powers that were not expressly contained in the Constitution and, further, that states could nullify federal laws within their jurisdictions.

---

[5]Versailles is the elaborate palace and gardens built for Louis XIV in the mid-seventeenth century. Versailles played an important role in the French Revolution, when Louis XVI was forced to move from Versailles to Paris in 1790. It is now a national monument.

BOX 3-5
The Shadow Founding Father

A good case can be made that the most influential of the American founding fathers never set foot in the new world. He is John Locke (1632–1704), the great British philosopher of empiricism and liberalism. Locke most eloquently expressed the Enlightenment's faith in man's goodness, in science, and in the middle class. Locke believed that man was in his natural state a creature of reason, tolerant, and happy. He argued that states have a social contract with their citizens and that the right to life, health, liberty, and possessions are guaranteed by natural law. If governments fail to accord their citizens these rights, then revolution is not only a right but an obligation. Locke also argued that religious toleration is essential to the just and harmonious society. Further, Locke advocated a system of checks and balances among the elements of government, as such a system deters tyranny.

Madison's accomplishments outside the influence of Jefferson were considerable. His role in the drafting of the Constitution was unequaled[6] (Jefferson was in France at the time). Madison's ideas are substantially represented in the Constitution. Two Madisonian elements are critical to understanding American politics. First, interests (factions) are the fundamental elements of politics, and while these interests may be potentially dangerous to the public good, they are in any case inevitable. This point we find especially interesting, as it illustrates important differences between Jefferson and Madison. Second, voters and public opinion are minor elements in the American political system—at least as viewed through the constitutional lens. As indicated above, Madison was a close follower of Jefferson. However, their views diverge when it comes to regarding political parties. Madison was probably the most effective advocate for the Constitution. His arguments for the federal system in the *Federalist Papers* were very persuasive. In particular, he argued in *Federalist Papers 10* and *51* that factions (interests) should not be legally restrained (a Lockean sentiment) and that the creation of a federal government would be the most effective means of controlling factional interests, because locally dominant factions would be less influential in a larger arena where competing factions would restrain their propensity to mischief making.

The constitutional Madison suggests his position with respect to the role of voting. A reading of the American Constitution reveals the limited role of

[6]It is worth noting in this regard that while the Declaration of Independence is the more poetic and memorable document, it is the Constitution that remains the government blueprint for the American political system.

the American voter (as a voter—not as a PAC contributor, an interest group member, or a social or political group leader) in the national political process. In the Constitution as originally drafted, and until the twentieth century, the only vote members of the public were granted in the federal system was a vote for their member of the United States House of Representatives. This vote might be cast every 2 years; in the meantime, there was no constitutionally designated means for that voter to express an opinion on matters of public policy. Three different election systems were devised with separate electorates for the U.S. House (eligible voters), the U.S. Senate (state legislatures), and the president (electoral college). This status has changed; a voter may now cast a ballot for their two U.S. Senators (since 1913). Presidential electors still meet separately in their own state capitols and may vote their own choice, but in practice they vote for the plurality popular vote candidate. The establishment of national supremacy with the victory of the North eliminated the possibility of strong states' rights advocacy. Yet, federalism still rules. Individual voters may elect a member of Congress, but they are not granted the right to elect the entire Congress.

The Jeffersonian/Madisonian Era[7] with its minimal role for voters ended with the creation of the Democratic Party and the inauguration of the Jacksonian era in 1828–1832. Now the misfortune of common birth could be overcome and access to elite political status gained. The conception of the voter had changed. It was organized political action that made the Jacksonian era democratic. New groups were brought into active participation and influence: the Scotch-Irish and Celts in the South, the urban poor and working class in the North, and the early settlers and small farmers in the West. This meant party politics,[8] the spoils system, and machine politics. Jackson was a man of common antecedents ("descended from an Irish family of obscure history"[9]) who early in his life experienced bankruptcy. The "gentlemen" of the earlier era—in the person of John Quincy Adams—stole the presidency from him in 1824, an event that was not to be repeated. Martin Van Buren,[10] Jackson's close confederate and successor as president, was a premier machine politician and founder of the Albany Regency (a political machine in New York). Interestingly from our perspective, he only received a simple schoolhouse education, and his writing was characterized as an illegible scrawl—a vivid contrast to Jefferson's elegant prose. The arrival of the Jacksonian era

[7]This era is usually termed the Democrat-Republican era, as we shall see in Chapter 5.

[8]A complete party system had to await the formation of the Whig Party. Once the Democrats, the party of the commoners, had acquired power (and thus the opportunity to abuse it), their opponents organized themselves into the Whig Party, representing more substantial citizens (Duverger (1954) calls this process the "contagion from the left").

[9]From Jackson's eulogy delivered by Jefferson Davis, future president of the Confederate States of America.

[10]Van Buren was Aaron Burr's second in the famous duel in which Madison's partner in the Federalist Papers was killed.

meant that the elite political class was now more open—more permeable—than before. *It was not voting that changed the system; it was party organization and the expansion of participation.* In the process, the development of party organization changed the popular conception of voting: from the 1830s until the Progressive era, the vote was thought to be the right of all white (male) citizens.

The Progressives and Voting

Progressives were so successful as organized reformers of party that they have an entire era of American politics named after them. The Democrat-Republicans were in their ascendancy at the start of the nineteenth century; the progressives at the end. The progressives were almost diametrically op-

---

TABLE 3-1
Major Progressive Reforms of Elections

Structural Reforms	Major Effect	Comment
Council-Manager Government	Reduce power of mayor, the most important elected official Power in hands of un-elected city manager	Management objective—efficiency "public interest"
Nonpartisan Elections	Destroys organized group interests •Weakens local parties •Encourages issue avoidance •Media role enhanced •Minorities hurt •Frustrates protest voting •No party discipline—difficult to develop governmental consensus •No mechanism to get out the vote	No party designation on ballots, however, does not rule out factions Prestigious civic organizations and local notables with well-known names advantaged Separates politicians into two groups: those who run for partisan office and those who run for nonpartisan office
At Large vs. Ward-Based Systems	Destroys geographic basis of groups Benefits candidates endorsed by prestigious civic organizations, and those with name recognition	Advantages of ward system: Similarity of views → gains representation Shorter Ballots → more information about candidate Candidates have stands on local issues

posed to the philosophy and program of the Democrat-Republicans. The progressives were not advocates of states' rights, nor followers of John Locke, and unlike for the Democrat-Republicans, voting is probably *the* principal element of progressive politics. This was true during what is formally known as the Progressive era (1890–1920) as well as during more modern episodes of progressive political activity. Three elements of the progressives' program are of particular interest here (see Table 3-1). First, the progressives were successful in amending the Constitution and state and federal laws in such a way as to increase the significance of voting. Second, the progressives effectively diminished (at least during the height of their influence) the power of various organized interests, not only interest groups, trusts, and monopolies, but also parties, party machines, and state governments. These interests represented wealthy industrialists as well as the working and immigrant classes. Finally, the progressives viewed themselves (and represented themselves to

Structural Reforms	Major Effect	Comment
Civil Service and Merit System	Undermines patronage Weakens party control over bureaucracy Lessens responsiveness of bureaucracy to officials	Impartial decisions made without regard for party support
City Planning Commissions	Professional management of urban problems Group interests not a factor	Removal of important public policy issues from public agenda
Initiative, Referendum, and Recall	Weakens government Benefits prestigious civic organizations and interests	Issues dominated by prestigious civic organizations
Direct Primary	Weakens party role in recruitment of candidates	Not insurmountable, actually a southern invention
Cross-Filing	Eliminated party role in elections	Progressive innovation— allows candidate to run as both the Democratic and Republican nominee
Secret Ballot	Recognition of candidates now a state responsibility	Required literacy Creation of parties as public utilities
Female Suffrage	Granted women full right to vote	Major argument and near effect was to dilute the voting power of immigrant men
Party Registration by State	Lists maintained by state	Artificial definition of party member

be) as disinterested and nonpartisan reformers, committed to transcendent values, in particular, the "public interest." Joseph Schumpeter (1942) wrote of this notion:

> There is, first, no such thing as a uniquely determined common good that all people could agree on or be made to agree on by the force of rational argument. This is due not primarily to the fact that some people may want things other than the common good but to the much more fundamental fact that to different individuals and groups the common good is bound to mean different things. (p. 251)

The concept of public interest in the literal sense assumed an undifferentiated public—a thing not found in American (or any other) society. In the absence of a mass public (or mass society), the progressives naturally represented their partisans and pursued their programs much as other organized interests did.

Among other things, voting was to the progressives a means to displace and undermine the power and values of their enemies. The progressives were anti–big business, anti–machine politics, and xenophobic. Their own appeal was largely to the English (Yankees), nativist, and educated middle classes. Their program suggested that reform was needed, and those who needed reforming were their enemies. There was need to control the unbridled excesses of big business, the corruption of party (machine) politics, and immigration with its unwholesome effects on American society. Big business represented the progressives' main enemy since this was an era when corporate America would unflinchingly use its muscle (primarily financial) to procure whatever it needed in the way of sympathetic local, state, and national governments. When the opportunity presented itself (after Theodore Roosevelt[11] became president), they pursued a course of action that diminished the power and influence of big business in two ways.

First, as noted above, constitutional changes increased the importance of voting. The U.S. Senate was popularly elected for the first time in 1914, and in 1920 the electorate was expanded to include women. The halcyon days of arranging legislative triumphs with suitcases of money were coming to an end; at least such activities would be more discreetly done in the future (a not inconsiderable thing, since appearances do matter). Other aspects of voting changed under the progressives' reformist zeal. Nonpartisan elections (as well as nonpartisan government), party primaries, referenda, at-large elections (a progressive idea to manufacture an undifferentiated electorate, notably in opposition to Madison) and the idea of voting for individual candidates on the basis of issues and policy began to spread. The press was, of course,

---

[11]Theodore Roosevelt became president in 1901 after President McKinley was assassinated. It is ironic that the Progressive movement gained such influence from an accident. Mark Hanna and William McKinley had selected Roosevelt (a person of growing visibility) to be vice president after McKinley's first vice president died. This was done with the firm conviction that he would never be president and that he would effectively be neutralized in such an ineffectual office.

interested in promoting the idea that voting involved issues, since it was the press that would introduce and ventilate those issues. Citizens were to participate and vote for candidates as *individuals*, regardless of party, and be informed of the issues of the day as individuals via the press, the then contemporary mass media. Voting was not to be based upon interests, especially short-term tangible interests. Voters should "vote the issues." The role of groups and interests (and the leaders of those groups and interests) was to be superseded by an independent body of individuals, "voters," acting as individuals, informed by the mass media as to the issues of the day and where candidates stood on those issues. Most important, the progressive theory of government had no place for group-based elites situated between individual voters and the government. Endorsements by newspapers in nonpartisan elections provided the only way for voters to tell the difference between the

> party-less—and for most voters, meaningless names on the ballot. . . . Newspapers are particularly important to the election of candidates in nonpartisan cities—especially the larger ones—and the nonpartisan system is therefore understandably dear to the newspapers. (You can't tell the players without a scorecard," a newspaperman remarked happily, "and we sell the scorecards.") (Banfield and Wilson, 1963, p. 157)

These changes and the ideas that accompanied them undermined the influence of big business as well as political machines.

The second element of the progressives' assault on big business involved the activities of trust-busting and corporate regulation (child labor and safety laws and food and drug regulation), which, together with the income tax, diminished at least somewhat the economic base of big business. Also, further civil service reforms continued to erode the capitalists' ability to use the government as an instrument to further their ends. All these changes were significant. Captains of industry, given their resources—economic, political, and intellectual—often relied upon the legal system, including loyal and compliant judges, such that these reforms were not used too often against their interests. The progressives could not so easily reform the federal judiciary with its system of life tenure. Nonetheless, Teddy Roosevelt's "malefactors of great wealth" felt the sting of the progressives' reforms. A further element of the progressives' program also harmed the major industrialists' interests; the progressives advocated restricting immigration, a policy that reduced the supply, and thus increased the cost, of labor.

Political machines were also high on the progressives' list of those in need of reform. The machines operated on the basis of a spoils system, where voters received jobs or other tangible benefits from the party machines in exchange for their votes. Machines did not represent individual voters so much as blocks of voters (Irish, Italians, Poles). Voters within these blocks voted to support their party, not on the basis of issues or policy considerations, but on the basis of a group-based alliance politics. The overall progressive program was in theory, as well as in fact, antimachine. Among the reforms sought (and achieved in many places) that were especially harmful to the machines were nonpartisan elections, expansion of the civil service, and primary elections. Primary elections, at least in principle, took the power of selecting the party's candidates from the party leadership and gave it to voters in primary elections. In those jurisdictions where the progressives were most successful, many leaders of the party machines were neutralized by the more direct method of arranging charges of corruption and then using the judicial system to unceremoniously deposit them in prison. As with the capitalists, the restrictions on immigration also harmed political machines; their supply of willing voters was reduced by immigration reform. Progressives viewed political parties as performing important public services and thus as "public utilities" (Epstein, 1986). As the province of all citizens, parties should thus be heavily regulated.

From a modern democratic perspective, one of the most repugnant of the progressives' traits was their xenophobia. The progressives consistently pursued policies hostile to the wave of immigrants who came to the United States starting late in the nineteenth century. This hostility can be traced to at least two sources. First, the progressives thought that the newcomers diminished the quality of American life. The immigrants were poor and largely non-Protestant, and their cultures were unpleasantly foreign. A second reason for the progressives' antipathy toward immigrants was the fact that these immigrants served the interests of both big business and machine politicians; since the progressives opposed both, their hostility not surprisingly extended to these immigrant masses. The immigrants were compliant workers ("fodder") for the mines and mills of big business. American capitalists had regularly sent their agents to Europe to encourage emigration to the United States, often (perhaps usually) under false pretenses concerning the conditions of their future employment. New immigrants suffered greatly, crowded into urban slums, their wives and children forced to work for subsistence wages. Speaking little English, they had little recourse to assistance in the face of abuse. One of the party machines' functions was to provide social welfare and assistance. In the process, they turned newcomers into citizens; if they secured their support in return that was only in the natural order of things. Because of the general poverty of their circumstances and the abuse that they suffered at the hands of their employers, the tangible spoils offered by the political machines were more than attractive enough inducements to ensure the loyalty of the immigrant classes. Hostility toward immigrants was exacerbated by the fact that the immigrants provided willing support to the machine politicians of the era.

Progressives elevated voting, yet in practice they restricted it to those like themselves. Even suffrage for women was touted as a way for the votes of white middle-class women to dilute the vote of immigrant men (Kraditor, 1965), as immigrant women coming from traditional cultures and working mothers as well were least likely to vote. Further, many poor or illiterate immigrant men were excluded from the newly introduced registration of eligible voters. This was not a painless process. Consider the following description of voting registration in the Virginia mountains under progressive innovations:

> It was painful and pitiful to see the horror and dread visible on the faces of the illiterate poor white men who were waiting to take their turn before the inquisition. . . . This was horrible to behold, but it was still more horrible to see the marks of humiliation and despair that were stamped on the faces of honest but poor white men who had been refused registration and who had been robbed of their citizenship without cause. We saw them as they came from the presence of the registrars with bowed heads and agonized faces; and when they spoke, in many instances, there was a tear in the voice of the humiliated citizen. (Kousser, 1974, p. 264)

Whole groups of people were disenfranchised by the progressives, a somewhat tawdry heritage for a movement with such lofty goals.

Pluralism and Democracy: Mass Society Theory

Pluralism developed as a major normative and empirical theory in political science in the 1950s. Pluralists feared the degeneration of American politics from a pluralistic group-based society into a mass society. To begin, it is essential to understand that the ideas central to mass society theory had their roots in Europe dating to the time when the influence of totalitarian philosophy and politics was in the ascendancy in places such as Italy, Hungary, Rumania, and most menacingly in the form of National Socialism in Germany. During this period, many European scholars fled to the United States, including some political scientists and sociologists who, not surprisingly, eventually directed their scholarship to studying what was to them "a crisis in Western Society" (Heberle, 1949).

In order to appreciate mass society theory, it is important to clearly define the concept of *mass*. In mass society theory, its meaning is not simply the intuitively plausible "large number of people." The mass in mass society refers to a society where there are a large number of *undifferentiated* individuals; specifically, undifferentiated by group or social category (e.g., where a large number of individuals are not differentiated by family, class, community, religion, ethnicity, or party). Mass society develops during times of social disintegration. Traditional social relationships based in intermediary groups (the workplace, church, neighborhood) and located between the nuclear family and the large modern state are diminished or nonexistent.

The undifferentiated individual is socially alienated, and being socially alienated he or she is also politically alienated. This is crucial for democracy. As Joseph Gusfield (1962) summarizes, he is also more likely to become the extremist activist than is a member of a structured interest group. He is no longer limited in his attack on rivals by the controls of a structured pluralist society. His resentments against opposing groups and against the existing institutions need not be confined to the calculative instrumental style of democratic politics. The mass man is a passionate supporter of democracy. (p. 24)

Mass society theorists view intermediary groups as essential to promoting proper citizenship values in electoral-based democracies. Politically egalitarian societies are always at risk because the mass might develop, a mass unattached to larger institutions and norms. In a society of normless individuals, the masses are vulnerable to demagogic movements. Unlike the progressives, who celebrated the media, pluralists feared the media. Probably the singularly most important source for concern regarding mass society in the United States is the pervasive and apparently profound influence of television on American society. Television is part of the mass media in the United States, and it is an institution of cultural uniformity, that is, a mass institution. Pluralists believe that individual attitudes are unstable. If a clever commercial can change an attitude, another equally or more clever can change it again. The individual in mass society attends to objects remote and distant from everyday life ("national issues"). While institutions in mass society, such as the mass media, can manipulate attitudes relating to these remote objects, they do not concomitantly influence the character or personal values of individuals in mass society.

Personal character and values are shaped only in proximate groups. As Joseph Schumpeter suggests,

> roughly, it consists of the things that directly concern himself, his family, his business dealings, his hobbies, his friends and enemies, his township or ward, his class, church, trade union or any other social group of which he is an active member—the things under his personal observation, the things which are familiar to him independently of what his newspaper tells him. (pp. 258–59)

Mass society theorists believe that national institutions build cultural uniformity, while only local institutions ensure cultural diversity. Because of this "cultural schizophrenia," mass organizations are incapable of ordering the electorate in a stable fashion, a critical failure in electoral democracies. Thus, there are alternating periods of mass apathy and mass activism. Because of this failing, such electoral democracies are sometimes replaced by totalitarian regimes.

It is clear from this description of mass society that pluralist mass society theorists in no way endorse the idea that democracy ought to be based in individual voters, nor do they regard the idea of a mass public as anything but a source for concern. On the contrary, mass society theorists are enthusiastic defenders and supporters of intermediary groups and organizations, or pluralism. They regard the conservative influence of such groups as being a very good thing. In contrast to progressives, pluralists and mass society theorists defend interests. Pluralists provide no analytical vantage point from which to understand parties except an historical one. The pluralist definition of party has been described as one defending *indigenous institutions* (Epstein, 1983, 1986). Pluralists did not conceive of political parties as much more than mechanisms through which interests bargained and compromised. Pluralists extol the very characteristics that party government theorists decry in American parties.

> They appreciate decentralization, limited ideological or programmatic appeals, porousness, relatively noncohesive legislative contingents, and the absence of mass-membership organizations as natural in American political development and often as party qualities especially useful in the social and constitutional circumstances of the United States. (Epstein, 1986, p. 23)

For pluralists, while interest groups are sharply delineated, political parties are not. Pluralists take an evolutionary perspective on parties: however parties have evolved in the United States defines appropriate party organization. As Theodore Lowi (1974) put it, in elevating "the pressure group system from power to virtue," pluralists advocated a *direct* relationship between elected officials and group leaders. Just as the progressives eliminated the political party by advocating a direct relationship between voters and elected officials, so too have the pluralists in their defense of interest groups as the only legitimate representatives of interests. For these reasons, the pluralist conception of party is *atheoretical*.

Party Government and Voting

In contrast to the previous theoretical positions on voting, party government theorists view voting as being related to party competition and democracy in complex ways. First, party government theorists oppose the progressive notion of voters having "membership" in political parties. As E. E. Schattschneider asserted, "whatever else the parties may be, they are not associations of the voters who support the party candidates" (1942, p. 53). The problem is that "membership in a political party has none of the characteristics of membership in an association" (p. 55). The major difference is that associations or interest groups may choose their members, while the party has no such control (see Box 3-6). Those who register with a political party assume no obligations to the party whatsoever, and the party has no control over its members. Party membership is thus a *legal fiction*, created by public registration of primary voters—a progressive innovation.

Second, unlike pluralists, party government theorists do not believe that voting should be the only form of mass participation. Competitive political parties expand participation, and as we shall see when we examine the special case of the South, noncompetitive parties may act to restrict participation. Even when voting is restricted, individuals are not excluded from participation

BOX 3-6
Why Parties Are Not Associations of Voters

Any legal voter may on his own initiative and by his own declaration execute legal formalities before a duly designated *public* official making himself a registered member of the party. The party as such is not consulted. It does not accept the application; it does not vote the applicant into the association; it may not reject the application; and finally, there is usually no recognized and authoritative procedure by which the party may expel a member.

Moreover, the member assumes no obligations to the party. He takes no oath prescribed by the party. He does not subscribe to a declaration of party principles and does not sign articles of incorporation. He does not pay membership dues, is not liable for debts of the party, and has no equity in its property. He has no duties whatever to perform as a condition of membership. He is not required to solicit votes, is not required to participate in the campaign, need not attend political rallies, and need not vote for the party candidates. In fact, he need not vote at all. If he wishes to leave the party he does not resign. He does not even notify the party.

Source: Schattschneider, 1942, pp. 55–56.

in party government. Parties need considerable resources—both financial and manpower or volunteer labor. Even those who cannot vote may work for a political party. For example, blacks in the South were effectively denied the vote (until the mid-1960s), yet they were not always doomed to political impotence. Donald Matthews and James Prothro (1966) found that voting was an inadequate index of black participation in the South in the pre–civil rights era, particularly when community factors were considered. Their study also indicated that southern blacks were *more* active than whites in political organization and association memberships. Thus, for party government theorists, voting should not be exaggerated to the exclusion of other, more meaningful, forms of participation.

Third, party government theorists believe that voting is extremely important for groups in politics *because the right to vote guarantees the right to hold political office.* The French party scholar Maurice Duverger (1954) defines democracy as liberty for all groups in society, "not only liberty for those privileged by birth, fortune, position or education, but real liberty for all, and this implies a certain standard of living, a certain basic education, some kind of social equality, some kind of political equilibrium" (p. 424). Duverger goes on to conclude that "liberty and the party system coincide" when it is no longer the case that "economic and financial powers alone disposed of the Press, of techniques of information and propaganda, and of a means of organizing the electorate" (pp. 424–25). Given the basis of elite power in the preparty era in property, the distinctive contribution of parties historically is that "they provided the necessary framework enabling the masses to recruit from among themselves their own elites" (p. 426).

This theoretical point is quite evident in American political parties. As J. Morgan Kousser (1974) explains in his study of the restriction of the franchise after the end of Reconstruction, as long as blacks had the vote, they also held government offices throughout the South. "Negroes sat in every Congress except one from 1869 to 1901. Hundreds of blacks were elected to the state legislatures. Thousands served as sheriffs, judges, magistrates, customs collectors, census officials, and clerks" (p. 228). Even the Democrats appointed blacks to patronage positions. With the restriction of suffrage in the South, blacks were dependent solely on Republican federal patronage for jobs. Even this decreased with blacks no longer able to offer votes to the party.

> Theodore Roosevelt's famous meal with Booker T. Washington, his nomination of a Negro as collector of the port of Charleston, and his refusal to dismiss a Negro postmistress in Indianola, Mississippi, immediately became causes celebres. Earlier, such events would have been dismissed as normal patronage politics, as similar acts by President Cleveland had been. And when an avowedly racist national administration [President Wilson] took over in 1912, the remaining blacks in federal employ were placed in humiliating segregation and relegated to minor duties. (Kousser, 1974, p. 228)

Fourth, the significance of the *collective vote* as opposed to voting as a form of individual or group participation has also been of concern to party theorists. There is some internal disagreement within the party government school over just how much policy guidance popular majorities can provide to those in government. Schattschneider's view stresses the role of the "opposition," with the public voting for two sets of potential leaders: those in office and those in opposition ("ins" versus "outs"). This vote is based on the "goodness or badness of the times," and thus provides somewhat vague policy guidance. The other view was expressed in the APSA report, *Toward a More Responsible Two-Party System*. The report expresses the view that the public is capable of a more sophisticated level of issue-based and ideological voting. By choosing from parties with different and clearly defined issue and ideological positions, the public is capable of producing a relatively clear policy mandate, which the government would then be obligated to translate into policy. Despite this disagreement, each side believes there is a need for unified and effective parties regardless of how they perceived the various capacities of the electorate. At a minimum, the parties must be cohesive enough to translate their platforms into policy and then fight the next election on the basis of their records. The opposition party should then serve as an organized critic of the "in" party.

In summary, party government theorists, while not placing voting as an individual act at the center of party theory, do consider voting a necessary element in party competition. Voters—particularly voters in groups who vote as a bloc—do play a critical role in enforcing party competition and responsibility. Another way that group or issue-based voting can influence politics is through realignments in a *critical election*. In particular, V. O. Key stressed the role of third parties in forcing a realignment. The development of third parties depends on voters who will vote for a new team of leaders. If electoral fortunes are at risk (at least among certain constituencies) due to less-than-popular positions, there is usually some manner of retreat. For example, the highly regarded late GOP chairman, Lee Atwater (1989–1991), as well as President Bush's choice for RNC chair during his reelection campaign, Richard Bond, (1992–1993) announced that the Republican party is a "Big Tent" under which all manner of divergent views can be accommodated, especially the pro-choice position on abortion. This more ecumenical Republican party is in response to two Supreme Court decisions—the "Webster" decision and, more recently, Planned Parenthood of Southeastern Pennsylvania vs. Casey. These two decisions have made abortion a voting issue for many women because these rulings place abortion rights at risk. Similarly, the Bush-Quayle campaign put considerable distance between itself and the family values crusade launched at the 1992 Republican National Convention in Houston. However, since the Supreme Court's *Webster* decision and the 1989 victories of prochoice Democrats over prolife Republicans in the New Jersey and Virginia gubernatorial races made the prochoice position suddenly more attractive, the party wished to limit possible electoral consequences over their apparently unpopular decision. The third-party challenge and the promiscuity of parties associating with groups in order to win ensures the representation even of those who may be disliked by the party leaders.

Voting, Theories, and Democracy

We have reviewed four theories on political parties and democracy. Two represent *political* positions found in American political history and culture—the Constitutional position and the Progressive era—while the other two represent mature theories in political science. All four have found their adherents in political science. Each has quite different views on the meaning of democracy and their concept of what constitutes a political party (see Table 3-2). Party government theorists have stressed competitive political parties—not voting—as the key to democracy. Yet party government theorists also believe that voting and an expanded electorate are necessary ingredients for effective party competition. To more fully flesh out the views of party government theorists, we need to consider the role of third parties in ensuring party competition and to examine a crucial case where party government has failed—in the South.

TABLE 3-2
Theoretical Positions on Democracy Compared

Theory	Concept of Party	Major Thesis	Position on Suffrage	Concept of Democracy
Constitutional	Dangerous factions	Voters should defer to their natural rulers (elites)	Restricted to property-holders	Undesirable, dangerous
Progressive	Public utility	Voters should have a direct relationship to elected officials	Restricted to educated and informed voter	Direct democracy via voting
Pluralist	Indigenous parties	Group leaders should intermediate between group members and elected officials	Limited suffrage desirable; low voter turnout increases stability	Competition between groups; countervailing group power
Party Government	Responsible parties	Parties should intermediate between elected officials and voters and groups	Expansive notion of suffrage; parties increase participation	Competitive parties; liberty for all groups

THIRD PARTIES IN AMERICAN POLITICS

There have been a number of third parties in American politics (see Box 3-7). True third parties are a nineteenth-century phenomenon. They occurred at roughly 20-year intervals and obtained considerable success until roughly World War I, when increasing restrictions were placed on the formation of new parties. In the twentieth century, what are popularly known as third parties have been either associated with a presidential candidate—Theodore Roosevelt in 1912, Robert La Follette in 1924, Henry Wallace in 1948, George Wallace in 1968, and John Anderson in 1980[12]—or have been single-state phenomena—such as the Farmer-Labor Party in Minnesota and the Progressive Party in Wisconsin in the 1930s. True third parties should have an organization at the state and local as well as the national level—an organization that nominates candidates for office which would allow them to *make a government.*

> In 1876, the Greenback Party . . . elected fourteen U.S. congressmen. In 1892, the Populist Party polled over eight percent of the vote for President, won twenty-two electoral votes, and elected several congressmen, three governors, and hundreds of local officials. In the elections of 1912 . . . former President Theodore Roosevelt's Progressive Party actually ran ahead of the Republicans in the popular vote for President and the Party elected fourteen congressmen. . . . Support for the Socialist Party peaked at six percent of the presidential vote in 1912. The Socialists elected a handful of congressmen, over 1200 local officials, and seventy-nine mayors. In 1911 no fewer than thirty-three cities were under Socialist administration, including Milwaukee, Wisconsin; Berkeley, California; Butte, Montana; and Jackson, Michigan. (Bradley Smith, 1991, p. 170)

Since 1944, only one Senator (James Buckley, elected as a Conservative in New York in 1970, but who ran for reelection as a Republican) and no members of Congress have been elected by a third party. In contrast, 128 congressmen were elected by third parties between 1896 and 1944. Since 1944, however—demonstrating the difficulties in mounting a third-party challenge—seven independents have been elected to the U.S. House and two to the U.S. Senate.[13]

Third parties are handicapped in large part by the electoral system, which provides for *single-member districts with plurality election.* This means that

[12]John Anderson ran for president in 1980 as an Independent candidate. At that time he was still a Republican member of Congress, and had run in several Republican presidential primaries in the spring of 1980. After doing poorly against Ronald Reagan, Anderson switched to an independent candidacy in April. In the fall election, he received 7% of the popular vote, enough to qualify him as a political party in terms of the Federal Election Campaign Act. This meant that he qualified for public financing of his 1980 campaign and for the 1984 election (which would enable him to receive funds during the election). Anderson did not run in 1984, and thus disappeared as a "party."

[13]Harry Byrd (VA) and Strom Thurmond (SC) were first elected as Democrats. Bernard Sanders, previously elected as a Socialist Mayor of Burlington, Vermont, was elected to the U.S. House as an Independent.

only one representative for the legislature is chosen from each district, and that this one representative is elected based on the most votes, even if it is not a majority. A second or third place is meaningless under this winner-take-all system of representation (Schattschneider, 1942). This means that the geographic distribution of electoral support is critical for attaining power. Over time, the electoral system has focused attention only on the top two candidates or parties. When one party obtains majority support, the second-strongest party monopolizes the opposition—even binding together disparate interests. Sectionally based third parties who dominate in their localities will profit by this system locally, but will be hurt in national politics when selecting the president. The presidency is the major prize in the federal system, and over time, a third party that can never attain the White House will lose influence. This has posed handicaps for new or third parties, but not insurmountable ones if there is widespread and serious dissatisfaction with the policies of the major parties. Even with the single-member plurality election system, third parties were common in the nineteenth century. Since the close of the Progressive era, no third party has provided any significant challenge to the Democratic and Republican Parties. There are three major reasons why third parties have declined as a threat to the current two majority parties: (1) the role of primaries as a nominating device, (2) the granting of privileged status in access to the ballot and in the receipt of public funding of elections to the Democratic and Republican Parties in state and federal laws, and (3) the more recent Federal Election Campaign Act (1971) and its associated amendments.

Primaries and the Decline of Third Parties

The right of a political party to decide who runs under its name is central to a strong party system. Yet this right contradicts the need for parties to be permeable. Boss Tweed of the New York–based Tammany Hall machine once said, "I don't care who does the electing so long as I do the nominating." Nominations in the preparty era (before 1830) were conducted by informal *caucuses* of like-minded elites. Caucuses are notably undemocratic—they work according to the principle of minority faction (see Box 3-8). Caucuses were replaced with the development of political party conventions, which democratized the process and resulted in a grass-roots modern party system. Conventions met in the hinterlands, not in the capitol; inside public buildings, not in the halls of the legislature; and perhaps most important included party activists officially delegated to represent different regions and all levels of government, not just federal elected officials. Primaries, a somewhat later democratization of the nomination process, did not originate with the progressives. Primaries were introduced in Crawford County, Pennsylvania, in 1842 (some still call it the Crawford County system). While it is often mistakenly said that the first statewide primary was introduced in Wisconsin in 1903 under the urging of Progressive Senator Robert La Follette, actually it was

BOX 3-7
Major Third Parties

Free-soil (1847–1854): The Free-Soil Party was opposed to the extension of slavery to new territories. In the 1848 presidential election, they nominated the ticket of Martin Van Buren and Charles Francis Adams, which polled enough votes to throw the election in New York state to the Whigs. The party eventually divided into two factions following the "Compromise of 1850"; the "Barnburners," a faction of the New York state Democratic party, which had supported the Free-Soil party, returned to the Democrats; the more radical members eventually joined the newly formed Republican party in 1854.

Know-nothing (Native American) (1843–1856): The Know-Nothing Party was so called because when outsiders asked about them, party members replied that they knew nothing. The party began in New York State with its motivating cause being opposition to increased Roman Catholic immigration into cities in the eastern United States. Their program included electing only native citizens to office and requiring 25 years residency for citizenship. The Know-Nothings did very well in New York, Massachusetts, and Delaware in the 1854 elections. The party split over the issue of slavery, with the antislavery faction joining the new Republican Party. In 1856, they nominated the former Whig president, Millard Filmore, who did poorly, winning only Maryland.

Populist (1892–1896): The Populist Party had its roots in the agrarian protests of the latter part of the nineteenth century. Tight money and low farm prices were the cause of the farmers' protest. The party was officially constituted in Omaha, Nebraska, in 1892. In the 1892 election James Weaver was the Populist candidate, running on a platform of free coinage of silver. He ran well in the distressed agricultural areas, polling over a million votes and receiving 22 electoral votes. By 1896 the Populist Party was a spent force with farm prices rising and William Jennings Bryan and the Democrats running on a program of loose money.

Socialist (1890s–present): The Socialist Party in the United States developed roughly (actually slightly later) alongside Socialist parties in Europe. The Socialist Party in the United States was first a party advocating the political agenda of organized labor, such as the right to associate and strike, together with the pacifist and internationalist ideals of socialism elsewhere. This was during the era of its first famous leader, and presidential candidate, Eugene Debs, who was imprisoned during the Pullman strike and immediate post–World War I (red-baiting) era. After organized labor achieved its primary program under Wilson and Roosevelt, its political agenda turned to more broadly humanitarian objectives such as feeding the poor and using the government to promote social justice. Their leader and presidential candidate during this period (1928–1948) was Norman Thomas. Many of the programs of the Socialists were realized during the Great Society era in the mid-1960s. Except for the year 1912, the Socialist Party was arguably more a minor rather than a third party according to the strict definition.

Progressive (1912/1924): The Progressive Party was a major third party twice: first as the Bull Moose Party in 1912 with Teddy Roosevelt as its candidate and second with Robert LaFollette in 1924. The two parties were quite different in program and composition. The Bull Moose Party primarily consisted of Republicans loyal to TR and supporting his reform program, most especially, the vote for women and "good government." The Bull Moose Party under Roosevelt received 88 electoral votes and superseded the Republican Party under Taft in 1912. The Progressives under LaFollette in 1924 were much more a "left" party advocating the rights of organized labor and government control and regulation in various areas. LaFollette carried 13 electoral votes, i.e., his home state of Wisconsin. The Progressives of the Bull Moose stripe have endured as a faction in Republican Party, while those of the LaFollette type have persisted in the Democratic Party.

Dixiecrat and **American Independent** (1948/1968): These two parties are alike in their programs—states' rights—and the motivations for their programs—civil rights and desegregation. Both parties were concentrated in the South with Strom Thurmond, who eventually became a Republican, running in 1948 and receiving 39 electoral votes, and George Wallace, running in 1968 and receiving 46. Wallace remained a Democrat. As the GOP became competitive in the South, these third-party efforts became unnecessary.

BOX 3-8
How the Party Caucus Magnifies Minority Factions

The practice of prior consultation in order to agree upon a unified front is an old one, usually described by the word "caucus." The caucus is the core of party politics; it makes political parties possible and distinguishes them from all other political organizations. The general principle underlying the stratagem is that, other things being equal, any unorganized group will exhibit a tendency toward dispersion of its voting strength, which can be overcome only by planning, consultation, and organization. The discovery that a few men, often acutely conscious of their lack of public influence, can by the use of the caucus technique and a little cool calculation acquire a wonder-working efficacy in town meetings and parliaments has never ceased to amaze and fascinate people.

To illustrate the process, let us take the hypothetical case of a committee of seven elected by an assembly of 300. It is assumed that each member casts seven votes, one vote for each of seven candidates, the seven candidates receiving the highest vote being elected. It is not unreasonable to suppose that one sixth of the membership could determine the outcome of the election by agreeing in advance on a carefully selected slate, provided that the remaining 250 did not consult at all. Assume that the 1,750 votes of the unorganized 250 members were distributed among the leading candidates as follows:

A—210	G—60	L—50	Q—40
B—140	H—55	M—50	R—40
C—90	I—55	N—40	S—35
D—75	J—50	O—40	
E—70	K—50	P—40	1,250 Unorganized
F—60			Voters

The remaining 500 votes cast by the members not participating in the caucus might reasonably be expected to be too scattered to contribute to the decision, i.e., they are obviously wasted. On the other hand, the caucus is able to add 50 votes to the total cast for each of seven candidates. That is, the caucus is able to take advantage of the fact that many nonparticipants will vote for caucus nominees unaware of the fact that a slate has been nominated. Thus, the unorganized participants not merely waste a high percentage of their votes but actually assist the caucus by casting unsolicited votes for the caucus nominees. It must not be imagined that the caucus would be so stupid as to align itself against the nonparticipants by nominating candidates who get no support outside of the caucus. Far from it; the caucus counts on its candidates' receiving substantial assistance from outsiders who know nothing about the conspiracy. In this way the caucus is able to make a few votes go a long way.

An analysis of the vote in the election described in the foregoing paragraph will show that the caucus could not defeat A and B who received a very large vote. On the other hand, the caucus could, with a little luck, determine which *five* of the remaining seventeen popular and respected members of the assembly would be elected. A wider distribution, very likely to occur in the vote of an unorganized group, would improve the chances of success, while a greater concentration of the vote of the unorganized would make the maneuver more difficult.

If we assume that the caucus nominated D, E, G, I, K, M, and O, the votes of these candidates would be:

	Unsolicited vote from unorganized members	Caucus vote	Total
D	75	50	125
E	70	50	120
F	60	50	110
I	55	50	105
K	50	50	100
M	50	50	100
O	40	50	90
	400	350	750

The successful candidate supported by the caucus thus might expect to receive more unsolicited votes from the outsiders than the caucus casts altogether.

Source: Schattschneider, 1942, pp. 40–44.

considerably earlier and for entirely different reasons. The first statewide primary was held in Louisiana in 1892, due to a bitter dispute between two Democratic Party factions. The Louisiana primary was a voluntary white primary, adopted to prevent a Populist or Republican victory against the divided Democratic Party. As J. Morgan Kousser (1974) points out, "the fact that its purpose was clearly to prevent party defeat rather than to allow popular control of nominations or wrench power from the bosses should give pause to those who describe the primary simply as a beneficial, progressive reform" (p. 74).

Other states, primarily in the South, also provided for the institution of primary nominations. State laws in Kentucky and Mississippi provided for optional primaries in 1892, followed by Virginia and Massachusetts in 1894, Delaware in 1897, and Ohio in 1898. Except for Massachusetts, the laws provided for primaries only in selected counties. By 1900, about two-thirds of the states had provisions for some type of primary for state or local offices.

The primary, while not a progressive innovation, was advocated and popularized by many progressives. As in the South, the primary was proposed in one-party dominant states to allow competing factions to have a chance at election. The progressives advocated the primary as a way to "democratize" the nominating system. Currently, 44 states and the District of Columbia require the use of the primary for major parties. During this era, the primary was also introduced as a vehicle for selecting delegates to the national nominating convention in a small number of states. By 1920, the movement to expand the use of the primary ended with close of the Progressive era. What was a progressive and antiparty innovation was the cross-filing system. Cross-filing allows a candidate to file in the primaries of *both* parties. This system was first instituted in California in 1911 as part of progressive prosecutor (later senator and governor) Hiram Johnson's "party-busting" package. As intended, this system proved insurmountable for the weaker of the parties— the Democratic Party in California.

The primary changed the strategic calculations of politicians. Nominations were made in conventions and in caucuses. If an enterprising politician did not like the outcome or the major party leaders were indifferent or hostile to his policy preferences, his only choice was to put together another slate *under a new party label* and run it in the general election. One either worked as a team within the major party, or else formed an opposing party. This simultaneously enforced party discipline, while providing an effective avenue for strongly dissenting groups to be represented. Third parties were extremely common in the nineteenth century. With the development of the primary, the strategic calculus was altered. Dissenting party leaders could obtain the party's nomination simply by appealing to the primary electorate over the heads of major party leaders. Groups require leaders. With the primary alternative available, potential third-party leaders could make an end run around hostile or indifferent major party leaders. With the primary escape valve, there was no need to organize a new party. The individual dissenting leader could obtain public office *without organizing a new party*. The problem was that he or she did not work as a team with other like-minded leaders, nor did they run on the basis of a common philosophy. Thus the linkage function was lost.

The decline of third parties was significant because it meant the decline of a method through which new groups with new issues could force the major parties to incorporate them into their programs. The spread of primaries during the Progressive era froze the current alignment of groups already represented by the major parties into place. Excluded groups—in particular, blacks, women, and youth—were not represented in either party. Electoral voting power of these groups did not always translate into representation. For example, women, who received the vote in 1920 as a major progressive innovation, did not achieve power or influence at the elite levels. Without the third-party option, the incentives to incorporate new groups were diminished. The United States is distinct among Western nations in its diverse array of interest groups, and its longstanding ethnic, race, and labor cleavages. Until the development of social movements in the 1950s and 1960s (see Chapter 8), there was no mechanism for forcing party leaders to incorporate new groups or issues. Thus, we believe the explanation for the current two-party system is not to be found in the *absence* of multiple cleavages, as the pluralists argued. Third parties were common prior to the Progressive era. Indeed, the party system the pluralists wrote about so glowingly had artificially been frozen into the progressive mold with limited participation. For all their criticisms of progressivism, pluralists built their theory on the remnants of the Progressive era.

Legislating the Election System

Not only did primaries prove a *disincentive* to third parties, but another progressive innovation gave the current two major parties—the Democratic and Republican Parties—an advantaged position. Originating in the Progressive era, state laws greatly regulate the organization and activities of political parties. The advent of the Australian secret ballot in 1888, the introduction of voter registration, and the widespread use of the primary election for party nomination meant that the state was responsible for determining who was permitted to vote, who should be listed on the ballot as a candidate, and which parties were to be recognized. Two methods were devised: (1) the certification of party nominations by "recognized" political parties, and (2) nomination petition. By the early 1900s, a confusing welter of political parties were listed on the ballots. Due to administrative costs, states sought to reduce the numbers of parties listed. However, because of the dominance of the two major parties, these state laws have largely been written by Democratic and Republican state legislators to grant them a legally privileged position.

The election system covers a wide range of laws, which advantage the Democratic and Republican parties (see Box 3-9). At the state level, these laws

---

BOX 3-9
Legislating the Election System

1. Administering the election system: includes the appointment or election of state and local election personnel, and the tasks necessary to implement legislative and regulatory requirements.
2. Drawing election boundaries: Defining the areas of representation (the geographic scope of each office) and the areas for voting (the geographic scope of individual voting districts or "precincts" where all voters vote at a single polling place).
3. Providing ballot access: Process by which candidates and political parties qualify for the primary and general election ballots.
4. Campaign monitoring and disclosure: The laws and procedures governing unfair campaign or elections practices and those regulating the financing of election campaigns.
5. Providing voter information: Providing voters with election-related information such as time, manner, and place of registering and voting.
6. Balloting: Designation and staffing of polling places, casting and recording of votes (including absentee ballots), and polling place rules and procedures.
7. Tabulating the votes: Counting, aggregation, and reporting of election returns.
8. Certifying the election results: Determination and declaration of election winners; resolution (including recounts) of any challenges of election process, outcome, or right of the winner to assume office.

Source: Feigenbaum and Palmer, 1988, p. 5.

---

limit ballot access to major party candidates and restrict the inclusion of third-party or independent candidates. A patchwork of laws govern ballot access, ranging from California's nearly impossible requirement that 1% of all registered voters sign petitions to Washington's minimal requirement of 155 signatures. The state government pays for the party primaries for the nomination of Democratic and Republican candidates. Third parties may hold conventions, which they must finance themselves, or else obtain ballot access via petition.[14] While many are critical of primaries for weakening parties,

[14]Independent candidates, who operate outside of party politics, do not, of course, participate in the nominating process. They obtain access to the ballot through payment of a filing fee or properly signed petitions (or both).

state-sanctioned primaries provide tremendous advantages to major party candidates. In effect a public subsidy of the Democratic and Republican Parties, they are conducted at no cost to the party, provide legitimacy to the candidate and party, give the candidate and party an opportunity for greater name recognition, and, by involving more grass-roots activity in the campaign at an early stage, increase interest the campaign. Further, candidates who obtain major party nomination via a primary are tested with the public, particularly when they face intraparty competition, and their campaign organization will be in place long before the general election. By contrast, ballot access by convention nominations or via petition produces less publicity for the candidate and party and insulates the candidates from the electorate for a greater period of time. In addition, primary states maintain lists of Republican and Democratic Party primary voters, while providing no such lists for other parties (Feigenbaum and Palmer, 1988).

In addition, federal laws exclude minority parties from access to equal time on television and radio debates and provide automatic public financing of presidential campaigns only to the major parties. Also, and most important, the federal government pays for the Republican and Democratic national conventions, an important subsidy not available to third parties. Other obstructions include the U.S. Post Office refusing reduced-rate postage to third parties. And in the early 1930s, a backlash against socialism and communism resulted in the enactment of explicit proscriptions against the Communist Party, candidate loyalty oaths, and bans against those parties advocating overthrow of the government. In addition, governmental harassment of "suspicious" groups and third parties greatly constrained party competition. These activities, of course, are characteristic of elites and of bureaucracies. As Michels (1962) pointed out, elites will act to protect their position.[15] A consequence has been the channeling of party competition within the two already existing parties, with no avenue for alternative party formation. These points are quite evident when we examine the South, an example of when party government failed.

WHEN PARTY GOVERNMENT FAILS: THE CASE OF THE SOUTH

Party scholars have been fascinated with the South because it presents an ideal set of negative cases where party government does not work. What many forget is that party politics was alive and well in the South prior to the Civil

---

[15]In Virginia, the law read that ballot access was permitted to parties that obtain 10% of the vote in the last two successive statewide elections. In 1990, the Democratic Party did not run a candidate against popular incumbent Sen. John Warner (R-VA), thereby violating the state provisions. The Democrats assumed that the Republicans would in the time-honored tradition not contest the matter. However, when there was some attempt to do so, the law was immediately changed to read *either* of the last two statewide elections.

War. Blacks (slaves) were not a political power. Partisan cleavages divided economic classes. The poorer classes were Democrats, while the southern "man of property"—the planter and slaveowner—was a Whig.

> A wide gulf in opportunity came to be fixed between the rich and fortunate, and the less advantaged groups of the South. It was important for the political expression of this social fact, that the two groups became geographically distinct. The planters exploited the Black Belts. Here also there were small farmers. This middle group and the agricultural proletariat (the "poor whites") shared the piedmont. In the upper piedmont, the infertile mountain regions, and the sandy pine barrens just back of the Atlantic coast, the poor whites and the frontiersmen eked out their existence. (Lewinson, 1933, p. 6)

The aftermath of the Civil War and Reconstruction in the South resulted in a one-party system dominated by leadership factions within the Democratic Party. Suffrage restrictions sharply reduced participation among poor and agrarian whites and all blacks. The only meaningful election in the South became the all-white Democratic Party primary. Southern Republicans contributed to corruption of the Republican Party, bargaining prospective votes for presidential patronage after Reconstruction ended. In effect, southern Republicans, powerless in the South, constituted a pocket vote for incumbent Republican presidents. Nationally, "both political parties fell substantially under the control of elites who favored industrial development and private enterprise." The result was the nearly "complete insulation of elites from attacks by the victims of the industrializing process" (Burnham, 1967, pp. 298, 301).

The "solid South," built on a racist foundation, had profound implications for American national politics, particularly after the New Deal realignment of 1932 made the Democrats the majority party. Because Democratic congressional representatives were more consistently reelected there than in other parts of the country, the solid South dominated the U.S. Congress in a committee system based on seniority. In effect, while the Democratic Party remained the majority in Congress, Congress was ruled by a de facto "conservative coalition" in which a majority of southern Democrats voted with northern Republicans, so long as the Republicans allowed the southern Democrats to run the South as they wished. This de facto agreement resulted from the challenged 1886 presidential election in which Democratic Governor Samuel B. Tilden of New York won the popular vote and seemed destined to win the necessary 185 electoral college votes for election. The Republicans challenged 20 electoral college votes. This dispute was resolved in the Hayes-Tilden Compromise of 1877, in which southern Democrats agreed to accept Republican Rutherford Hayes as president if the Republicans would agree to remove federal troops from South Carolina and Louisiana. The solid South also had enormous clout in the nomination of Democratic presidents. Because of the two-thirds rule, which required any Democratic Party presidential nominee to obtain at least a two-thirds vote of the nominating convention delegates, the conservative South exercised an effective veto over all Democratic Party presidential nominations until 1936. The solid South had devastating effects on the possibility for responsible party government at the national level, and party scholars like Key and Schattschneider were understandably preoccupied with the demise of party competition in the South.

Democracy, as French party scholar Maurice Duverger (1954) has argued, is "liberty for all groups." Political parties represent competing social formations—groups with competing values, norms, and ways of life. It is important to understand the development of southern one-partyism as a suppression of internal group conflict. For this reason, to understand the South is to understand the different social formations within southern politics. Southern one-partyism did not develop as a consequence of the Civil War, but via a suppression of opposing groups by the dominant social class in the late 1800s. Many scholars have viewed the South more akin to a third world country than a region of the United States with some similarities to other regions. Certainly, the racism of southern politics—the rise of the Ku Klux Klan and lynchings and intimidation of blacks following the end of Reconstruction—seems foreign to many northerners. If southern culture is ill-understood by many scholars,[16] it is because the southern culture has traditionally been an oral culture, not a written one, and consequently few southerners have described their culture in books. But that tells us little about the social formations that comprise southern culture and the basis for party conflict. To understand the South, it is important to compare the different settlement patterns in the United States prior to the American revolution. The South was settled predominantly by "Crackers" or those of Scots-Irish origins.[17] Historian Grady McWhiney (1988) terms this "Cracker culture." A Cracker is someone who, in the Scotch-Irish dialect, talks boastingly. The South was settled primarily by those of Celtic heritage—the hilly uplands of Scotland, Ireland, and Wales—rather than of English heritage. As McWhiney tells us, the Old South prior to the Revolution was sparsely settled, yet rich with untouched forests, vast grazing lands, and a temperate climate.

> Such a region was ideally suited for the clannish, herding, leisure-loving Celts, who relished whiskey, gambling, and combat, and who despised hard work, anything English, most government, fences, and any other restraints upon them or their free-ranging livestock. (p. 8).

[16]Many scholars compare southern culture to the rest of the United States without discussing its nature by comparing the "native-born" to those not born in the South. Even recent works, such as a study by Merle and Earl Black (1987), approach the South in this way.

[17]It is important to note here that the Irish who settled in the South came prior to the Revolution, primarily because of the settlement and enclosure of the Celtic fringes in Great Britain. This immigration is distinct from the immigration in the 1840s during the Irish potato famine, in which many of the Irish settled in Boston because they had no money to travel further. One important distinction is that the Irish who settled in Boston retained their Catholic faith, while the earlier immigrants took whatever religion offered itself.

The Celts who migrated to the United States brought with them the old antagonisms, as did the English. The difference was that the Celts settled predominantly in the South, while the English settled primarily in the North. The South proved quite hospitable to the traditional Celtic culture, which was based on the herding lifestyle. In the 1790 census, it was found that about three-quarters of northerners were English. New York had a large Dutch minority, having been a Dutch colony, but even there, the English were still about two-fifths of the population and the largest single group. Pennsylvania was more heterogeneous: two-fifths Celtic, a third German, and less than a fifth English. Elsewhere, Celts became the dominant group the further south and the more frontier the region, comprising from 60 to 100% of the inhabitants. Because the environment of the South was so suited to the traditional Celtic culture, most southerners were assimilated into Celtic ways.

Cracker culture was in conflict with English or Yankee culture, and conflicts from the Old World were transported and continued in the New one. English culture was based on mixed agriculture with intense cultivation of the land, while Cracker culture was based on the herding of livestock on the open range. The herding of livestock was incomparably easier. "Aside from marking or branding their animals, Southerners had little more to do than round them up in the fall and either sell them to a local buyer or drive them to market" (McWhiney, 1988, p. 67). Because of the sparse settlement and the open forests, it was even possible to raise livestock without owning land—something impossible in the North. Typical of herding cultures were an emphasis on the narrative and storytelling and a clannish devotion to family ties. The herding lifestyle also fostered idleness and gaiety, disapproved of by the hard-working Yankees. Indeed, one Yankee complained that life was so easy in the South that "one could live here forever and dream away his existence as if he were indeed in Mohommed's . . . paradise" (McWhiney, 1988, p. 94).

Cracker culture provided more time for leisure and hospitality. Visitors were always made welcome, because a premium was placed on socializing. Illiteracy was high, but primarily because southern Crackers valued the skills of the hunter, fisher, fighter, fiddler, and storyteller, not those of the scribbler, reader, and figurer—skills necessary for trade and industry. Indeed, it was a sensual culture, which favored the spoken word over the written word and fostered such pleasures as dancing, singing, drinking, smoking, fighting, gambling, hunting, fishing, and loafing. Crackers disdained the written word.

> The aversion to reading extended to reading music. A New Englander, who visited a southern "singing school," wondered "how music could be taught, where so many of the people could not read." He discovered that the teacher used no books; sixty pupils were "taught by rote," and they sang "Remarkably well," admitted the visitor, who "was indeed surprised to hear them sing so well." When he asked why no books were used, the teacher replied "in a tone of decided prejudice against *book* knowledge: 'We don't believe in this blind note-singing here.'" (McWhiney, 1988, p. 206).

The South was not totally homogeneous, however. In particular, lowland Scots, Scotch-Irish Presbyterians who took their religion seriously, and Germans, who were found in the towns and larger plantation areas, reflected an alternative culture. These nonassimilated groups were more English than Celtic, often in business as "storekeepers or taverners, millers, ferry operators and surveyors as well as planters" (McWhiney, 1988, pp. 18–19). What business there was in the antebellum South was conducted by "some combination of Yankees, Englishmen, Germans, Jews, Lowland Scots, or the southern-born sons of Northerners or foreigners" (McWhiney, 1988, p. 258). Cracker culture was the dominant culture, however. As southern secessionist Louis T. Wigfall explained the South to an English reporter in 1861:

> We are a peculiar people, sir! We are an agricultural people; we are a primitive
> . . . people. We have no cities—we don't want them. We have no literature—
> we don't need any yet. We have no press—we are glad of it. We do not require
> a press, because we go out and discuss all public questions from the stump with
> our people. We have no commercial marine—no navy—we don't want them.
> We are better without them. Your ships carry our produce, and you can protect
> your own vessels. We want no manufactures: we desire no trading, no mechanical
> or manufacturing classes. (McWhiney, 1988, p. 267).

Crackers did not value trade or the making of money, but the finer things in life. In the words of one southerner,

> Yankees are a 'go-ahead,' energetic enterprising people, full of vim and vigor,
> and shrewd, smart, and calculating, the very sort of people to get along in this
> world, the ways it is 'put up' at present; but it seems to me they lack a something
> that the Southerners have, that is necessary in the making up of a number-one
> gentleman. (McWhiney, 1988, p. 266)

Crackers also valued their freedom. This characteristic was in evidence in the debate over ratification of the Constitution. Jackson Turner Main (1974) notes that the Scots-Irish were, for the most part, anti-Federalist because they feared the growth of federal power would constrain freedom. In his eulogy of Andrew Jackson, Jefferson Davis, the president of the Confederacy, described him as "descended from an Irish family of obscure history but as far as I can learn distinguished by a love of liberty, a hatred of tyranny, and a defiance of oppressions" (McWhiney, 1988, p. 35). This love of liberty was one of the downfalls of the Confederacy. Jefferson Davis was the president of a *confederation* of southern states and had none of the powers exercised by Abraham Lincoln, the president of the Union. Unlike Lincoln, Davis had no compulsory draft and was unable to institute martial law and requisition needed resources.

The Reconstruction of the South is usually divided into two phases: Presidential Reconstruction (1856–1867) and Congressional Reconstruction (1867–1877). Presidential Reconstruction provided few bans on the political participation of former Confederate officials, and the early governments accordingly instituted "black codes," which regulated freedmen in a status similar to their former servitude. After the impeachment of President Andrew Johnson, political reconstruction and black suffrage became the lynchpin of Congressional Reconstruction. The Reconstruction Act of 1867 provided for the temporary disenfranchisement of 10 to 15% of whites (those active in the Confederacy), while granting suffrage to over 700,000 black freedmen. In five states, blacks gained voting majorities and were essential to Republican majorities, with blacks providing 8 out of 10 Republican votes in the South. Yet neither Reconstruction era destroyed the planter classes; while the political system was reconstructed, no land reform was attempted—a significant fact, which allowed the planter classes to reassert themselves when Reconstruction ended. The Democratic Party now included many former Whigs (the party replaced by the Republicans), drawn from the planter and business classes.

Growing election fraud, the rise of the Ku Klux Klan, and the Democratic lynchings and intimidation of blacks resulted in a modest decline in black voter turnout, sufficient to deprive the Republicans of a majority. However, the Republicans and a third party—the Populists—still posed a significant threat should the Democrats split into warring factions, a not uncommon phenomenon in a factional party. The 1876 elections ended Republican rule in the southern states. By 1880, the Republican label had lost much of its appeal in the South, with only blacks and the hill country whites remaining Republican. The "Redeemers" sought to reestablish white rule. High Reconstruction era taxes and a depressed economy led to the development of sharecropping among both white and black farmers, a system that reinforced plantation-based wealth. Tenant farming and the attendant poverty was only reinforced by the development of the textile mills, which were based in rural areas and employed whole families. Class distinctions became more prominent, as rural poverty gripped both poor black and white families.

Cultural conflicts between traditional Cracker culture and Yankee culture, and economic conflicts between the planter and business classes resulted in considerable third-party activity. The alliance movement of poor farmers in the South and the West first began in Texas in the late 1870s. In 1887, Charles Macune assumed leadership and merged several regional farmers' organizations into the National Farmers' Alliance and Industrial Union in 1889, with about 3 million members. A parallel organization, the National Colored Farmers' Alliance, also was organized in the South, with about 1.2 million members. The Northwestern Alliance, based in the Plains states, also developed in the early 1880s as drought and blizzards bankrupted many farmers. In 1890, Alliance leaders turned to politics, endorsing Democratic candidates who supported their agenda of tariff reduction, graduated income tax, public ownership of the railroads, federal funding for irrigation research, and free coinage of silver. Once in office, the endorsed Democrats proved disappointing. In 1892, Alliance leaders gave up working within the Democratic Party and formed a third party—the Populist Party. The Populist Party focused on class issues, and sought to include both blacks and whites. "Populists were engaged in a crusade to unite both races upon a platform of democratic reform in behalf of the common man" (Woodward, 1951, p. 322). In some southern states, a "fusion" slate between the Populist and the Republican Parties produced opposition majorities in the state legislatures. In 1896, the Populists endorsed Democratic presidential nominee William Jennings Bryan, a "fusion" slate along with their own vice-presidential candidate. After the demoralization of Bryan's overwhelming loss to Republican William McKinley, former white Populists were brought into the Democratic party as progressivism in the South expanded.

The central Democratic and progressive appeal was racism, and they drew their greatest support in counties composed of majority or near-majority blacks, the former center of slavery and the slave-owning aristocracy. Black-belt whites had the most to lose if a party based on hill country whites and blacks won the election. Any government elected with black votes would have to appoint some blacks to office in black majority areas, which meant that whites in these areas would "then have to pay taxes to Negro collectors, argue cases before Negro juries and judges, [and] apply to a Negro legislator for favors" (Kousser, 1974, p. 17). The southern progressives were predominantly drawn from those least assimilated into Cracker culture—particularly the educated, business, and former planter classes.

> Not only did the vast majority of the leaders reside in the black belt, almost all of them were affluent and well-educated, and they often bore striking resemblances to antebellum 'patricians.' Indeed, almost every one was the son or grandson of a large planter, and several of the older chiefs had been slaveholders before the war. (Kousser, 1974, p. 247)

There were important similarities between northern and southern progressivism. In the words of one southern progressive, qualifications for suffrage should be raised high enough to "leave the ballot only to those who have intelligence enough to use it as an instrument to secure good government rather than to destroy it" (Kousser, 1974, p. 253). Progressives disenfranchised not only blacks, but also poor whites.

The Redeemers made sweeping changes, including the calling of constitutional conventions to roll back Reconstruction Republican-majority era laws. Key among these changes were the suffrage restrictions such as the institution of the poll tax, the grandfather clause, secret ballots, voter registration, and the eight box law.[18] Where Populism was strong, the Democratic Party delayed disenfranchisement. Both parties sought to appeal to blacks, so long as they had the vote. Party competition required appealing to all eligible

---

[18]The eight box law was an extension of using separate ballot boxes for federal and nonfederal elections. The boxes were used for each major state office. While each was labeled, their order could be mixed up to confuse illiterate votes. If ballots were dropped in the "wrong" box, the ballot was not counted.

voters in order to win. The situation was extremely fluid. The Democratic Party was by no means a united party, peopled as it was by former Whigs (drawn from the upper socioeconomic strata). Not only was the Democratic Party threatened by internal dissension, but they faced significant electoral challenges from Republicans and Populists. These different parties reflected different social formations. In considering this, it is important to remember that the progressives were *not* Crackers.

> The ephemeral victories of the White Ribboners[19] over the saloons, like those of the shippers over railroads, independent oilmen over pipelines, policyholders over insurance companies, and righteous amateurs over political bosses, constituted satisfactions of a tangible sort to a considerable class of Southerners. But there were other Southerners, many of them, who were relatively unmoved by these triumphs of the righteous and whose political urges were not fulfilled by progressivism. They had nothing to ship by classified freight rates, no oil wells to protect against pipelines, and no insurance policies to bother about. Perhaps they were also deficient in righteousness, for come Saturday night they wouldn't mind if they had a drink. (Woodward, 1951, p. 392).

The white primary was not introduced in the South until *after* suffrage was restricted. The primary was open not only to Democrats, but also white Populists and Republicans. In Georgia, as in most southern states, many Democrats thought that exclusion would "divide the white people of the state into two parties, rather than to build up the [D]emocratic party by obliteration of the factional lines" (Kousser, 1974, p. 78). The effect of suffrage restrictions was to reduce the number of voters; the institution of the white primary then channeled them into the Democratic Party. There were dramatic declines in turnout and strength of opposition parties following the institution of suffrage restrictions. Prior to the legal disenfranchisement of blacks—when the Redeemers were limited to tactics of violence, intimidation, and fraud—the proportionate decline in turnout was 18%. After disenfranchisement, the proportionate decline in turnout was 62%. The suffrage restrictions did not merely reflect a fait accompli[20] achieved principally by intimidation. The most serious declines in turnout were due to the suffrage restrictions. Suffrage laws made it possible for the majority Democratic Party to eliminate party competition through legal means.

> Although the relatively small declines in Negro voting previous to disfranchisement were enough to enable restrictive laws to pass, the laws did not simply mirror already established conditions. They had very large impacts on black and white turnout and voting for parties opposed to the Democrats. (Kousser, 1974, p. 246)

[19]White Ribboners were prohibitionists, symbolized by the wearing of a white ribbon.

[20]V. O. Key assumed that the effect of the suffrage laws was a fait accompli in southern politics, occurring after suffrage had already been restricted by intimidation. Kousser (1974) conclusively shows that the suffrage laws did have an independent effect, much greater than the declines due to intimidation.

Voter turnout overall declined markedly. In the 1880s, average turnout in the South was 64%, rising to 73% in the 1890s in states where no restrictive legislation had been enacted. Where restrictions on suffrage had been enacted in the 1890s, turnout in those states fell to an average of 42%. In the early 1900s, turnout fell even more, to an average of 30%.

One-party rule *dampens* turnout, and election laws *do* restrict suffrage. The substitution of intraparty conflict for interparty conflict, along with the declines in voter participation, greatly affected the representation of interests. If one can assume that no blacks voted, "the average primary winner gained the support of less than one potential voter in four even among the whites" (Kousser, 1974, p. 227). The fewer the voters one needed to appeal to for victory greatly magnified the power of interest groups and party machines. Among those few who voted, the lack of a party label made issues appeals impossible and resulted in a politics of personality and minority faction. The solid South represents a classic case where the decline of party competition results in a diminution of democracy. Moreover, it is important to note that democracy happens not because of what a single party does, but in spite of them when two parties compete for power. In E. E. Schattschneider's words, "democracy is not be be found *within* the parties, but *between* them" (1942, p. 64). Political party theorists have told us much about how parties uniquely contribute to democracy. Yet the rich, complex theory of party government has rarely found its way into textbooks, as we shall see below.

THE TEXTBOOK MODEL OF PARTY

Textbooks represent conventional wisdom about political parties, and political party textbooks are no exception. Conventional wisdom is probably what most students look for in a textbook. The problem is that the conventional wisdom about political parties reflects neither the views of traditional party theorists like V. O. Key and E. E. Schattschneider, nor the range of contemporary changes currently being discussed by recent party scholars. For example, the classic definition of political parties as a social group comprising a social formation that links leaders and followers rarely finds its way into textbooks. If it does, it is presented only as one of many different—and apparently equally valid—ways of defining political parties. One of the biggest problems with this approach is that with so many competing definitions proffered, the student can only conclude that there is no settled way of looking at political parties. Yet as we have seen, political party scholars *do* agree on what comprises a political party. It is only when we broaden our scope to include other nonspecialist political scientists working from competing theoretical paradigms that we end up with a disagreement over what constitutes a political party. What is particularly unfortunate about this is that without a clear theoretical understanding of what constitutes a political party, we cannot understand the dramatic changes in the party system in the past 20 years. To clear up this confusing state of affairs, we turn to a review of the *textbook model of political parties* (see Box 3-10).

A key problem with the textbook model of political parties is its *American bias*. Textbook writers have treated American political parties as *sui generis*—unique entities unlike those of other countries. Leon Epstein, a widely respected *comparative* party scholar, has been a proponent of this approach. In 1967, his well-known book *Political Parties in Western Democracies* surveyed party systems with a deliberate "Americanist" bias.

> The aim is to show that American parties, so often regarded as underdeveloped by European standards, are really responses to American conditions which cannot, in their entirety, be regarded as marks of a backward nation supposed eventually to resemble Europe. (p. 6)

Certainly it is true, as Epstein argues, that American parties developed under unique circumstances, and it is also true that modern political parties developed *first* in the United States in the 1830s. However, any theory that provides general explanation must be comparative in nature, and there are important similarities between American parties and parties in other countries. The work of traditional party scholars has always treated political parties not as a singular American phenomenon, but as one found in any system that purports to be democratic. The Americanist bias found in so many texts means that the comparative theory of party government theorists is ignored as "foreign," while the distinctly American political views of progressivism and pluralism dominate descriptions of party.

The mechanistic, atheoretical textbook model of political parties provides little purchase for understanding the complex relationship between political interests and political parties. V. O. Key, a distinguished scholar of political parties, considered parties inseparable from political interests. So did E. E. Schattschneider, who considered interest groups as the "raw material

---

BOX 3-10
Textbook Model of Political Parties

- Political scientists disagree on what constitutes a political party.
- There is no difference between an interest group and a political party—only a label.
- Responsible parties are impossible in U.S. constitutional system.
- Voters are the most important element in the party system.
- Party coalitions are dealigning.
- Party system is seriously in decline.
- Party reform does not democratize the party system.
- Party reform weakens the parties.

of politics." But in recent years, it has become commonplace to treat political parties and interest groups in separate texts and in separate courses. This is ironic because most introductory texts as well as more sophisticated treatments in advanced texts tell the student that there is little difference between a political party and an interest group except for the *label* by which political parties seek to organize government.

For party scholars, the critical component of a political party is the *organization*. The organization circumscribes all those who work for the party. This means that those who contribute money to the party, who work for the party, who attend political rallies, who solicit votes, and who subscribe to the principles of the party comprise the party association. It is useful to consider the party organization as comprised of two parts: (1) the permanent organization and (2) the temporary organization. The *permanent organization* consists of the elected party officials and governing groups (the Republican and Democratic National Committees, Republican and Democratic state central committees and local parties and committees) who make decisions on a day-to-day basis. The *temporary organization* consists of activists who are selected to attend party conventions and meetings during election years. Political party scholars consider those who do no more than identify with a political party to be important because political parties, unlike associations, are *permeable* to new political and social movements. It is through the temporary party organization that activists may redirect the focus of the party. Interest groups are not structured like this—one either is or is not a member of an interest group.

To get around the atheoretical approach to party found in the textbook model, the definition of political parties is often given cafeteria-style, with definitions from many different writers. Commonly, these different definitions are divided into the mechanistic *tripartite model*: the party-in-the-electorate (the voters), the party organization (party leaders), and the party-in-office (elected officials). Party then becomes an abstraction—a theoretical amalgamation of these three different parts. What the political party actually *is* never becomes concrete. In particular, the views of party scholars are rarely highlighted. Joseph Schlesinger, a party scholar who has pioneered the view of candidate ambition as a driving force in party organization, has recently argued that we cannot even address questions like "Are parties declining?" because our party scholarship has been "piecemeal" (1984, p. 372). The "dominant textbook mode of analysis" separates political parties into different pieces.[21] We agree with Schlesinger that this is misleading. Yet, while apparently untheoretical, the textbook model of political parties does represent an amalgamation of the pluralist and the progressive strains in political science.

From progressivism, the textbook model assumes that the most important element of the party is the party-in-the-electorate. Thus, one finds dis-

---

[21]Ironically, Schlesinger commits the same "sin," characterizing parties reductionistically as nuclear and multinuclear units comprised of organized pursuit of office.

cussions of participation in the party system limited to discussions of voting. As discussed earlier, this image is quite misleading from the perspective of party government theorists, who also stress other forms of participation. In particular, it is difficult to conceive of political parties as groups in Ralf Dahrendorf's terms *if* we include the party-in-the-electorate as a true component of the party. The concept of party member in reality is an artifice of the progressive innovation of the state maintaining lists of primary voters. These individuals do not meet as a group, nor do they maintain group norms or channels of communication. Instead, they may identify themselves as Republicans or Democrats based solely upon attitudes they hold—as measured by a statistical aggregation. Anthony King (1969) has expressed this criticism quite succinctly:

> It is common in the United States for writers on parties to refer to "the party-in-the-electorate," sometimes as if it were on a par with the party in Congress or the party organization. The notion of party-in-the-electorate seems a strange one on the fact of it. It is rather as though one were to refer not to the buyers of Campbell's soup but to the Campbell-Soup-Company-in-the-Market. (p. 114)

What is missing from the "Campbell-Soup-Company-in-the-Market" approach to parties is the concept of parties as organized groups. It remains true, as Frank Sorauf noted many years ago (1963), that " 'party' as an organized recruiter and elector of candidates has been conspicuously missing in many of the recent excellent studies of American voting and electoral politics" (p. 2). Students of national parties Cornelius Cotter and Bernard Hennessy proposed some time ago (1964) that parties be understood more like the "organism-in-the-environment" or a "group-in-the-systems" approach because parties are not "usefully analyzed as discrete units" such as implied by the tripartite approach.

> The national party system . . . is, to use an anatomical analogy, rather like the lymphatic apparatus as contrasted to the more wholly self-contained parts such as the heart, the muscles, or the lungs. The entire body politic would suffer— indeed, die—without some processes for doing the work of political parties. Yet the forms and devices by which this work is accomplished defy generalization and regularity. (p. 11)

From pluralism, the textbook model draws the notion that there is no difference between political parties and interest groups and that responsible parties are impossible under the American Constitution. In sum, the most serious failing of the textbook model of political parties is that it interprets the work of traditional party theorists as advocating a foreign system of government. Pluralists did not conceive of political parties as much more than mechanisms through which interests bargained and compromised. While interest groups are sharply delineated, political parties are not. Pluralists believe that however parties evolved in the United States was what political parties were—indigenous parties. As discussed in Chapter 2, pluralists were sharply critical of the contemporary (post-1968) Democratic Party reforms. Because pluralists have so closely linked *any* reform of the parties with the Progressive era, they have been unable to distinguish the difference between the progressive reforms and the contemporary era reforms. Further, the pluralist interpretation is inconsistent with recent party scholarship (see Table 3-3).

The pluralist or indigenous parties conception of party, however, was only adumbrated in response to a specific document—the 1950 APSA report *Toward a More Responsible Two-Party System*—and in substantial ignorance of party theory. Indeed, the pluralists were not theorists of party or of party government. The foes of "responsible" parties view the American party system as adapted to the uniquely American constitutional system, and, for the most part, they support the preservation of the party system as it evolved since the early nineteenth century. The problem with this normative preference is that it idealizes a system built on progressive foundations—the limitation of participation, constraints on third party organization via the primary "escape valve," and the unresponsiveness of dominant party coalition. As E. E. Schattschneider pointed out in 1960, well before party reform initiatives were developed, "theories of power and political organization get themselves related to what people want to accomplish." Pluralist theories with their weak conceptualization of party were developed during an artificially stable era, based on the "assumption that the community is so well established and so stable that no one needs to think about its future." Yet, the 1960s and 1970s were tumultuous times—and times that called for "ideas about conscious control of events by the community and [placed] . . . a high value on the public interest, majority rule and political parties." (p. 60). Pluralist theory— particularly its politicized version—was incapable of understanding the vast changes in American politics during the previous 30 years. The pluralist interpretation was based on the partisan alignment frozen in the post-Progressive era. They are like those disenchanted by the words of Heraclitus; they still long to "step in the same stream twice," that is, they wish for the American party system to conform (or return) to its former self, to a party system that they would find more satisfying for personal or other reasons. Unfortunately for them, a mirror held up to the contemporary American party system will not reflect back the faces of Andrew Jackson, Marcus Hannah, Jim Farley, or Sam Rayburn—but in its own fashion, it serves democracy as much as, and probably more than, its predecessors.

In contrast to the alternative ideas on voting discussed above, we believe (along with Key and Schattschneider) that open and competitive political parties are essential to democratic governance. Both Key and Schattschneider wrote substantially before the contemporary Democratic Party reforms and the decline of the one-party South. While we believe that they both would be cheered by the contemporary changes, the field of political science has been dominated by the pluralist theorists who defend the old indigenous political

TABLE 3-3
Characteristics of the American Party System

Characteristic	Pluralist Interpretation	Contemporary Changes
Two-Party System		
•Duality of Interests (Key, 1964)	Two-party system provides for moderate conflict	Two-party system even more entrenched with the Federal Election Campaign Act (1974) Institutionalization of Democratic and Republican parties increases competition and partisan cleavage and conflict (Herrnson, 1990; Baer, 1992)
•Single-Member Plurality Districts (Schattschneider, 1942; McRae, 1967)		
•Legal Recognition of Democratic and Republican Parties Since Progressive Era (Ranney, 1975)		
Party as a Coalition of Interests		
•Voters Identify with Parties based on Groups, not Issues (Campbell et al., 1960)	Voters are weakly interested in politics Elite similarity moderates conflict Only during rare critical elections do voters switch habitual, group-based voting patterns Interest group relationship to parties is weak—groups bargain with both parties Interest groups articulate interests, parties aggregate them	Parties now based on distinct coalitions at the elite as well as the mass levels (Baer and Bositis, 1988) Democratic and Republican Parties distinct political cultures at elite levels (Freeman, 1986) Interest groups more partisan Conflict is more open New groups formed, older groups more active (Berry, 1984; Baer and Bositis, 1988)
•Party Identification learned during Childhood Socialization—not Issue Based (Easton and Dennis, 1969)		
•Critical Elections (Key, 1955, 1959)		
•Realignments (Burnham, 1970; Sundquist, 1973)		
•Role of Interests in Parties		
•No Structural Relationship with Union or Labor Group (Epstein, 1967)		
No Socialist Parties		
•Ideological Character of U.S. (Hartz, 1955)	U.S. nonideological No class consciousness, limits party conflict Sectional conflicts based on sectional leaders predominate	Parties more ideologically distinct (Schlesinger, 1985; Baer and Bositis, 1988; Jackson, Brown, and Bositis, 1982; Miller and Jennings, 1986) South has changed dramatically (Black and Black, 1988)
•Granting of Suffrage Before Parties Formed (Epstein, 1967)		
•Sectional Conflicts over Class Conflicts (Alford, 1963)		

Characteristic	Pluralist Interpretation	Contemporary Changes
Decentralized Power Structure		
•Separation of Powers •Federal System •Electoral College	Party responsibility is impossible Prohibited by U.S. Constitution	Conflict becoming nationalized (Baer and Bositis, 1988)
Party Organization		
•Cadre not Mass Style of Organization (Duverger, 1954) •Stratarchy, not Hierarchy (Eldersveld, 1964) •Power lies in state parties	Emphasis on competing leadership teams who alternate between the ins and the outs, not very different in philosophy	National parties resurgent (Cotter et al., 1984; Herrnson, 1988; Reichley, 1985)
American Ambivalence over Parties		
•Party Viewed as a "Public Utility" (Epstein, 1986; Ranney, 1975) •Reformism as a Tradition (Banfield, 1980; Ranney, 1975)	Americans not devoted to use of party system Attacks on party system occur in reform cycles—all reform is progressive and anti-party in nature, weakens parties	Decline of straight-ticket voting (DeVries and Tarrance, 1972) actually strengthens parties (Schlesinger, 1985) Advent of social movements, party reform benefits and strengthens parties (Baer and Bositis, 1988) Advent of public interest groups increases party regulation "Common Cause" (McFarland, 1984)

parties. It is ironic that pluralists—no longer dominant in the study of interest groups—would dominate the study of political parties, while the theory of party government has been disparaged. One of the major criticisms lodged against contemporary reforms has been the changing relationship of elites and nonelites. To more fully understand contemporary political parties, we need to revise our theoretical understanding of elite theory, a task to which we turn in the next chapter.

chapter 4

Intermediation: Linking Elites and Masses in Democratic Politics

It is an essential characteristic of democracy that every private carries a marshal's baton in his knapsack. It is true that the mass is always incapable of governing; but it is no less true that each individual in the mass, in so far as he possesses, for good or for ill, the qualities which are requisite to enable him to rise above the crowd, can attain to the grade of leader and become a ruler.

Roberto Michels, 1962, p. 172

Intermediation refers to how elites and masses are linked in politics. For many political scientists, the concept of intermediation refers to a specific theory of linkage: it incorporates both the notion of political parties and interest groups and the idea of two-way communication between elites and nonelites (see Chapter 3). According to pluralist scholar Nelson Polsby, intermediary groups are supposed to interpret the desires of ordinary people to leaders and to inform publics of alternatives available to them, thus tutoring their expectations about the activities of government (1983a, p. 138). The concept of political linkage, however, is somewhat broader than that of intermediation. In this chapter, we examine a wide variety of concepts of political linkage and the significance of elites in democratic politics, survey theories of elite behavior, and introduce a party elite theory of democracy.

INTERMEDIATION AND SOCIAL CHANGE

Political linkage can occur through a wide variety of mechanisms (see Table 4-1). These alternative forms of linkage include the rational informed voter (the progressive ideal) who votes on the basis of issues, belief sharing between elites and masses involving a common socialization, elite representational roles in which leaders respond to constituent preferences in specific ways, and

TABLE 4-1
Concepts of Political Linkage

Theory	Concept of Linkage	Prominent Proponents/ Theorists	Institutions Providing Linkage
Constitutional I	Federalism/Trustee role Dispersal of interests	James Madison	Three separate election systems for Presidency, House, and Senate
Constitutional II	Federalism/Delegate role Concentration of interests Concurrent majorities	John C. Calhoun	States (regional interests)
Constitutional III	Federalism/Delegate role Constituent public opinion	None	Elected officials with varying constituencies
Progressive I	Informed voter (based on concept of limited suffrage)	Rex Tugwell	None—posits a direct relationship between voters and elected officials
Progressive II	Informed voter (based on concept of expanded suffrage)	David Broder	Press interprets true opinion of voters via opinion polls and superior judgment
Fascist	Elite control of public opinion	None	Government manipulates opinion via press and schools
Pluralist	Coalition of interests	David Truman Nelson Polsby	Interest group leaders bargain and compromise
Party Government	Representation of majorities	V. O. Key E. E. Schattschneider	Parties appeal to majority, not limited to group

government manipulation of public opinion (Luttbeg, 1981; Weissberg, 1976). Not all of these concepts of political linkage involve two-way communication between elites and nonelites, nor do all of them assume essential roles for political parties and interest groups as agents of intermediation. Some theories predicate linkage via the mass media. For example, progressive notions of linkage presume a *direct* relationship between voters and elected officials based on educated opinion, while fascist notions of linkage presume a one-way relationship in which elites manipulate and create public opinion. Both perspectives place a high value on the media, but with different ends.

There have been dramatic changes in the party and pressure group systems in the past 30 years. As we have seen in the past two chapters, many theorists have disagreed over the significance of these changes. Walter Dean Burnham (1985), for example, has argued that the contemporary change in the party system represents elite manipulation of the masses, while Joseph Schlesinger (1985) has used rational choice theory to develop a theory of the party organization that *excludes* voters from the concept of party. Kay Lawson (1978) has introduced the term "truncated party" to refer to an elite organization divorced from its mass base. Yet like Mark Twain, who once complained that "word of my death has been greatly exaggerated," one group of party scholars has noted that

> for at least twenty years, political scientists and journalists have been conducting a death watch over the American parties . . . [with] some of the more impatient watchers . . . [conducting] the obsequies without benefit of the corpse. (Cotter et al., 1984, p. 168)

In sharp contrast to those bemoaning the decline of party, others were either identifying a resurgence of party (e.g., Cook, 1986; Frantzich, 1989; Herrnson, 1986; Kayden and Mahe, 1985) or arguing that parties had never really declined, but instead evolved from "episodic voluntary associations" to "modern institutionalized parties" (Cotter et al., 1984, p. 168).

How can one unravel this complex debate? Key theoretical issues are the ability to explain change, and the type of linkage between elites and nonelites. As we have seen in the previous chapters, interest groups and parties practice two different types of politics: parties mobilize majorities, while interest groups specialize in circumventing majority opinion. These are two entirely different political strategies. Theories also differ depending on the political climate. As Schattschneider (1960) puts it,

> In the end, theories of power and political organization get themselves related to what people want to accomplish. Automatism and theories of the disintegration of politics grow out of the assumption that the community is so well established and so stable that no one needs to think about its future. On the other hand, concern for the survival of the community in tumultuous times calls for ideas about conscious control of events by the community and places a high value on the public interest, majority rule and political parties. (p. 60)

These two issues are intertwined. Depending on the level of analysis—elite or mass—contemporary party theorists have come to widely divergent conclusions on the health of the party system (see Table 4-2).

Party theorists do not monopolize explanations of contemporary politics. Indeed, there are also widely varying explanations of social and political change (see Table 4-3). Party theories include those explaining change via critical and secular realignments. *Critical realignments* occur when the stable voting patterns of groups are permanently altered in a single critical election. They are unusual—thought to occur about every 30 or 40 years—and develop out of periods of intense controversy over political issues. Critical realignments are based in changes at both the elite and mass levels. *Secular realignments* occur through slow secular (i.e., non–issue-based) demographic changes at the mass level, such as when individuals move from the city to the suburbs, thereby switching from the Democratic to the Republican Party. Both the *resource mobilization* and the *logic of collective action* (or *rational choice*) *theories* focus on elite level conflict to explain social change. *Pluralist theory*, as discussed in Chapter 3, is based on stability, not tumultuous times, and is ill-equipped to explain changes except through a degeneration of groups into mass society. By contrast, other contemporary theories—*class* and *social group conflict theories*—stress the opposite trend: the expansion of group conflict. Theories stressing *socialization* and public opinion focus on mass level generational change, but ignore other types of group conflicts. By contrast, the theory of *relative deprivation* includes both elite and mass levels of analysis, but focuses on values and discontinuities between achieved and ascribed status, particularly among outgroup elites. As is evident from this very brief review, the contemporary political context cannot be understood without an integrated theoretical understanding of elites and nonelites. As we shall see, the study of elites has been a foreign topic to most American theorists.

ELITE THEORY

The United States is characterized by a democratic ethos: participation in politics is thought to be open and available to all. This sentiment can be traced to the era of Thomas Jefferson. M. Ostrogorski observed that "the triumph of Jefferson, in 1801, without effecting a democratic revolution in habits, gave an extraordinary impulse to the propaganda of democratic ideas, made them the object of an almost ritual cult" (1902, p. 27). The propaganda remains and so does the gulf between habit and belief. It is a fundamental fact that even during the peak seasons of political activity in the United States, only about half of the American public bothers to vote. Even fewer citizens participate at more elite levels. Since participation is open, many observers have concluded that if few participate, then it is the fault of the many who choose not to become engaged, the masses or nonelites, rather than the few who do,

TABLE 4-2
Traditional Party Theory Unraveled: The Views of Contemporary Party Theorists

Level of Analysis	Party Strata	Assessment of Party Strength	Explanation of Party Change	Source
Mass	Party-in-the-electorate	Party system is in decline	Elites have changed Mass public has only responded to a changed elite	Wattenberg (1980) Burnham (1985)
Elite	Party-in-office	Party system is stronger—and it never declined	Mass public has changed Elites have responded to this change to strengthen their position	Schlesinger (1985)
	Party organization	Party system is in decline Performs fewer functions	Mass public has changed Democratic party elites have responded to their disadvantage	Schlesinger (1984) Cotter et al. (1984) Kirkpatrick (1975) Polsby (1983a)

Source: Baer and Bositis, 1988, p. 49.

the elites. Jeffersonian propaganda aside, we need not assume that *everyone* is or should be interested in politics. The American democratic ethos—the belief that "before the majesty of the people everything should bow" (Ostrogorski, 1902, p. 27)—has led many people to accept *as an article of faith* that a democratic political system like the United States is not an elite-dominated one.

Political science—the study of "who gets what, when, where, how"—has done little to redress this popular misunderstanding. The study of elites in political science has been overshadowed by an unfortunate interdisciplinary dispute between sociologists and political scientists beginning in the 1960s. Sociologists like Floyd Hunter (1953; 1959) argued that an elite subtly controlled all important political decisions (i.e., a cumulative elite), while political scientists, led by Robert Dahl (1963), countered that if one studied political decisions, one found a plurality of groups in conflict, a finding that contradicted the notion of a "cumulative" elite. Each theory was associated with a different methodology: Hunter utilized the "reputational" approach (identifying power-holders by their reputation in the community), while Dahl (in the only major empirical study of his career) relied on the "decisional" approach (identifying powerful actors by their influence on a particular decision) (see Chapter 3). This dispute somewhat obscured (in an era of mass voting studies) the point that sociology's elite theory and political science's pluralist theory were both predicated on the same basic assumption that an elite (or sets of elites) existed and controlled political decision-making while the majority (the nonelites) were inactive in politics.

The irony of this dispute is that both elite and pluralist theorists built their theories on the assumption that elites who dominated politics were fundamentally different from nonelites. The similarity of pluralist and elite theories of politics becomes quite evident upon a close reading of one of the best known American works on elites, sociologist C. Wright Mills' *The Power Elite* (1959). Mills identified a new development in American society: the rise of a "power elite" in politics. Mills' work has been described as using the "institutional" approach—focusing on identifying the top persons in major societal institutions. Those who comprise the power elite have attained their power not through an elite "conspiracy," but because of four structural changes in American politics and society: (1) institutional trends such as the growth of the military-industrial complex; (2) the social similarities and like-mindedness of elites; (3) the rise of professional organizers and the decline of political parties; and (4) the transformation of American society from a heterogeneous one of many publics to a mass, i.e., undifferentiated, society. This last point is most instructive. Mills does not disagree with Dahl that a pluralistic society is preferable. Rather, it was his conclusion that the pluralistic society was already in decline (in the 1950s) and that a mass society based on the development of large impersonal bureaucratic organizations was already in evidence. Mills' analysis was originally dismissed as too extreme by most political

TABLE 4-3
Major Explanations of the Changing Pressure System

Fundamental Cause	Theory	Source	Mechanism of Change	Comment
MASS LEVEL SECULAR CHANGE	SECULAR REALIGNMENT	Key (1959)	Demographic Change	Explains Gender Gap
	SOCIALIZATION	Inglehart (1971, 1981, 1986)	Generational Replacement	Explains Change, but Ignores Group Conflict
EXTENSION OF	LOGIC OF COLLECTIVE ACTION	Olson (1971) Walker (1983)	External Group Sponsorship	Explains Difficulties of Social Movements, Not Their Successes
ELITE LEVEL CONFLICT	RESOURCE MOBILIZATION	McCarthy and Zald (1973) Salisbury (1969)	Professionalization of Reform and Political Entrepreneurs	Explains Public Interest Groups, not Social Movements

↑ Consensual

MASS AND ELITE LEVELS STRUCTURAL CHANGE AND DISLOCATION

↓ Conflictual

Theory	Citation		
RELATIVE DEPRIVATION	Gurr (1969)	Value Discrepancies	Explains One Important Precondition to Change, But Only One
PLURALISM	Truman (1958)	Equilibrium Disturbance	
MASS SOCIETY	Kornhauser (1959)	Social Disorganization	Counterfactual—Socially Atomized Individuals Do Not Participate
CLASS CONFLICT	Garner (1977) Piven and Cloward (1977)	Lower Class Revolt	Class Consciousness Declining
SOCIAL GROUP CONFLICT	Tilly (1979) Oberschall (1973) Gamson (1975)	Social Movement	Explains Civil Rights and Women's Rights Movements, but not Public Interest Groups
CRITICAL REALIGNMENT	Key (1955) Schattschneider (1942, 1960)	Third Parties	Third Parties are Difficult and Unlikely Since Progressive Era

Source: Adapted from Baer and Bositis, 1988, p. 117.

scientists.[1] Yet, as we saw in Chapter 2, pluralism as a political theory has since been discredited, and many political scientists today make arguments quite similar to his.

In recent years, the study of elites has been dominated by a particular theory of elites—the *power structure approach*. This approach is most closely associated with sociologists C. Wright Mills and Floyd Hunter. There are a wide variety of views among sociologists on this issue, although this is not generally recognized in political science texts on elites.[2] Within political science, one of the more widely read contemporary power structure researchers is G. William Domhoff, who has argued for the related concept of the governing or ruling class.

> A governing class is a social upper class which receives a disproportionate amount of a country's income, owns a disproportionate amount of a country's wealth, and contributes a disproportionate number of its members to the controlling institutions and key decision-making groups in that country. (1967, p. 142)

Domhoff's institutional approach in *Who Rules America?* emphasizes the power of private economic elites and assumes that the political system is dependent on the institutionally based economic power of private elites, such as is found in elite men's clubs and upper-class–dominated policy planning organizations, for example, the Committee for Economic Development (CED) and the Council on Foreign Relations (CFR) (see Box 4-1). This approach to elite theory ignores the critical roles of interest groups and political parties in democracy, as discussed in Chapters 2 and 3. In particular, given the basis of elite property in the preparty era, the distinctive contribution of parties historically is that "they provided the necessary framework enabling the masses to recruit from among themselves their own elites" (Duverger, 1954, p. 426). Political parties allow for the possibility that the political sphere may dominate the economic sphere.

The separate roles and interdependence of elites and nonelites in the domain of politics has been greatly obscured by this historical debate between sociologists and political scientists. On the one hand, party and interest group theorists have ignored the greater role of elites in governing. Yet, power structure researchers have ignored E. E. Schattschneider's theoretical insight about the conflict between the socialization and the privatization of conflict. These are critical issues for democratic practice. If, for example, elites are inevitable, does that make democracy impossible? Answers to this question cannot be formulated in the absence of political party theory, a theoretical

---

[1]Four years after the publication of *The Power Elite*, Dwight David Eisenhower, warrior and president, warned against the dangers of the military-industrial complex as he was leaving office.

[2]Two of the more well-known texts include Kenneth Prewitt and Alan Stone, *The Ruling Elites* (1973), and Thomas R. Dye and L. Harmon Ziegler, *The Irony of Democracy* (1984).

BOX 4-1
Who Really Rules America?

Domhoff does not assume an elite consensus on all issues, but does argue that elites are cohesive on basic issues and that liberals have little influence. Domhoff combines a class and an institutional analysis. For Domhoff, there are three major groups of the ruling class:

> The first is the CFR-CED-Business Council wing of the power elite, which is rooted in the largest corporations and has great influence in the centrist wings of both political parties. The second is the NAM [National Association of Manufacturers]-Chamber of Commerce-American Enterprise Institute wing of the power elite, with its economic base in smaller corporations and its political influence among ultraconservative Republicans and Southern Democrats. The third is the loose-knit liberal-labor coalition rooted in the trade unions, middle-income liberal organizations, university communities and the independent wealth of a few rich mavericks; its connections are to the liberal wing of the Democratic Party. The major strength of the CFR-CED conservatives is in the Executive branch through its numerous ties to the White House. The major strength of the ultraconservatives is in Congress. The liberal-labor coalition does not have any major stronghold. (1978, pp. 117–118)

In his recent work, Domhoff (1990) argues that neither the national state nor the military have been dominant in American history until the past 50 or 60 years, thus allowing the corporate and private elites greater scope in governing. In making this argument, Domhoff is responding to critics who argue from the perspectives of structural Marxism and state autonomy.

> ... most evidence suggests that the American ruling class has had more influence over its government in the twentieth century than any counterparts in other advanced European capitalist nations. Perhaps there is irony in the fact that the most celebrated pluralist nation may be the least pluralist of the major democracies when it comes to political power on major issues. (1990, p. 185)

Source: Domhoff, 1978; 1990.

---

void in the work of power structure researchers who *by assumption* view the political realm subservient to the economic realm. To consider this issue, we will examine in detail the views of the classical elite theorists—Gaetano Mosca, Vilfredo Pareto, Max Weber, Roberto Michels, and Maurice Duverger—(see Box 4-2), who antedated the developments of twentieth-century sociology and political science as well as various twentieth-century party theorists. In this

---

BOX 4-2
Classical Elite Theorists

- Vilfredo Pareto (1848–1923)
- Gaetano Mosca (1858–1941)
- Max Weber (1864–1920)
- Roberto Michels (1876–1936)
- Maurice Duverger (1917–   )

All of the classical elite theorists have been criticized at various times for their apparent sympathy to fascism, in part because they believed in charismatic leadership as an antidote to plutocracy (the sovereignty of wealth) and the factional and antidemocratic tendencies to be found in traditional and bureaucratic forms of leadership. This charge is a mostly false one. Weber and Michels are arguably ardent democrats. Mosca was a supporter, albeit a somewhat reluctant one, of parliamentary democracy, and Pareto, while a critic of parliamentary forms, was more truly an "agnostic" than anything else. According to Joseph Schumpeter, "to his last day Pareto refused this ism [i.e., fascism] as he had refused to embrace any other" (Meisel, 1965, p. 65).

---

section, we introduce each of the elements of elite theory and discuss their significance for understanding American political parties and organizations. The elements of elite theory discussed here include the nature of leadership[3] and inevitability of elites; the source, recruitment and socialization of elites; the permeability of elite classes; the variability of elites; the circulation of elites; and the interrelationship of elites and nonelites.

The Nature of Leadership

Leadership has undergone important transformations in modern society. The elite theorist who wrote the most enduring and insightful analyses on the nature of elite leadership was the German social theorist, Max Weber (1947). Weber was first and foremost a theorist of *bureaucracy*. Bureaucracy is a type of authority based upon rationality and legal rules. It developed as a result of several causes: the development of a money and capitalist economy, the general trend toward rationality (e.g., science), the rise of democratic opposition to the traditional rule of notables, population growth, the devel-

---

[3]In contrast to pluralist theorists, who have stressed the term "leadership," elite theorists have generally used the terms "leader" and "elite" interchangeably and have focused instead on the prospects for democracy within organizations.

opment of modern forms of communication (the mass media), and the emergence of especially complex administrative problems. Weber also identified two opposing forms of leadership: *traditional* and *charismatic*. In approaching Weber's analysis of leadership, it is important to remember that Weber advanced these concepts as *pure types*, which are an abstraction from empirical reality. These three types can be used to characterize both historical and modern leaders. In Weber's work, the nature of leadership is inseparable from the nature of the social order.

TRADITIONAL LEADERSHIP. Traditional claims to authority rest upon personal relationships and personal respect for authority that has always existed. It is based on *deference* to natural leaders. The most important type of traditional domination Weber identifies as *patriarchy* or patrimonial authority.

> Patriarchalism means the authority of the father, the husband, the senior of the house, the sib elder over the members of the household and sib; the rule of the master and bondsmen, serfs, freed men; of the lord over the domestic servants and household officials; of the prince over house- and court officials, nobles of office, clients, vassals; of the patrimonial lord and sovereign prince (*Landesvater*) over the "subjects." (Gerth and Mills, 1946, p. 296)

Such leadership closely corresponds to intuitive notions of monarchy and aristocracy, which have never been established in the United States.

Traditional leadership, based as it is on family and bloodlines, is mostly irrelevant to American party politics. In the early years of the American republic there were leaders—economic and social notables—somewhat corresponding to Weber's traditional type. In the seventeenth century, the Stuart kings

> made a series of seigniorial grants which conferred large parts of Maine, New Hampshire, and the lower Connecticut valley and all of New York, New Jersey, Pennsylvania, Maryland, Carolina, and the northern neck of Virginia to such favorites as Sir Ferdinando Gorges, the Duke of York, William Penn, Lord Baltimore, the Earl of Shaftesbury, Lord Culpepper, and others. (Barker, 1970, p. 35)

These grants meant an early transplantation of the whole system of medieval property rights to the United States. Tenancy and subtenancy of land, along with the introduction of slavery and the creation of a class of indentured servants, gave form to early distinctions of social class. Josiah Quincy observed about Washington society in 1826 that "the glittering generalizations of the Declaration [of Independence] were never meant to be taken seriously. Gentlemen were the natural rulers of America after all" (Ostrogorski, 1902, p. 18, note 1).

The advent of party politics in the 1820s contributed much to the demise of this traditional leadership; after all, political parties in the United States and elsewhere have had as their historical mission the expansion of political participation at the expense of this traditional leadership. Because slavery existed in the United States until the Civil War and African-Americans were treated as a separate caste, traditional forms of leadership at least in terms of race persisted somewhat longer in the states of the Old Confederacy. There is one important feature of traditional leadership in the United States that differentiates it from the European experience. Settlement of the United States occurred too late for Americans to develop an indigenous American conservatism rooted in feudal traditions. While some feudal arrangements were transplanted to the North American continent, these early social distinctions did not long survive the American revolution. Apart from the related issue of nepotism (to be discussed below), traditional leadership is absent from American party politics.

CHARISMATIC LEADERSHIP.   The concept of charismatic leadership is based in Christian spiritual experience, and so, not surprisingly, charismatic leaders are often prophets, for example, Christ or Saint Francis of Assisi. Weber is explicit in noting that charismatic (meaning Christ-like) leadership is temporary and revolutionary and based in the "sanctity or the value of the extraordinary" (Gerth and Mills, 1946, p. 297). Another common type of charismatic leader is the warlord and hero. Weber's charismatic leadership type is not only different from traditional and bureaucratic types, but in opposition to them. Such leadership is naturally unstable and is inevitably transformed into one of the other types, either traditional, which values the sanctity of the everyday routine, or bureaucratic, which values rational discipline. It is perhaps more proper to speak of charismatic *movements*[4] than charismatic *leaders*, for charisma binds leaders and followers. According to Weber,

> in order to do justice to their mission, the holders of charisma, the master as well as his disciples and followers, must stand outside the ties of this world, outside of routine occupations, as well as outside of the obligations of family life. . . . All this is indicative of the unavoidable separation from this world of those who partake . . . of charisma. . . . Modern charismatic movements . . . represent "independents without gainful employment." (Gerth and Mills, 1946, p. 248).

Weber characterizes the charismatic leader as follows: unlike the bureaucratic leader, he knows no appointment or dismissal, no career, advancement, or salary; such leadership has no supervisory or appeals body, no local or technical jurisdiction, or permanent institutions independent of the (char-

---

[4]Weber's conception of charismatic movements subsumes social, political, and religious movements, which we will discuss in Chapter 5.

ismatic) leader; charisma is self-determined, and the leader sets his own limits and seizes upon the task for which he is destined and demands that others follow by virtue of his mission; finally, when the followers do not recognize charisma—it must constantly be proven—it does not exist (although the claim is *not* based upon the will of the followers).

Two brilliant portrayals of charismatic leaders that are entirely consistent with Weber's type can be found in the work of the Greek novelist, leftist political leader, and Christian spiritual figure, Nikos Kazantzakis. Kazantzakis' portrayals of Christ (1960) and Saint Francis (1962) personify Weber's type: they are intensely isolated and spiritual figures from ordinary backgrounds, who because of their personal gifts attract large followings, including many who are at first uncertain or hostile toward them. Further, toward the end of their lives, others (for Christ, it was Saint Paul) seek to transform their unique, spiritual, and unstable charismatic leadership to enduring bureaucratic institutions, such as the Roman Catholic Church and the Franciscan Order, an outcome that Weber would describe as inevitable. In the modern political domain, the ideal charismatic type leaders are Napoleon, Mussolini, and Hitler. They all were very ordinary in their antecedents, rising to positions of substantial but temporary political power solely due to their personal attributes. In the political domain, the significance of charismatic leaders can *only* be understood in juxtaposition to traditional and bureaucratic forms of leadership. It is essential to a genuine appreciation of elite theory to understand that traditional and bureaucratic leaders distrust and generally despise charismatic leaders—from Christ to Hitler.

Weber's characterization of charisma is apparently unfamiliar to most scholars writing on American parties and politics, since it is often used to describe leaders who are clearly not charismatic according to Weber's description. In American politics, the orthodox understanding of charisma seems to be derived from Theodore White's work, *The Making of the President, 1960* (1961). Following White, John Fitzgerald Kennedy is often cited as the model of a charismatic leader in American politics. White stressed the imperial powers of the president and the personal nature of presidential influence (see Box 4-3). Kennedy's appeal to all Americans and his telegenic appearance during his televised debates with Richard Nixon were, to White's mind, the source of his success on election eve. Charisma, according to this view, is a personal quality that is communicated over television. White was a popular journalist, and many have followed his analysis in examining presidential leadership, despite the fact that Kennedy in no way resembles Weber's charismatic type. Let us examine the reasons why.

Political leaders who are telegenic or who appear attractive or personable on television are *not* charismatic leaders. Contrary to popular fancy—especially those nurtured by television and the movies—American politics is based almost entirely upon organizational and bureaucratic activity, not on individual activity. Any individual, like Kennedy, who is acceptable to those bureau-

BOX 4-3
The Making of The President, 1960

The blast effect of this explosion on American culture in the single decade of television's passage from commercial experiment to social menace will remain a subject of independent study and controversy for years.

In these debates, before this audience, there could be no appeal to the past or to the origins of any ethnic group—there could only be an appeal, across the board, to all Americans and to the future.

. . . What cannot be reconstructed is the visual impact of the first debate. . . . For it was the sight of the two men side by side that carried the punch. . . . All this [Nixon's illness, fatigue, and poor make-up], however, was unknown then to the national audience. Those who heard the debates on radio, according to sample surveys, believed that the two candidates came off almost equal. Yet every survey of those who watched the debates on television indicated that the Vice-President had come off poorly and, in the opinion of many, very poorly. It was the picture image that had done it—and in 1960 television had won the nation away from sound to images, and that was that.

The forces that run in American politics in our age are many and varied; they run in strange ways in our times of general education. . . . Yet one man must make them all clear enough for American people to vote and express their desire.

He is the President.

It is an entirely personal office. What the President of today decides becomes the issue of tomorrow. He calls the dance.

Source: White, 1960, pp. 279–90.

---

cratic leaders is not charismatic[5] according to Weber's conception. Further, as to the communion between leader and follower on television, it is *not* a relationship based in charisma. Marshall McLuhan (1964), who is probably the foremost theorist of television, has characterized television as being a "cool" medium where the intense, passionate, and spiritual leader will appear

---

[5]John F. Kennedy came from a distinguished political family. His wealthy father was head of the Securities and Exchange Commission (SEC) and ambassador to England; his grandfather was mayor of Boston. He pursued a traditional political career including attending an Ivy League College, serving in the U.S. Navy and then in the U.S. House and Senate, and eventually becoming president. His support when he ran for office in Massachusetts consisted of his co-religionists and Irish ethnic kin, and when he ran for president his support was based in similar kinship, co-religion, and party support groups including labor and white southern segregationists. Kennedy won by less than one-half of one percent of the vote. In close elections, almost any group

frantic and unattractive. The formal, albeit not the popular, conceptions of telegenic and charismatic are most dissimilar.

Traditional leaders are an historical artifact of traditional societies. In modern society, which lacks an hereditary aristocracy or other "natural" elite, leadership is organized along bureaucratic lines. Except perhaps in times of great crisis when bureaucracies are ineffective and charismatic leaders may arise from those outside normal authority, modern leadership is bureaucratic. As Weber makes evident, bureaucratic and charismatic leadership are irreconcilable—they cannot co-exist. Even among mass protest movements, as we shall see in Chapter 5, charismatic leaders are exceedingly rare, and when they do develop, they are commonly defeated by bureaucratic tendencies within their own organization.

BUREAUCRATIC LEADERSHIP. Bureaucratic leadership is the most modern, significant, and powerful form of leadership. Modern society is ordered by organizations and institutions that are bureaucratic in form. When introducing Weber's characterization of bureaucratic leadership, it is important to define what Weber means by organizations and a subset of the general class of organizations, namely institutions. Organizations are based in social relationships and are generally corporate in form. *Social relationships* indicate situations where two or more individuals are engaged in conduct where each takes account of the behavior of the other in a meaningful way. In the political domain, such relationships are primarily "role" relationships, that is, individuals occupy roles in organizations and behave toward one another according to the consensually understood meanings of the roles, including the expected behaviors associated with organizational roles.

Corporate groups are social relationships that are either closed to outsiders or that restrict admission by statutes, regulations, or other devices. These regulations are enforced by individuals within the organization whose role and function is to do so. By contrast, a voluntary organization, which is characteristic of a political party or an interest group, is a corporate group based on a voluntary agreement among its members to comply with its regulations. An institution, or compulsory organization, is a corporate group whose laws and regulations can be imposed within a given jurisdiction on every individual behavior that conforms to certain prespecified criteria. Institutions describe the character of governments and their constituent parts. A corporate group is characterized by an *administrative staff*, whose activity is oriented exclusively

---

or any electoral district can be advanced as providing the margin of victory. For example, some of Nixon's advisors suggested that he should challenge the election because of the large number of repeat graveyard voters ushered to the polls by Richard J. Daley, Sr. (one of Kennedy's Irish Catholic kinsmen) in Chicago. It stretches the imagination to believe that poor whites from Georgia who did not own a television were so influenced by the Kennedy-Nixon debates and JFK's personal magnetism that their votes carried the state for Kennedy.

and continuously to achieving the objectives of the organization. According to Weber, this administrative staff, their characteristics, and the functions they perform are essential to the bureaucratic model (see Box 4-4).

Bureaucracy is based on the principle of official jurisdictional areas, ordered by rules and regulations. Thus, regular activities are transformed into official duties, authority is distributed in a stable and regular fashion, and methodical provision is made for the regular and continuous fulfillment of official duties. Further, official duties are regulated by the principles of office hierarchy, ordered through channels of appeal based on a clearly es-

---

BOX 4-4
Weber's Model of Bureaucracy

1. *Fixed authority within official jurisdictions*: Authority only attaches to the office—not to the person; authority is therefore limited to official duties and does not result in the formation of notables.

2. *Hierarchy of offices*: Hierarchy submits administration to central planning, coordination, and discipline. Each office is under the supervision and responsibility of higher offices.

3. *Written formal rules*: Application of rules requires trained experts and results in standardized application—any bureaucrat would (theoretically) provide the same interpretation.

4. *Impersonality*: Bureaucracy is based upon the "leveling of status" and objective criteria. All written rules are applied the same—without favoritism or discrimination.

5. *Career civil service*: Administrative staff are appointed and have tenure for life. They possess specialized skills and receive their positions by virtue of specialized training and expert examinations. They have a fixed salary, are promoted by seniority or achievement (or both), and have job security (protected from arbitrary dismissal and provided pensions for old-age security).

6. *Permanence*: Because bureaucracies rationally order societies, they give rise to a "power instrument of the first order." Once in place, bureaucracies are "practically unshatterable."

7. *Secrecy*: Bureaucracies seek to keep their knowledge and intentions secret from all but the professionally informed (the trained expert). "The absolute monarch is powerless opposite the superior knowledge of the bureaucratic expert."

Source: Weber quotes are from Gerth and Mills, 1946, pp. 230, 234.

tablished system of super- and subordination in which there is a supervision of the lower offices by the higher ones. Management is based upon general rules and written records (i.e., the "files"), which require thorough training and specialization. Knowledge of these rules represents a special technical expertise.

Political parties, interest groups, and government bureaus are all subject to the bureaucratic tendency. Yet, there are two important differences. First, the election of public officials substantially modifies the element of hierarchical subordination. "An official elected by the governed is not a purely bureaucratic figure" (Gerth and Mills, 1946, p. 200). Second, the political principle upon which parties are based differs from the fundamental bureaucratic principle. In bureaucracies, the specialization of functions and increasing vocational training will result in a "caste" of experts as closed to the masses as were the traditional notables that preceded them. For Weber, all genuine mass parties are bureaucratized, but it is a bureaucracy based upon political support and the economic benefits of office rather than technical expertise. Weber traces the bureaucratic development of political parties in the United States to the innovation of the spoils system during the Jackson administration. The appointment of followers and supporters rather than trained experts to administrative posts constitutes an antidote to bureaucratic rationality and a specialized caste. This use of the political principle opposes the bureaucratic principle. The Pendleton Act of 1883 establishing the Civil Service and the Hatch Act in 1939 prohibiting federal employees from engaging in partisan politics even during their nonwork hours substantially limited the ability of parties to serve as the antidote Weber desired:

> Those American workers who were against the "Civil Service Reform" knew what they were about. They wished to be governed by parvenus of doubtful morals rather than by a certified caste of mandarins. But their protest was in vain. (Weber, in Gerth and Mills, 1946, p. 71)

Democracy, for Weber, is based on the equal rights of the governed. The democratic principle opposes feudal subordination of serf and vassal to superior, patrimonial heritage, lordly prerogatives, and plutocratic privileges (e.g., sinecures, prebends) in administration. While political parties are bureaucratic in form, it should be clearly understood that various bureaucracies are constituted in different ways with some rigidly conforming to the model described by Weber and with others—particularly political parties—configured with less structure. The federal civil service is probably the bureaucracy in the United States most closely conforming to Weber's ideal type. American political parties are more personal and less hierarchical (see "stratarchy" below) than the civil service; also, unlike the civil service, parties have no career service and relatively little permanence in office.

The development of bureaucracy for Weber thus involves an irony: democracy requires the bureaucratic principle to defeat traditional elites, but bureaucracy—particularly in its pure form resulting in a closed caste—is a threat to democracy. Weber distinguishes between participatory democracy found in small homogeneous units and *mass democracy* found in large modern societies. Note that Weber finds bureaucratic organization an inexorable tendency in large populations. Because "democracy" has different meanings, Weber stresses that the term "democratization" is often misleading when considering the real influence of nonelites.

> The *demos* itself, in the sense of an inarticulate mass, never "governs" larger associations; rather, it is governed, and its existence only changes the way in which the executive leaders are selected and the measure of influence which the *demos*, or better, which social circles from its midst are able to exert upon the content and the direction of administrative activities by supplementing what is called "public opinion." (Weber, in Gerth and Mills, 1946, p. 225)

For Weber, the pure bureaucracy cannot serve as a source of leadership. Unless leadership arises from some other source (such as a political party), mass democracy is leaderless—and a leaderless democracy is ruled by a bureaucracy.

Are Elites Inevitable?

Classical elite theorists all agree that elites are an *inevitable* feature of any society. As we shall see below, this assumption does *not* mean that all elites are the same. The inevitability of elites is based in two general propositions: (1) individuals differ and some individuals have talents and drives that cause them to seek and achieve power while most people lack these talents and drives; and (2) organizations are inevitably run by a few individuals (Michels' iron law of oligarchy).

THE APTITUDE FOR POWER AND LEADERSHIP. Mosca, Michels, and Pareto suggest in different ways that in every society there are individuals who possess relevant aptitudes for power and leadership and that these individuals achieve influence and recognition. To Pareto, the relevant aptitudes depend upon the nature of the society, such that "if it is one of thieves, the nimblest thief will become chief" (1935, p. 2028). In the study of American political parties such a view might be subsumed under what is called *ambition theory*.[6] Different aptitudes are required for achievement in presidential or executive branch politics, in legislative politics, in party politics, or in organized group politics. For example, consider the aptitudes of a famous legislative leader like Sam Rayburn (D-TX) and compare them with the talents of Franklin Roosevelt as

---

[6]For example, see Joseph Schlesinger, *Ambition and Politics: Political Careers in the United States.*

national chief executive or Ed Kelly or Richard J. Daley as mayors of Chicago. The talents necessary for achievement in the legislative branch are not necessarily those needed for success in other political domains. The general nature of the proposition is that in particular political domains, individual qualities are necessary for leadership, and those who possess them become the elites in those domains. However, these talents do result in important differences.

ELITES DIFFER FROM NONELITES. The most basic point made by all elite theorists is that elites *do* differ from nonelites. As we shall see below, elites and nonelites are interdependent, but retain their own independent spheres of action. It is the elites, for example, who decide party organizational policy, write party platforms, write and promote proposed legislation, and recruit their own for party and public offices. As many power structure theorists have argued, elites do share a common background. A consistent conclusion of party elites is that in terms of status, profession, educational background, and income, elites in both parties have more in common with each other than they do with the mass public. Similarities in education, status, and background have important effects on elite behavior. However, the major criterion of elite status is not a common experience in an Ivy League college, but a difference in their sophisticated understanding of politics. First, elite attitudes are more stable than those of nonelites (Kinder, 1983, p. 397) and are relatively constrained when considered as a belief system (Converse, 1964). Elites thus tend to be more extreme ideologically and more consistent in their belief systems. This elite-mass difference was first delineated within the party system by Herbert McCloskey, Paul J. Hoffman, and Rosemary O'Hara in 1960, and has been replicated in many subsequent studies (Montjoy et al., 1980; Jackson et al., 1982; Miller and Jennings, 1986; Baer and Bositis, 1988). This is known as the *McCloskey distribution.*

Elites differ from the mass public as well in their media use. A major research finding is that the ability to acquire and use information differs between the elites (generally higher income and better educated) and the mass public (generally lower income and less educated). Elites are more likely to rely on *multiple* (and national) media sources rather than a single (and local) media source than the mass public. Further, elites tend to rely more heavily on the print media than the broadcast media. Compared to the broadcast media, the print media provides a greater volume of higher quality and more current information (Graber, 1984, pp. 136, 145).

In the contemporary era, with the *increasing* amount of information now available, the result is an increasing gap in knowledge between elites and the mass public (Tichenor et al., 1984). This allows elites, who have access to more information and a greater variety of good information, to respond more immediately to changes in government policy. The similarity that elites share in terms of attitudinal constraint, information access, and processing vis-àvis nonelites results in a phenomenon known as *elite agenda setting* (Graber, 1984). That is, elites as a class determine the issues (or issue agenda) that are debated. Due to their greater advantages, elite influence tends to be greater than that of nonelites. However, the ability to gain information is not limited to the genetic stock of current elites; therefore, the talent and aptitude for leadership may appear among both elites and nonelites.

THE IRON LAW OF OLIGARCHY. Of more interest for the study of political parties is the second proposition, namely Michels' "iron law of oligarchy," for "Who says organization, says oligarchy" (1962, p. 365). As reviewed in Chapter 3, Michels argues that even those political parties whose primary purpose is the advocacy of democratic principles are oligarchic in nature. Political parties are antidemocratic in character because they are organizations, and organizations give rise to oligarchies. Michels articulates the nature of this problem by analyzing the character of organizational behavior. He starts with the premise that organizations have specific objectives, which is certainly true for political parties—their objective is to gain power. In the United States this is done by the party's candidates winning office. Michels' analysis has been given wide credence among social scientists, even those who reject elite theory,[7] because his case study was based on the German Social Democratic Party (Karl Marx was one of its founders), which was organized precisely to defeat traditional authority. At the turn of the century, the socialist workers parties were thought to be the best hope for genuine democracy—if oligarchy occurred here, then it occurred everywhere.

In order to accomplish their organizational objectives, political parties must perform certain tasks that are essential to achieving them. Further, there are different tasks to be performed, and for reasons of economy and efficiency, there is task *differentiation*. For the organization to operate efficiently, different individuals perform these various tasks, that is, task *specialization*. Some tasks are more important to the organization than others, and thus, they are more valued by the organization. Those individuals who perform the more valued tasks achieve special positions within the organization, and they are accorded more privileges and obtain more power. Eventually, the few—the oligarchy—dominate the organization.

As noted, Max Weber identified the knowledge of rules and procedures governing organizations as being a special expertise. Once a particular clique or oligarchy is in power, however, Michels stresses that this insider group benefits by virtue of their leadership position because they control the information necessary to turn them out of office. Michels observed that "the leaders, those who already hold the power of the party in their hands, make no concealment of their natural inclination to control as strictly as possible the

---

[7]As indicated in Chapter 1, our position is that one cannot combine theories piecemeal— if one accepts Michels' thesis, then one has accepted one of the most essential elements of elite theory, and one from which the remaining elements of elite theory mostly follow.

freedom of speech of their colleagues from whom they differ" (1962, p. 177). What Michels is identifying here are the efforts by the leaders of party organizations to control the various channels of communication, including official party bulletins and newspapers and, more generally, the flow of information out from the party as a means of controlling the organization. These two factors—the knowledge of party rules and procedures together with the control of organs of communication—contribute substantially to maintaining the leadership of party organizations in power. Finally, Michels notes that "the leaders of the government [meaning the party] arouse in the minds of the masses (in the American context, this would be within the minds of the party followers or partisans) distrust of the leaders of the opposition by labeling them incompetent and . . . demagogues" (1962, p. 179).

What Michels has identified here, in a study published over 70 years ago, is a fairly accurate description of the activities of interest groups and political parties, although there are some important differences. Information about failures in an organization usually only becomes available to the average member when two leadership factions oppose each other. Such a battle developed in 1985 when Eleanor Smeal, the former president of The National Organization for Women (NOW), challenged her hand-picked successor, Judy Goldsmith, for the NOW presidency. NOW was organized in 1966 as feminist group working to end patriarchal privilege (see Chapter 5). Smeal had been president of NOW since 1977 until stepping down and endorsing Goldsmith in 1982. In 1985, Smeal argued that it was necessary for her to return because Goldsmith's pragmatic stewardship of NOW had cost the organization membership, money, and militant zeal. Widely varying figures were disseminated to back or refute these claims—NOW membership and finances had been closely guarded secrets.

> When Smeal left office in late 1982, she said NOW had 220,000 members and $13 million budget. She boasted at the time that NOW would have a million members by the 1984 election. NOW's current budget is $5.4 million.
>
> Asked the size of NOW's membership, Goldsmith last week said "Comfortably, a quarter million." But an aide later said NOW has 166,000 members . . . compared with 181,000 members . . . when Goldsmith took office.
>
> The only other public source for NOW's membership are circulation figures published once a year in the National NOW Times. In October 1982, the newspaper claimed a circulation of 290,000. By December 1984, the last time it published a figure, that number had dropped to 178,000. (Peterson, 1985a, p. A20)

The campaign for the NOW presidency was acrimonious. Smeal's backers claimed that Goldsmith supporters on NOW's paid staff had packed meetings at which NOW convention delegates were elected, while Goldsmith supporters claimed that Smeal partisans had distributed erroneous sample ballots. In her final campaign speech, Goldsmith told the assembled NOW members "You deserve better than hysterical misrepresentations of reality. You deserve better than duplicity, character assassination and the ward-boss mentality" (Peterson, 1985b: A3). Smeal won her bid and resumed the presidency of NOW, only to step down again in 1987, when she again picked her successor, Molly Yard, a NOW official who shared Smeal's militancy and preference for the use of large-scale demonstrations to achieve political objectives.

These behaviors likewise hold for political parties, although there are critical organizational differences between parties and interest groups. For example, in several state and local Republican organizations in 1988, this is exemplified by party leaders' responses to the challenges of the Pat Robertson candidacy. Christian right activists associated with the Robertson campaign sought to take over various party organizations throughout the country, most notably in Georgia, Michigan, and Washington state (where the party regulars were ineffective and the Robertson forces were eventually successful.[8] The regular party leaders withheld (and controlled) information, manipulated party rules, and procedures and publicly (and privately) characterized Robertson and his followers as being "religious nuts." In some instances, such as in the Michigan caucuses, despite the superior numbers of Robertson supporters, the party regulars dominated the eventual outcome of the proceedings.

Elite tendencies hold whether the organization is an interest group or a political party. Michels argues that the leaders of organizations come to regard their domination as right and proper. He writes of a "psychological transformation"—not only is there an actual gulf between leaders and followers in organizations in terms of actual skills and powers, but there is a perceived gulf between the two with the oligarchic leaders believing that they are especially gifted and chosen: "the vanity of power." While this tendency is apparent in both interest groups and parties, their organizational characteristics differ. Pressure groups are small, while parties are large organizations. As E. E. Schattschneider (1960) noted,

> the problem of party organization is so different from that of smaller associations that it is often misunderstood. Parties are usually compared with smaller organizations nearly always to the disadvantage of the parties, but parties cannot be judged by the standards used to measure other organizations. . . . The parties establish their own standards of adequacy. Most of the organizational problems of the parties are unique. The party system is by a wide margin the largest mobilization of people in the country. The parties lack many of the qualities of smaller organizations, but they have one overwhelming asset of their own. *They are the only organization which can win elections.* (pp. 58–59)

[8]In political parties, which are more permeable than interest groups, leaders may be less successful in maintaining control over the organization. Many party leaders must be elected and some (e.g., delegates to the national conventions) are elected in public elections. In some instances, the rules by which this process takes place are widely known.

Political parties are constrained by a unique organizational imperative unfamiliar to interest groups—they must outbid the opposing party. Michels makes a similar point. Electoral competition and the party's need to outbid its opponents results in the loss of "political virginity" "by entering into promiscuous relationships with the most heterogeneous political elements" (1962, p. 341). Thus, only in those cases where a group can be kept out of *both* parties via a gentlemen's agreement (such as occurred in the case of blacks in the South after Reconstruction) do parties exempt themselves from the "promiscuity" imperative unique to party organizations.

Samuel Eldersveld (1964) proposed a revision of Michels' iron law of oligarchy for the American party system because of the federal character of American political parties. Since there are not actually two major parties but rather two national committees, 50 state committees, and literally thousands of local party organizations for *each* party, a simple hierarchy or oligarchy model would not be sufficient to describe the American party system. Eldersveld introduced the concept of *stratarchy*. A stratarchical system is one where the individual party organizations are organized hierarchically (i.e., an oligarchy) at all levels—national, state, and local—but such a system is also characterized by a system of *mutual deference* across levels. That is, because of the federal nature of the party system, which complements the system of government, the national party organizations cannot dictate to state and local party organizations; rather they must take into account the individual leaders and character of state and local parties. The state and local party leaders must take similar account of the national organization.

In the 1970s, the national Democratic Party adopted a number of new rules and procedures for delegate selection that state and local parties were *required* to implement. These changes are collectively known as *party reform*, and these reforms represent a special case in the history of relations between the national, state, and local parties. Many observers believed that since these originated at the national level, they represented a top-down nationalization of the Democratic party. We would argue that the changes did not result in a nationalization of party but rather a democratization of the party insofar as they permitted participation in party affairs for those who had previously been excluded. Women, African-Americans, and others have gained access to party positions because of these changes, and while the reform rules may have *anticipated* the eventual social and political changes that altered the status of women and African-Americans, the parties have not become national hierarchies, and the concept of stratarchy remains a useful one. To the extent that there is a nationalization of group conflict, Democratic Party reforms only reflect changes initiated at the grass-roots level.

The Source and Permeability of Political Elites

The processes of recruitment and socialization of elites is critical in determining the source and permeability of elites. The *source* of elites refers to the types of interests represented. Gaetano Mosca in *The Ruling Class* (1939) refers to the various important interests in society as the "social forces" in a society. He identifies these social forces as being based in land (i.e., landowning), education, labor, religion, and in the military. For the United States in the late twentieth century (and for the American party system), we would add economic interests based in industry and manufacturing (more generally, based in production), in communications, and in racial, ethnic, and gender-related groups (e.g., women's groups, gay and lesbian groups). For each of these interests, political elites represent them in some manner in the political parties.

The quality of *permeability* with respect to an elite group refers to what type or category of individuals may or may not become a member or part of the elite. This is a most essential element of elite theory as it relates to democracy. It is a logically *necessary* condition for a democracy that the elite class be permeable. Duverger suggests that democracy involves liberty for all groups: "not only liberty for those privileged by birth, fortune, position or education, but real liberty for all" (Duverger, 1954, p. 426). Included in this is the liberty to enter various elite classes and not be excluded on the basis of social *category*, either race, gender, or sexual orientation. A more democratic political system requires that the various political elite strata in the society be open to all persons of talent, judgment, and ambition regardless of their social category. There has been substantial debate on internal party rules[9] since the mid-1960s with regard to the representation of certain of these interests. In particular, the debate has focused on quotas and demographic representation. Using Mosca's terms, the issue is this: Can political elites adequately represent "social forces" (or interests) to which they do not belong? The debate has revolved around the questions of whether male elites can genuinely represent women, whether white elites can represent African-Americans, and whether heterosexual elites can truly represent gays and lesbians.

RECRUITMENT.   The recruitment function for political elites can be a formal one—part of the bureaucratic milieu described by Weber. There are positions to be filled, and individuals are recruited (the jobs are advertised, or subordinates are recruited by their supervisors) based upon some prespecified criteria. Of course, organizations differ: an "ideal" bureaucracy recruits those

---

[9]Many politically active individuals, including many party scholars, have represented the manipulation of party rules as being somehow a new and unwholesome development in the history of American political parties. This is entirely untrue; it is merely one variation on an endlessly repeating theme. Ostrogorski (1902) observed the following about early nineteenth-century American politics. "It was the eternal craving for domination, which in American political society, ... [based] on the legally expressed will of the majority, adapted itself to the new circumstances; deprived of the use of brute force, it set up from the very beginning, majorities and minorities seeking to circumvent one another by devices of vote counting. The divergent views on the Constitution and its interpretation, which broke out from this early date, gave the sanction of principles and convictions, often sincerely held, to these efforts to supplant the other side by expedients of electoral legerdemain" (pp. 19–20).

with demonstrated expertise, while parties stress political loyalty. In these circumstances, there is usually the appearance of some "objectivity" in the recruitment process, although recruiters usually have extensive latitude in evaluating credentials. This latitude is, of course, consistent with the position of Weber, Pareto, Michels, and Mosca, since the new recruits are selected according to their value to those who select them. Kenneth Prewitt defines recruitment as "a process which legitimates claims to political office" (1970, p. 11). In most circumstances, political recruitment favors those from the dominant social classes and groups. Social and political notables constitute the class of "eligibles" from which most political elites are recruited. In some circumstances, elites are self-recruited. This is especially important for social movements groups and political parties, which are, using Michels' characterization (1962, p. 341), the most "promiscuous" and therefore "democratic" of groups, since they are voluntary organizations. Self-recruiters are important to parties and other groups since they often represent the most capable of individuals. All of the elite theorists discussed here suggest that there are people of talent, creativity, and ambition who are capable of putting themselves forward (i.e., "every private carries a marshal's baton in his knapsack") and achieving positions of genuine power in organizations.

The last type of recruitment to be discussed here is nepotism, that is, the recruitment or, more generally, the preferment of family members and other close kin (see Box 4-5). Nepotism can be viewed in two ways, one benign and the other less so. The benign view is that politics is like any other business: fathers and mothers pass their trades along to their offspring, so plumbers' offspring become plumbers, doctors' sons and daughters become doctors, and the children of political elites become political elites as well. In Alabama, for example, Agriculture Commissioner Albert McDonald ran for the U.S. House, while his son Stan, who got his start in politics working in his father's campaigns, ran for McDonald's job.

> "Every one of us has run Dad's campaign at some time," says Caroline McDonald, 22, who is taking her turn this year. "The whole family runs when Dad does. It shows he brought up a good family. And he's such an outstanding example that we want to be a part of that. Like any kid, if your dad is a doctor, you want to be a doctor. It's not just a job to us. It's what the family does together." (Radcliffe, 1990, p. B4)

The less benign view is that nepotism represents something of an aristocratic tradition in the United States. Thus, those who already possess power attempt to hoard it when possible by recruiting—or causing others to recruit—their children and spouses for elite positions. There are numerous children and spouses of political elites who have succeeded their parents or spouses to elite positions. In some families, politics is the family business. Representative Lindy Boggs (D-LA), the first woman elected to the U.S. House of Representatives from Louisiana, succeeded here husband, Hale Boggs, who

BOX 4-5
Nepotism Circa Election 1990:
Political Hay and The Family Name

Mondale, Humphrey, Taft, Wallace, Brown, Chiles, Udall.

Sound familiar, don't they? And they are only a sampling of the famous names from America's political past that voters around the country will find on their ballots when they go to the polls tomorrow.

In Ohio, the great grandson of America's 27th president is running for secretary of state. In Minnesota, the sons of two former vice presidents are in races for state offices. In New Mexico, the son of a former U.S. Cabinet officer want to be attorney general. In California, a woman who is both the daughter and sister of former governors is campaigning for state treasurer.

What sets them apart from their opponents is one plum they are born with: name recognition. They don't underestimate it, not in the world of pollsters, approval ratings, prime time and sound bites where they have chosen to live.

Neither do they take it for granted. They talk about pride of family and respect for the legacies of their famous forbears. Politics for them is as much a family career field as entertainment, medicine, or law can be in other families.

Tom Udall, son of former Arizona congressman and interior secretary Stewart Udall, is out to capture the up-for-grabs post of attorney general of New Mexico. He likes to quote another attorney general with a famous name, Hubert H. Humphrey III of Minnesota, running for his third term.

"Skip Humphrey said, 'I'm not going to trade on what I haven't earned but I'm going to build on what I've been given.' For me, that really says it," says Udall, who is also the nephew of Rep. Morris Udall (D-Ariz). "You can't go around running on your name, but you have been given something, something's been passed on to you that people respect."

---

was the Democratic majority leader in the House at the time of his death in 1972. Lindy Boggs, the daughter of a wealthy sugar planter and longtime Democratic party activist, is the mother of Cokie Roberts, congressional correspondent for ABC News, and Thomas Hale Boggs, Jr., one of the foremost lawyer-lobbyists in Washington. Among those currently in high political office in the United States are many close relatives and children of elite parents. These include George Bush, Ted Kennedy and Joseph P. Kennedy II, Jay Rockefeller IV, John Heinz, Nancy Kassebaum, Jim Baker, Sam Nunn, Albert Gore, Claibourn Pell, Richard J. Daley, Jr., and Lloyd Bentsen. These names

. . . In California, Kathleen Brown, 45, gets right to the point in her stump speech for state treasurer. "I have three great assets: I am a woman, I am a Democrat, and I am a Brown," she tells voters. . . . As with other offspring of famous politicians, Brown is proud of being the daughter of former governor Edmund G. "Pat" Brown Sr. (1959–67) and sister of former governor Edmund G. Brown Jr. (1975–83).

. . . In Florida's State Senate District 24, ballots will list two Democratic candidates named Chiles. One is Lawton, the former U.S. senator now trying to unseat Gov. Bob Martinez. The other is Ed, Lawton's son, who is running against Republican John McKay for the District 24 seat.

. . . In Ohio, among the better names in the news [is Robert A. Taft II]. . . . Taft himself says it's "a tremendous advantage" that people remember his grandfather, the late Sen. Robert A. Taft, and his father, former senator Robert A. Taft Jr. because it "strikes a responsive chord and creates enthusiasm." . . . Bob Taft says that nobody in his family pressured or even encouraged him to follow in the footsteps of his father, grandfather, and great-grandfather—President William Howard Taft. . . . "You can't grow up in a family without being aware of its traditions."

. . . When Rep. Thomas Luken (D-Ohio) announced this year that he was stepping down after seven terms in the House, his preferred successor came as no surprise: his son Cincinnati Mayor Charles J. Luken, 38.

. . . Alabama is also the land of the Folsoms and the Wallaces, two names nobody takes lightly. George Wallace, Jr., whose father served four terms as governor between 1963 and 1986, is running unopposed for his second term as state treasurer.

Source: Racliffe, 1990, pp. B1, B4.

are offered only as a small sample of a much larger number. Even within outgroups, being the child of an elite family is quite significant. As will be noted in the next chapter, the Reverend Martin Luther King, Jr., was the son of an elite family. Mike Espy, the first black U.S. congressman elected from Mississippi in this century, comes from a prominent family; his grandfather built Mississippi's first black hospital, and his family owns a chain of funeral homes.

SOCIALIZATION. Socialization to elite roles is an important element of elite theory. We are concerned here with *adult* socialization of specific attitudes and behaviors—not the diffuse value learning (e.g., trust, efficacy) described by most works on childhood political socialization. Organizations have specialized needs and very specific value systems. Further, organizations impart

---

BOX 4-6
Dress in The Republican Party

Different factions are held together by their common ideology, but this is not what holds the party as a whole together. The fact that the party is not ideologically homogeneous is a potential source of fragmentation. Instead, the party is held together by social homogeneity. Party activists share membership in common social strata, with common rules of behavior and a common definition of who is acceptable. These rules of behavior or acceptability create an informal language and style that is hard for outsiders to learn and thus operates as a barrier to their assimilation. . . . A crowd of traditional Republicans can be identified by their common dress and their unspoken understanding that someone who dresses differently is not one of them. A crowd of Democrats cannot be identified by a common appearance; indeed they are so diverse that a few Republicans in their midst would not even be noticed. [Despite this proclivity for sartorial conformity, Republican convention delegates show much more originality and creativity than Democrats in indulging in the personal expressionism that the convention atmosphere permits. Delegates to both conventions often wear costumes and/or hats decorated with political paraphernalia. Those worn by Republican delegates are considerably more numerous and picturesque.]

. . . Entire groups seeking to become Republican activists who do not share the common style find acceptance difficult because their presence threatens the social homogeneity that holds the party together. A

---

these values to their members—they are learned within the organization. In fact, the socialization of these values represents a formal task for the organization—it is not, as is often the case with childhood socialization, a matter of serendipity. Childhood socialization takes place informally in the family and among peer (i.e., same age) groups and more formally in the schools. Adult socialization to elite roles can take place informally in social interactions or more formally in training workshops offered by the organization for its members.

The values taught to elites represent a coherent world view, or *political culture*. This political culture is most evident in exclusive organizations like political parties, and less obvious in interest groups, which are characterized by overlapping memberships. Andrew McFarland, who has studied the organization Common Cause, concludes that most members share a world view he terms "civic balance." This is the belief that " 'special interests' control some areas of governmental policy and that 'public interests' ('the people')

frequent reaction by traditional Republicans to the New Right supporters of Reagan is to assert that they are "not real Republicans" and thus do not deserve to exercise power within the party. This claim was first made at the 1976 convention. When Reagan delegates dominated the 1980 convention it was muted, but still there. Reagan's political success curbed the expression of this sentiment, but not its existence. The 1984 convention saw many traditional Republicans present as Reagan delegates, but in eight years their opinion of the newcomers there with them had not really changed. One reporter [Molly Ivans] described the women delegates as coming "in two main flavors: Ultrasuede and polyester."

> The Ultrasuedes . . . look down on the polyesters. . . . Some Ultrasuedes are feeling outnumbered by the polyesters this year as though their party has been taken over by people they would never allow to join the country club. Not the right sort. . . . As though someone had let some tacky girls into a Kappa chapter. I guess it is a simple class distinction, but along with having more money, the Ultrasuedes tend to be more sophisticated and also more liberal on social issues than the polyesters. They are frankly embarrassed, if not mortified, by the party's Jerry Falwell connection, but only in a social sense.

Democrats would not seriously accuse someone of not being a real Democrat, because a Democrat is anyone who claims to be one.

Source: Freeman, 1986, pp. 349–50.

must organize to balance the power of those special interests" (1984, p. 3). This world view is not unique to Common Cause, but is one shared by progressives, generally, and other organizations like the League of Women Voters, Ralph Nader's Public Citizen, American Civil Liberties Union, and environmentalist groups.[10]

In the Democratic and Republican Parties, the political cultures extend not only to beliefs, but also to behavior and even to the manner of dress (see Box 4-6). Jo Freeman (1986) has detailed these differences based on her extensive observations of both parties. One of the more distinctive differences has to do with the way Republicans and Democrats manage conflict: "Democratic party politics are open, loud, and confrontational, while those of the Republican party are closed, quiet and consensual." Unlike the Democrats where "speaking out is a means of access," in the Republican party, "Maneu-

---

[10]McFarland notes that there are overlapping memberships between these organizations: "there seem to be 100,000 households in the country that contribute a total of at least $75 a year to three or more of the following: Common Cause, Nader's Public Citizen, LWV, ACLU, public television/radio, and environmentalist lobbies" (1984, p. 45).

vering is acceptable. Challenging is not." According to Freeman, "these contrasting styles were exemplified by a description of the battles over replacing the Massachusetts state party chairs in 1956" (1986, pp. 338–340).

> In the Democratic party the affair could best be called a brawl all the way—at least as the press reported it, no doubt with some gleeful exaggeration. Statements and counter-statements to the press, accusations of falsehood mutually tossed back and forth, gave the dispute most of the elements of an Irish donnybrook, minus only the swinging of fists. There were threats of that too. While the Democrats were having their fracas, the heir apparent for the Republican nomination was carrying on a quiet war against the incumbent Republican chairman, but with a very different tone and with very different procedures. A dispatch to the *New York Times* illustrated the differences of approach. It noted that the Democrats had allowed the reporters in to hear their showdown on replacing their chairman; it then went on to describe the Republican methods: "Following a brief exchange of statements in the newspapers, a characteristic hush fell over the Republican headquarters. It has been the experience of political reporters in Massachusetts for years that the Republicans promote publicity, and hire press agents to carry out the program so long as it is favorable. Anything unfavorable is carefully thrashed out behind closed doors of private social and dining clubs. The participants then walk out smiling at each other, each trying to ignore political knife handles protruding from their backs. So it was Tuesday night. . . . Reporters were barred from the meeting until after the balloting was finished. They were admitted in time to hear [the defeated chairman] make his valedictory." (Freeman, 1986, p. 339)

The parties also have different concepts of legitimacy in the organization, cohesion, commitment, and disloyalty.

Among party theorists, Roberto Michels (1962) stresses the inevitable psychological transformation that occurs when individuals attain positions of power.

> The consciousness of power always produces vanity, an undue belief in personal greatness. The desire to dominate, for good or evil, is universal. These are elementary psychological facts. In the leader, the consciousness of his personal worth, and of the need which the mass feels for guidance, combine to induce in his mind a recognition of his own superiority, and awake, in addition, that spirit of command which exists in the germ in every man born of woman. (p. 206)

Social learning theory describes the elite socialization process. New recruits in an organization observe the behavior of others, especially those in superior positions, and in some manner imitate that behavior with the expectation that such imitation will engender positive reinforcement (reward). New recruits in a law firm will dress and comport themselves like their superiors, perhaps read the same newspapers and magazines, and probably play the same sports, racquetball or tennis here and squash there. If asked they will probably voice opinions not unlike the opinions of their superiors in the organization; if they do otherwise it will be only rarely and apologetically. When this process is successful, the new recruits to an organization eventually become much like those who preceded them. This socialization process is not always descriptive of elite recruitment since, as noted above, there are challengers who defy leaders in organizations and if they are successful they will be co-opted or, more rarely, they will supplant those in superior positions to them (e.g., when Jesse Jackson and William Singer replaced Richard J. Daley as leaders of the Chicago delegation to the Democratic National Convention in 1972). Both co-optation and the replacement of those in superior positions are very significant for politics, since this represents an essential part of the process of political change.

The recruitment and socialization processes are essential to the establishment and maintenance of political organizations and elite cadres. The processes involved can be used to explain both continuity in organizations as well as change. It is impossible to understand the politics of an organization without understanding the source of its elite cadres and its recruitment and socialization practices. Political parties are critical to the recruitment and socialization of the ruling political elite. While independent candidates are occasionally elected to office, this is exceedingly rare. The Republican and Democratic Parties share an exclusive monopoly on political recruitment and even those who are self-recruited must ascend through one party or the other.

While parties are private voluntary organizations[11] like interest groups, political parties as organizations are quite different from all other organizations. In particular they are, as Michels says, promiscuous—seeking power by combining many and diverse support groups together without undue regard to principles. After all, the first priority of political parties is to win elections. This means that recruitment to political parties has been more open and indiscriminate than in other elite organizations. The French party scholar Maurice Duverger observed that the distinctive historical contribution of political parties was that "they provided the necessary framework enabling the masses to recruit from among themselves their own elites" (1954, p. 426). This was true for the United States. In this sense, the first genuinely modern democratic leaders in the United States were unquestionably Andrew Jackson and Martin Van Buren. Ostragorski observed that "Jackson's name was not merely the rallying-cry for the battle of the 'democratic principle against the theory of the Constitution' but also for the battle of the 'people' against the caste of men of intelligence, of culture, of wealth, of social refinement, of historical traditions" (1902, pp. 45–46). It is important to note here that while the processes of recruitment and socialization are critical to understanding

---

[11]While the U.S. Supreme Court considers parties to be private associations, they are heavily regulated at the state level in terms of their internal party organization. Recent cases in the Supreme Court have resulted in some of these regulations being overturned.

conflict, continuity, and change in elite institutions, it is also important to understand that this process differs somewhat from organization to organization, with political parties being the most open of elite organizations.

The Circulation and Variability of Elites

The *variability of elites* refers to the variety of these types or more particularly the presence of different types of elites in a particular political system. Elite types can be conceived of and idealized in a number of different ways. A system that is characteristically pluralist, democratic, or based in groups will have a variety of competitive elites. The concept of the *circulation of elites* is critical to an understanding of democratic practice. While it is necessary for democratic practice that no individuals be excluded from elite status based upon race, gender, or other social category (permeability), it is equally necessary that the ruling elites be replaceable. A number of theorists have discussed this concept, each offering a somewhat different perspective. The term circulation of elites is first and foremost one associated with Pareto; however, Pareto's formulation does not correspond to the simple intuitive sense of the term, i.e., one group of elites replacing another.

Self-recruits represent an important aspect of the variability of elites. Self-recruiters often represent a challenge to the leadership of organizations, and in some circumstances when the leadership is incapable of diverting their challenges, they are "bought off" (i.e., their challenge to the leadership and organization is withdrawn) with positions, and the benefits consequent to the positions, within the organization. In elite theory this is referred to as *co-optation*. While co-optation may engender change within an organization, its fundamental purpose is to minimize such change by an accommodation with opposition elements. Michels argued that the struggle between the old leaders and the new will mostly result in a *reunion des elites* rather than a *circulation des elites*. What he meant is that when the leaders of organizations face serious challenges, they compromise with their challengers rather than face the prospect of being replaced by them. And of course this strategy is especially appealing to the old leaders, since the new elites may soon be much like the old elites who preceded them.

Both the Republican and Democratic Parties have had women as the national party chairmen: Mary Louise Smith for the GOP and Jean Westwood for the Democrats (although for only a brief time). Party rules in the Democratic Party require equal representation for women in a number of party bodies, including the national conventions and on the national committee. Republicans do not have formal quotas for women, but there are a number of formal positions within various GOP organizations, such as the state parties, that are reserved for women. There are no formal quotas in either party requiring black or Hispanic[12] representation, but the Democratic Party has fairly strict affirmative action guidelines with respect to black delegate positions at the national conventions (also many of the women under the women's quota, i.e., the 50% rule, are black), and these rules were made even more comprehensive for 1992 because of the successful efforts of Jesse Jackson in 1988.

A distinction has to be made between positions in the party that are reserved for members of outgroups and positions that are genuinely competitive. There is some uncertainty as to the significance of many of the positions reserved for outgroup elites in the parties. Over 20 years ago, Cornelius Cotter and Bernard Hennessy observed that "while the national committee*men* were judged to be quite important figures in their respective state parties, nearly one-third of Republican women and one-half of Democratic women were rated as quite unimportant." They conclude that "if *these* women have little influence, then no women have much influence in the state parties" (1964, p. 58). More recently, during the 1988 presidential campaign, a prominent Democratic congressman suggested that women and blacks "shut up" until the presidential election was over, and then "if Dukakis won, they would get all that they wanted." If Cotter and Hennessy are correct, and we believe that their observations were both astute and correct, and if the statements of this Democratic congressman (Peter Kostmayer [D-PA]) are representative of the male leadership of the Democratic Party, then it is possible that the main purpose of these reserved positions for women in various Democratic Party organizations (both temporary and permanent) is to deflect them from a more serious *organizational* challenge to the male leaders—local, state and national. That is, if party positions reserved for women were eliminated, then perhaps women's organizations would seek to compete for, and perhaps win, those positions in the party that represent genuine influence.

The most important of the various typologies of elites was introduced by Pareto in *Mind and Society* (1935). Being an economist, he differentiates two ideal types found in both the economic system and the political system— the *rentier*[13] and the *speculator*. Pareto introduced these two types to explain consistent patterns of political change that have occurred throughout history. The rentier type is typically conservative, timid, averse to change, and wishes to preserve what has already been gained. Rentier types in government are referred to as "lions" by Pareto, who maintains that they govern primarily by means of force, religion, and similar sentiments. The speculator type is im-

---

[12]There are no formal requirements for gay representation in either party, although the Democrats have made great efforts to court organized gay interests. The only openly acknowledged gay members of the U.S. Congress are Massachusetts Democrats Gerry Studds and Barney Franks.

[13]The *rentier* as an economic type is one who seeks to cautiously invest in safe (and thus low yield) investments. The rentier mindset is a defensive one reflecting doubt and anxiety about the future and a desire to shield one's existing capital from risk.

aginative, expansive, and eager for new ideas, experiences, and enterprises. The speculator is venturesome and confident and eager to try something new. Pareto refers to speculators as "foxes" when they are the ruling elite, and they rule by means of intelligence, manipulation, cunning, and demagogic appeals to the various interests in society.[14]

Mosca (1939) also defines a somewhat similar typology, but his is based more in traditional class differences. He differentiates a "democratic tendency" and an "aristocratic tendency." Elite cadres or political systems based upon a democratic tendency are permeable to members of the lower classes. Systems displaying an aristocratic tendency reflect the desire to "stabilize social control and political power in the descendants" of the governing elite. Since American party politics has represented since its inception Mosca's "democratic tendency," his typology is less useful than Pareto's in understanding American politics and parties.

Pareto's formulation of circulation of elites starts with his division of society into ruling elites, nonruling elites, and the masses (nonelites). Political change, i.e., circulation, occurs depending upon the relative proportions of rentiers and speculators in the two elite classes. After a ruling elite of one type has been in power for some time, superior elements accumulate among the nonruling elites and inferior individuals begin to predominate among the ruling elites. Thus, energies wane and errors abound among the ruling elements, and they are eventually replaced by elites from the nonruling elite class. Thus, speculators are replaced by rentiers, only to be replaced at some later time by a new group of speculators. The nature of politics at any given time (liberal or conservative) depends upon which type predominates among the ruling elites.

The most interesting aspect of Mosca's thinking with respect to circulation of elites is his endorsement of the *democratic tendency* as a means to ensure gradual (and progressive) change. Mosca believes that the addition of new elements (and of course these are the *superior* elements for the nonelite classes) from the lower classes is essential to a stable politics and that it "prevents the exhaustion of the aristocracies of birth that is wont to bring on great social cataclysms" (1939, p. 127).

Weber was quite pessimistic about the prospects for change in completely bureaucratized institutions. Change occurs in response to the appearance of charismatic leaders and movements, which—if successful—inevitably (in modern

[14]It is tempting and quite natural to relate Pareto's rentier and speculator types to liberals and conservatives in American politics, but such an equation would be most incorrect as there is no necessary relation between the two. In fact, in 1980 when Ronald Reagan and a large number of conservative Republicans were seeking office, it was arguably they who were the speculators and the Democrats who were in power in the executive branch and in the U.S. Senate who were the rentiers. The Conservative Opportunity Society (COS), a conservative group in the U.S. House of Representatives formerly led by Jack Kemp (now secretary of Housing and Urban Development) and Newt Gingrich (now House minority whip), while motivated by conservative principles, is also arguably a speculator group.

societies) become routinized and transformed into bureaucratic entities. However, Weber did not anticipate the decline of the party machine, which traded jobs for votes (this was his ideal party bureaucracy), or the development of social movements, which arose from outgroup organizations rather than through the efforts of charismatic leaders.

A third perspective on the circulation of elites or rather the *noncirculation of elites* comes from Michels. Michels was quite deterministic in believing that organizational dynamics were central to party politics and further that "the struggle between the old leaders and the new" will result "not so much [in] a *circulation des elites* as a *reunion des elites*, that is to say of the two elements" (1962, p. 182). Michels proposes that change primarily occurs as the leaders of organizations incorporate new and somewhat different elements into their ranks (co-optation) rather than by the replacement of one group of elites with another. Michels (1962) observed that

> if the leaders of the opposition within the party are dangerous because they have a large following among the masses, and if they are at the same time few in number, the old party leaders endeavor to hold them in check and to neutralize their influence by . . . conceding posts . . . to its most conspicuous leaders, thus gaining control over the revolutionary [i.e., opposition] impulse. (pp. 181–182)

This of course remains a standard practice for the leaders of American parties. Both Jesse Jackson and Pat Robertson were opposition leaders within their respective parties in 1988. Among other things provided to these two opposition leaders was the appointment of Jesse Jackson's son to the Democratic National Committee (DNC) and the appointment of Pat Robertson's campaign manager, Marc Nuttle, to an important post in the national Republican Party hierarchy.

Political parties have been considered an essential element of democratic societies. Max Weber, who was a close friend of Roberto Michels, laid great emphasis on political parties as the only antidote for a bureaucratized government. Despite Michels' identification of the iron law of oligarchy, he still valued democracy—as "a treasure which no one will ever discover by deliberate search" (1962, p. 368). French party scholar Maurice Duverger criticized Michels' conclusion and abiding pessimism about discovering this treasure. While Duverger agreed with Michels that the socialist parties *did* create another elite separate from the masses, he believed that the socialist parties did expand democracy because they resulted in "government by the people by *an elite sprung from the people*" (1954, p. 425).

A final perspective of circulation of elites that we would offer is from Schattschneider,[15] who suggested that in a two-party political system, "the

---

[15]Other American party scholars have also attempted typologies in order to distinguish various types of elites, although their efforts have proved much less fruitful than Pareto's. The best known of these typologies is James Q. Wilson's (1962) conceptions of *amateurs* and *regulars*

monopoly of the opposition is the most important asset of the second major party" (1942, p. 82). In effect, Schattschneider identifies a system where there is a "party-in-power" and a "party-in-opposition." Party competition—requiring at minimum two parties—is an essential component of Schattschneider's model. The one-party system found in the South prior to Democratic Party reforms prevented the development of stable competition. Factions within the Democratic Party were fluid and new slates of candidates denied responsibility for the previous administration, even though they all belonged to the same party. V. O. Key observed in his classic study, *Southern Politics* (1949), that "the voter is confronted with new faces, new choices, and function in a sort of state of nature. . . . [The electorate] has no way of identifying the 'ins.' . . . There is really no feasible way of throwing the rascals out" (pp. 303–304).

This division of elites into the "ins" and the "outs" is similar to Pareto's conception of a ruling elite, a nonruling elite, and a mass. The nonelites, i.e., the mass, decide which group of elites will hold power, and when they are dissatisfied, they will replace one group of elites with the opposition group. Schattschneider's conception of circulation of elites is closest to the common intuitive sense of circulation of elites.

---

in the parties. Wilson studied club politics in New York, Chicago, and Los Angeles in the early 1960s and identified an amateur democratic type of political activist. According to Wilson, these amateurs were characteristically as committed to "internal party democracy" as to promoting any particular set of interests. They were committed to programmatic action, an expanded base of political participation, presenting clear alternatives to the other party, and basing action upon the merits of issues rather than on gaining partisan advantage. These amateur democrats were juxtaposed to party regulars, individuals like Mayor Richard J. Daley of Chicago, who were committed to their largely undemocratic and oligarchic party organizations.

We do not find Wilson's typology particularly persuasive because he acknowledges neither Pareto's nor Mosca's ideal types, and quite frankly we believe he fundamentally misreads the nature of elite politics. His contention that the promotion of internal party democracy is an important motivation of political elites we find inconsistent with elite theory and party politics. We certainly would agree that under some circumstances, there are elites who promote their *interests* under the *guise* of expanding internal party democracy, and further, we would even acknowledge that many of these elites sincerely hold to these principles while using them in pursuit of their own ends. This is of course precisely what Ostrogorski observed about American politics in the early nineteenth century and later (1902, pp. 19–20). The manipulation of majorities and minorities, electoral legerdemain, and devices of vote counting are all means to satisfy a craving for domination. There is no reason to believe that these amateur democrats were seeking anything else.

One of the amateur democrats that Wilson identified was Dan Walker, then a lawyer associated with the Committee on Illinois Government (CIG). This "amateur democrat" later walked the state of Illinois ("Walkin Dan Walker") as part of his campaign for governor and he was eventually successful. Thus, his association with the CIG and club politics was quite helpful to his personal career. Later, after he became governor, Dan Walker was not noticeably more concerned with democratic practices than were his predecessors, and his political career eventually ended with Walkin' Dan Walker being inmate Dan Walker, a temporary retirement not unlike that of numerous "undemocratic" party regulars who came before him. Perhaps, the same can be said for these amateur democrats as was said about the missionaries in Hawaii—"they came to do good, and they stayed to do well."

The Interrelationship of Elites and Nonelites

The final perspective on elites and nonelites that we offer is on the nature of the relationship between them. Elites and non-elites are *inter*dependent. They have separate spheres of action, yet they can influence each other. Elite theorists have consistently stressed that elites influence nonelites more than vice versa. However true this may be over the long run, elites—even in systems without popular elections—cannot ignore the views and preferences of nonelites. In the extreme case, elites may be overturned by a revolution. The historian Charles Tilly has stressed that nonelites acted independently of elites even before the advent of modern political parties and participation—or, in his terms, "speaking your mind without elections, surveys or social movements." The critical difference in the modern world is the "actions [of nonelites] are relatively *autonomous*: instead of staying within the shadow of existing power holders, users of the new repertoire [of political action] tend to initiate their own statements of grievances and demands" (1983, pp. 465–66).

This is a most important (and interesting) element of elite theory since the responsiveness of elites toward nonelites is one of the most central and crucial elements of "popular" democracy. The other elements of elite theory emphasize the dominant role of elites in society—that is, the ways in which elites influence nonelites. Here we are concerned with the influence of nonelites on elites. Because competition among elites is so critical to the circulation of elites—as opposed to recruitment and socialization of individuals—the accountability of elites to nonelites is related to the nature of circulation in the system. One way to distinguish them is to consider circulation as a horizontal relationship between peers, while the interdependence of elites and nonelites as a vertical relationship. This is an important distinction for democracy, since it is possible that all nonelites could be subject to comprehensive elite control—an ideal type of totalitarian society—and yet there might still be competition between elites, albeit a competition with no necessary relevance to nonelites. In considering the views of classic elite theorists, it is important to remember that they were writing about the birth and early years of European political parties, and before the development of modern social movements. Thus, it is important to consider the views of contemporary party theorists as well as the classical elite theorists on this. The mechanisms through which elites and nonelites exercise influence include elections, political parties, interest groups, social movements, the mass media, and public opinion.

Pareto's position on the interrelationship of elites and nonelites primarily involves an analysis of the preferences of nonelites by competing bodies of elites, i.e., the ruling and nonruling elites. When it is useful to them, these calculations are followed by political appeals directed toward nonelites and intended to gain some advantage from having the support of popular sentiment. If both sets of elites appeal to the nonelite domain, then it becomes the stage for the competition of elites. For Pareto, the interests of nonelites are both material and nonrational (what Pareto terms "residues"). This limits the utility of elite appeals. Thus, the nearness of elites and nonelites depends upon the calculated appeals of elites. In effect, one group of elites seeks to either maintain itself or displace the other group of elites by relying upon, at least in part, the support gained from appeals to the much larger class of nonelites. The role that the mass, i.e., the nonelites, play in this process depends upon the nature of the competition between the two elite groups. Thus, their role is a mostly passive and reactive one. Pareto's contribution lies in his stress that the interests and inclinations of nonelites are largely independent of elite control. This is an important point because elite theory does not postulate that an elite can control social change. Even in societies without elections, nonelites are not mere automatons—they can influence elites. In the extreme case, i.e., a revolution, an entirely new elite group may arise displacing all other elite groups. According to Pareto's oft-quoted conclusion, "history is the graveyard of aristocracies."

   E. E. Schattschneider provides the most profound analysis of the process through which parties contribute to democracy. In *The Semisovereign People* (1960), Schattschneider laid great emphasis on parties as defining the alternatives for political conflict: "Democracy is a competitive political system in which competing leaders and organizations define the alternatives of public policy in such a way that the public can participate in the decision-making process" (p. 138). The people do not participate either through special interest groups, which Schattschneider argues shut out 90% of the public, or through "public opinion." The problem with a simplistic definition of democracy for Schattschneider is that "a hundred million voters have a staggering number of opinions about an incredible number of subjects" (1960, p. 131). Public opinion is inchoate, and measuring opinion by virtue of what questions public opinion pollsters happen to ask cannot simplify the alternatives. In fact, *"the definition of the alternatives is the supreme instrument of power"* (1960, p. 66). Different groups, including pollsters, attempt to define the appropriate issues for the public based upon their *own interests*. Weber, of course, would suggest that polling of the public is a technique requiring expertise and thus is a handmaiden of bureaucratic power. For Schattschneider, political conflict depends upon social conflict: "What happens in politics *depends on the way in which people are divided* into factions, parties, groups, classes, etc." (1960, p. 60).

   There are two opposing tendencies in politics: one toward the privatization of conflict, and the other toward the socialization of conflict, which expands public participation and uses government to achieve what individuals cannot. Schattschneider stresses that *"the most powerful special interests want private settlements* because they are able to dictate the outcome as long as the conflict remains private" (1960, p. 39). Recourse to government and attempts to expand or socialize conflict is the lot of the have-nots and the least powerful interests. Schattschneider concludes that it is the political parties that have assisted the least powerful, and they have done so through expanding political participation: "Every major change in public policy (the Jefferson, Jackson, Lincoln, and Roosevelt revolutions) has been associated with an enlargement of the electorate" (1960, p. 97).

Schattschneider accords the nonelites a much larger political role in politics inasmuch as the choice of ruling elite is theirs. As noted above, he defines democracy as a system where there is a ruling party and an alternative party that holds a monopoly on the right to opposition. The primary decision that the nonelites make is a choice between the two groups of competing elites—they vote to keep one party in office or to replace it with the opposition party. This is not an especially issue-based choice, but rather a ratification or repudiation of the party in power (office). Nonetheless, the nonelites play an *active* part in the political process because it is through political parties that conflict is widened, and thus there is greater participation by the public. Party competition is *dynamic* because parties continually seek to displace and substitute conflicts for partisan advantage. Parties seek power by defining the "conflict of conflicts." Thus, Schattschneider accords the public (nonelites) a much greater role in the political process than does Pareto. The people may not be sovereign, but they are at least semi-sovereign.

chapter 5

Social Movements: An Antidote to Elite Oligarchy

It cannot be denied that the masses revolt from time to time, but their revolts are always suppressed. It is only when the dominant classes, struck by sudden blindness, pursue a policy which strains social relationships to the breaking-point, that the party masses appear actively on the stage of history and overthrow the power of the oligarchies.

Roberto Michels, 1962, p. 170

Nonelite populations can engage in autonomous political action via mass movements. Elite-mass interdependence means that both elites and nonelites have their own independent spheres of action. Elites and nonelites are interdependent because actions initiated in one sphere can influence the other. Mass movements are unique in that they are the one method of participation in which political alternatives are determined by the masses.

There are a variety of means by which nonelites can influence elites—through public opinion, mass media, and voting, as well as through other traditional forms: participating in political campaigns, donating money, working for an interest group, writing letters, and so forth. These methods, however, all share the drawback of being constrained *by the alternatives that elites have already determined.* One can vote or donate money to a candidate or work in a political campaign, for example, but only for those candidates on the ballot. One can participate in interest groups, but one is limited by the existing types of groups. And, as we saw in Chapter 3, where competitive parties are lacking (e.g., in the postbellum era), political party elites may be indifferent to voters' selection of limited alternatives.

If nonelite populations or groups were limited by the alternatives presented to them by elites, then elite oligarchies would continue without challenge. But that has not been the course of history: even those societies without the outward forms of democracy (e.g., the vote and freedom of association) have been punctuated by revolutions. In societies with democratic forms of participation, mass movements of all types intimately influence permeable organizations such as political parties and result in the formation of new interest groups. In democratic societies, mass movements represent an advance on mob rule and revolts—nonelites can reformulate policy alternatives that would otherwise be ignored by the existing elites. For this reason, mass movements generally, and especially one particular type of mass movements, social movements, represent an *antidote* to elite oligarchy.

MASS MOVEMENTS IN AMERICAN POLITICS

Mass movements represent an autonomous form of participation by nonelite groups. Mass movements (unknown in premodern societies) are ways in which masses can force elites to change. While the United States has been an extraordinarily stable society, mass movements have comprised the crucible in which new groups have formed and existing interest groups and political parties have been transformed. Contemporary party reform and competition and the current configuration of interest groups cannot be understood without a working knowledge of contemporary mass movements.

Mass movements are distinctively modern forms of participation. The development of mass movements in the 1800s created a whole new repertoire of political actions: strikes, planned public meetings, marches, and rallies. For this reason, many define mass movements as forms of *collective protest*, classified as nontraditional or illegitimate political participation (involving potential violations of law). Yet mass movements developed in tandem with the development of electoral politics, special purpose associations (or interest groups in more modern terms), and political parties. The advent of elections provided for choice between two or more leadership groups, as opposed to the traditional form of leadership. Interest groups introduced new forms of communication between ruling elites and nonelites through lobbying and group-based endorsements. And political parties introduced a permeable organization, which allowed for the recruitment of new elites.

Mass movements are critical because they introduced new repertoires or patterns of political action, which allowed for collective protest and autonomous actions on the part of nonelites. Earlier repertoires of political action were parochial in scope, focusing on local elites and depending on their voluntary patronage to resolve personal disputes and settle immediate grievances. The earlier repertoire would be the turnout, in which workers in a given craft would march through town and send a delegation to the local employer (e.g., a family-owned business) with their grievances asking for relief. A turnout would never threaten traditional leadership; instead it depended on the favor and personal largess of an individual employer. Key to the turnout's success was *not* offending the employer. By contrast, a strike consists of independent and potentially threatening action on the part of nonelites. Strikers usually threaten not to return to work unless their demands are satisfied, and through moral suasion and violence inhibit the hiring of permanent replacement workers ("scabs"). A strike essentially differs from a turnout because it focuses on an entire town, industry, or country and represents a demand for action on general problems (Tilly, 1983). Strikes thus have the potential for *socializing conflict* because they target a class of individuals rather than a specific individual. In the early era of mass movements, all mass movements were social movements *organized by the disadvantaged.*

In Europe, the birth of parties developed alongside the birth of social movements. It is noteworthy that the first European parties to organize at the mass level were the socialist parties that organized the working class. In Europe, widespread suffrage for males was granted after significant industrialization took place. Suffrage to most urban males was granted in Great Britain in 1867 and extended to rural males in 1885.

> Most other European nations also lacked the crucial basis for modern parties until at least fairly late in the nineteenth century. Many were even later than Britain. Belgium did not significantly extend its franchise until 1893. . . . Denmark's manhood suffrage dates from 1901, Norway's from 1898, and Sweden's from 1909. Perhaps France is the nearest to a major exception. It introduced manhood suffrage in 1848, but, save briefly, voting did not take place in a nonauthoritarian environment until 1875. Elsewhere there is nothing approximating universal manhood suffrage before 1867. Canada, Australia, and New Zealand were not yet nations before that date. (Epstein, 1967, p. 25)

Because widespread manhood suffrage was granted so late, the socialist parties that sought to represent the working class had to first fight for political freedom for the workers. This resulted in a different set of environmental factors than was true in the United States.

The U.S. party system differs from the European in four important respects:

1. There was widespread adult male suffrage by about 1830 (property restrictions were abolished in most states by about that time)—before industrialization had taken place and an urban proletariat had developed.
2. The United States has been more or less consistently a two-party system, which emphasizes the role of majorities.
3. Newly active political groups and social movements have been able to attain influence by forming a third party, which was then absorbed into the majority parties through the threat of losing major party status.
4. With the demise of third party viability with implementation of progressive reforms, Democratic and Republican parties no longer face any threat to their major party status.

Political parties organized in the United States during the Jacksonian era well before industrialization occurred and there was a labor social movement. For this reason, social movements in the United States have usually not resulted in the formation of permanent freestanding parties, rather they have worked through or were incorporated into the existing two major parties via the third party route. As discussed in Chapter 3, farmers who comprised a distinct social class in the late 1800s, organized first the Grange movement in the 1860s, and then the Populist Party, which was then absorbed by the Democratic Party in the 1896 campaign, which nominated William Jennings Bryan. Historically, of course, violent armed farmer revolts have been frequent in American politics since Shay's Rebellion in 1786–87. Prey to the vicissitudes of weather, bankers, and markets, farming through most of American history constituted a distinct way of life for most Americans. In recent years, however, the family farm is fast disappearing. Until about 1920, a majority of Americans derived their livelihood from agriculture. Today, more than two out of three Americans live in urban areas. Even among those living in rural areas, few actually work on farms. For this reason, it is increasingly difficult to consider farmers a distinct social group with a social identity and culture derived from farm life.[1]

Labor was early incorporated into the existing party system. Urban workers of the 1890s, offended by Democratic President Grover Cleveland's use of federal troops to break the 1894 Pullman strike and the anti-industrial stance of the Democratic Party symbolized by Bryan's nomination, and wooed by Republican Party support for recognition of trade unions, supported Bryan's opponent, William McKinley. In 1932, labor—and urban workers—already part of the party system, realigned their party support and became a key constituency of the Democratic Party, attracted by Franklin Roosevelt's provision of urban relief programs and the passage of the Wagner Act in 1935.

The incorporation of labor and farm interests into the party system did not mean that all politically active groups were welcomed with open arms into the parties. The decline of third parties during the Progressive era meant the eclipse of the major route through which new groups with new issues could force the major parties to incorporate them into their programs. Women and blacks, in particular, were groups whose vote was sought, but were systematically excluded from elite levels of power. The widespread progressive adoption of primaries proved a disincentive, and extensive progressive regulation of party organization by the states gave the Democratic and Republican Parties an advantaged position in state politics. In the early 1970s, the passage of the Federal Election Campaign Act on the national level permanently accorded the Democratic and Republican Parties a privileged position in presidential

---

[1]In fact, most farming today is not worker-intensive, but technological and dominated by commercial enterprises—"agribusiness." It is also difficult to locate a common identity even among producers. Agriculture is characterized by fierce competition: competing crops (e.g., alternate sources for fats, oils, and shortenings), supplier-consumer relations (e.g., higher grain prices hurt beef and hog farmers), new versus old producers, competing varieties and grades, and differing proximities to markets.

politics—the major prize—by funding their nominating conventions and granting funding to all candidates seeking their party's nomination. In recent years, many a prospective third party has crashed upon the shoals of the twentieth century institutionalization of the Democratic and Republican parties.[2] For this reason, mass movements, and particularly social movements that reflect the interests of disadvantaged social outgroups, are the only mechanism for transformation of the American party system. To consider this more fully, we turn to a discussion of the varieties of mass movements in contemporary politics.

Types of Mass Movements

A movement is more than a trend that is the result of many similar but independent actions. A movement requires the organized, *collective* action of large numbers of people who, working together, seek some sort of institutional change. There are four major types of movements, one of which is not a mass movement. An *intellectual movement* occurs *only* among elites. Examples of intellectual movements include modern art, schools of architecture, and behavioralism in political science. Participation in an intellectual movement requires prior initiation into the skills and expertise of an intellectual and creative discipline—a precondition available only to an elite few. Intellectual movements never expand to nonelites because their significance is circumscribed by the intellectual discipline or "high culture" with which they originate. While lacking grass roots, intellectual movements nonetheless incorporate organized activity and bring innovation to their disciplines, which challenges the contemporary orthodoxy.

The three types of *mass movements* include *religious movements, political movements,* and *social movements.* In contrast to intellectual movements, each is characterized by collective action at the grass-roots level. Social and religious movements arose first. Social movements were not widely recognized in terms of social science theory (even though they occurred in earlier eras) until the advent of the civil rights movement of the 1950s. The civil rights movement has provided a model for political activism and influence among the have-nots that has been widely imitated by all groups—even the haves—a process that has increased the incidence of more purely political movements. Not all

[2] Lenora Fulani, a 1988 candidate for the presidency on the New Alliance Party ticket, ran in the 1992 Democratic Party primaries. While the Libertarian Party is organized separately, many Libertarians remain sympathetic to the Republican Party, as evidenced by the national organization of the Libertarian Republicans, whose newsletter was inaugurated in 1988. Ron Paul, 1988 Libertarian Party presidential candidate, announced that he intended to run in the 1992 Republican Party primaries, withdrawing only when Pat Buchanan announced his candidacy. True third parties are sharply limited by restrictive laws in the states. *Ballot Access,* a nationally distributed newsletter, tracks recognition by states of the major new third parties. The Libertarian Party, the most well-organized party, was only qualified to be on the ballot in 24 states as of December 1991. By contrast, the New Alliance Party was only qualified in 2 states, the Green Party in 1 state, and the Populist Party has not yet qualified in any state.

BOX 5-1
Types of Movements

ELITE MOVEMENTS

- Intellectual movements

MASS MOVEMENTS

- Social movements
- Political movements
- Religious movements

---

interests can organize at the mass level,[3] but those who do are advantaged by their ability to demonstrate their grass-roots *mass* support.

Political movements may appear indistinguishable from social movements in terms of their political activities (including marches, protests, rallies), but they are distinct by their representation of middle-class interests—the politics of the haves. These interests would have had a hearing in the two-party system even without organization as a movement. However, their preferred policy alternatives are granted more credence *because* they are able to demonstrate growing public support. Elites use political movement strategies just as they would use public opinion polling to demonstrate that their personally preferred policies are preferred by the public at large. Social movements represent those social outgroups who have no representation in the two-party system. Thus, their positions and recruitment of group members to political office would not have occurred in the absence of a mass movement demanding representation.

Social and political movements, which we will consider in some detail, are both directed toward political change, while religious movements seek new forms or objects of worship and remain in the nonpolitical and nonpublic spheres of society. Social and political (sometimes characterized as citizen's groups) movements are extremely common in contemporary politics. Politically influential social movements have been led by blacks (civil rights move-

---

[3]Certainly all interests can organize at the grass-roots level as opposed to the mass level. The Chamber of Commerce, for example, utilizes an "outside" lobbying technique of targeting key members of Congress for contact by Chamber of Commerce members who live in their district, who personally know the member, and have contributed to his or her campaign. This is organized lobbying at the grass-roots level, but not mass-level politics or organization. Consider the thought experiment of trying to imagine a mass demonstration in favor of a Chamber of Commerce position (such as opposition to parental leave or minimum wage)—business does not have mass support of this type.

ment), women (women's rights movement), and homosexuals (gay rights movement). Politically influential movements have been organized by conservatives ("new right"), consumers and environmentalists. Before turning to an in-depth discussion of social and political movements, let us consider religious movements.

Pure religious movements focus on changing the objects, forms, or practice of worship and have been common in the Western world since Catholicism as the universal church became beset by Protestantism. Specific examples of religious movements include sixteenth-century Lutheranism and Calvinism, eighteenth-century Methodism, and twentieth-century Pentecostalism. Each of these movements sought institutional religious change, not changes in secular public policy.

Two of the more contemporary examples of religious movements include Methodism and Pentecostalism. Methodism, now an established Protestant denomination, no longer is an active religious protest movement. Originally based upon evangelistic preaching, Methodism began with the organization of a group at Oxford for religious exercises. Stressing "rule and method" (hence, Methodism), John Wesley, George Whitehead, and their followers withdrew from the Church of England in 1791 to become the Wesleyan Methodist Church. In America, the Methodist Episcopal Church was formed in 1784 under the leadership of Francis Asbury. Newly independent from Wesley following the revolution, Methodism "was a Bible-studying, hymn-singing, enthusiastic movement." Centrally organized under Asbury, the Methodists remained a "people's church," which alone among the American Protestant churches "was designed as much for large-scale missionary work as it was for the care of established congregations." During the religious renewal known as the Second Great Awakening, which began in 1787, Methodist circuit riders were particularly effective in recruiting new members at revival meetings held in weekend camps which up to 25,000 people would attend, an innovation introduced in 1801 (Barker, 1970). During this phase, Methodism was extremely permeable to new members. Methodism, now one of the largest denominations, is considered "mainstream" religion in the United States. Seeking new church members through conversion and proselytizing is now uncommon for the Methodists.

Pentecostalism has its roots in fundamentalist American Protestantism, which developed in the early twentieth century as a reaction to the effort to recast Christian teachings in light of scientific knowledge (e.g., paleontology and evolutionary theory). Pentecostals accept a literal interpretation of the Bible and personal salvation through the experience of being "born again." Like other fundamentalist churches, Pentecostal churches differ from liturgical churches (e.g., the Lutheran church), which emphasize form, and hierarchical churches (e.g., the Catholic church), which emphasize centralized church authority. Pentecostalism diverges from fundamentalist Protestantism by articulating beliefs in baptism with the Holy Ghost and the imminent second coming of Christ, and they engage in such practices as speaking in tongues (glossolalia) and faith healing.

Pentecostalism is of interest because it remains an active religious movement in the contemporary era, and therefore continues to actively proselytize for new recruits. This is crucial to understanding Pentecostalism as a movement. Pentecostals actively recruit new members, and thus they are open to those who are unsatisfied or feel unwanted by other denominations. Thus, Pentecostal churches are growing as they incorporate these new members. Many Pentecostals are organized in independent churches; the Assemblies of God is the largest affiliated group of Pentecostal churches. The movement has spread beyond Protestant churches to such unlikely faiths as Catholicism, resulting in prayer groups of "charismatic Catholics."

Speaking in tongues and faith healing are only a few of the practices that sharply differentiate fundamentalist Baptists like the Reverend Jerry Falwell (founder of the former Moral Majority) and Pentecostals such as the Reverends Jimmy Swaggart, Pat Robertson (1988 Republican candidate for president and founder of the Christian Coalition), and Jim Bakker. Pentecostalists are much more permissive about the use of make-up, dancing, and music. Many fundamentalists view Pentecostalists as engaging in practices forbidden by the Bible. Yet these religious leaders are often lumped together as interchangeable proponents of the "new right." It is more useful to separate their religious movement directed toward reshaping denominational religious practices and the establishment of new religious institutions from their political activities directed toward governmental policies and activity. In the United States, the separation of church and state means that purely religious movements with their emphasis on other-worldly ideas and nongovernmental and nonsecular institutions have very direct little impact on politics.[4] Once religious-based activism expands beyond simple proselytizing and becomes political activism (lobbying, campaigning, donating money, and running for office), it is transformed from a religious to a social or a political movement. We turn now to three competing theories on the origins of mass movements.

THREE COMPETING THEORIES OF MASS MOVEMENTS

The effect of mass movements on politics is a matter of controversy. Recall that conflict in the public sphere is contagious: while religious movements only seek new converts, social and political movements seek political change. Because both social and political movements seek political changes, many consider social and political movements interchangeable terms for the same

---

[4]Certainly, religious movements may have substantial indirect impact on politics because of their influence on a society's culture. Also, in a theocracy, religious movements become by their very nature political protest movements.

dangerous phenomenon. This is unfortunate, since they differ in a number of important ways. Political movements, like religious movements, are often associated with a single leader and his or her organization; this not true for social movements. Social movements, unlike political movements, develop a comprehensive ideology, while political movements do not. This is because social movements seek change in the social and private spheres as well as in politics. For example, feminists stress the "politics of housework"—an extremely personal conflict outside the reach of government regulation. Contrast this with political movements advocating handgun control or a nuclear freeze, which seek a change in a single government policy. The significance of these differences between social and political movements turns on which theory one uses to explain—and evaluate—mass movements. We examine mass society theory, resource mobilization theory, and social movement theory, each of which offers differing explanations of how social movements arise and the meaning of mass politics.

Mass Society Theory and Mass Anarchy

Mass society theory is the oldest and best-established theory that we consider. It developed in the post-World World II era as an intellectual response to the apparent breakdown of society following World Wars I and II. To many American scholars, the instability of many governments represented a crisis in Western society. Others, including many European scholars who had emigrated to the United States, were concerned about the experience of two world wars, the revolutions in Russia and Germany, the rise and fall of Mussolini and Hitler, and the postwar tensions between the West and the Soviet Union. Major theorists of mass society (including Hannah Arendt, Erich Fromm, Karl Mannheim, Robert Nisbet, and Phillip Selznick) were preoccupied with the factors causing crisis and social disintegration. The body of mass society theory formed the basis of the new behavioral research in political science and sociology.

Mass society theory assumes that the "mass" is found only in "mass society." Whether the ordinary individual lives in a mass society or a pluralist society, mass society theory assumes that the "normal" individual is not interested in politics. Most individuals learn political opinions and information indirectly. In pluralist society, this usually occurs through the political socialization process in the family or, for adults, through what is termed the "two-step flow of information." The first step is when local group leaders (elites who are interested in politics) synthesize political information from a variety of sources. The second step is when they initiate political discussions with their families, friends, and fellow workers and shape their political opinions because of personal friendship and respect. These local elites are termed "opinion leaders," and the groups they lead are called "intermediary groups."

Mass society is created when intermediary groups become disorganized and no longer mediate between the individual and government. Intermediary groups arise from traditional social categories such as family, class, school, community, and region. In pluralist society, they mediate by absorbing the emotional energies of ordinary people in immediate concerns so that nonelites remain uninvolved in such remote and distant things as politics. The communication that occurs through these intermediary groups contributes to the development of the proper citizen values among nonelites. The stability of intermediary groups results in a stable society: only these locally based groups both properly socialize nonelites and safely insulate elites from the political demands of ordinary individuals.

The mass society develops when communication occurs via large national or bureaucratic organizations and the mass media, and not through local community groups. Mass organizations of this type cannot really touch the personal lives of individuals. Political information is not learned in a face-to-face situation among those with a personal relationship. Instead, mass communication is a one-way affair from a centalized noninteractive medium like television to atomized and isolated individuals listening separately in their homes. As such, attitudes formed in mass organizations are unstable, and the masses are vulnerable to charismatic and demagogic leaders. The mass society is characterized by mass apathy punctuated by episodes of unstructured and dangerous mass activism. In pluralist society, mass activism is improbable because ordinary people are completely absorbed in their personal lives and are uninterested in politics. To theorists of mass society, all mass movements are similarly undesirable where masses make unreasonable demands and elites are incapable of responding appropriately.

Can mass society theory explain the rise of new social and political groups? Certainly television has expanded its presence in the political domain since the 1950s (see Box 5-2). Many mass society scholars believe that previous theories of political socialization and the two-step flow of information have been rendered obsolete by the advent of the television age. Most people do not watch television for political information. The television audience for political information is an inadvertent audience who happens to hear political information while they listen to their favorite entertainment programs, the weather report, or the sports results. As political scientist Austin Ranney (1983) concludes, the learning of political information from television is passive: "Unlike people who read about politics in newspapers, books, and magazines, they do not get it because they are actively seeking it" (p. 12). Because many public opinion polls have found that about two-thirds of Americans say that television is their primary source of news, and more say that they find television more believable than newspapers, radio, and magazines when news reports conflict, many political scientists have assumed that intermediary groups and political parties have declined. Mass society theorists link the rise of television to the increase in interest groups and the rise in importance of nonoccupationally based voluntary groups (e.g., Common Cause, NOW) that

BOX 5-2
The Advent of the Television Age

Although television by the projection of all-electronic scanning was first developed by the 1920s and regular television broadcasting began in the United States in 1941, it did not become a truly mass medium of communication until the 1950s. But when it came, it came with a rush! In 1947, less than 1 percent of American homes had a television receiver, and there were many areas of the country in which no television signal could be received. In 1950, the percentage of homes owning a set rose to 9, and in the next five years it shot up to 65 percent. By 1960, more than 87 percent of American households had sets, and by the 1970s the proportion rose to 95 percent. In the 1980s there is no part of the United States in which some television signal cannot be received. About 98 percent of all American homes have at least one television set and nearly half have two or more sets. Indeed, there are now more television sets in America than there are telephones, bathtubs, and flushing toilets!

Source: Ranney, 1983, p. 8.

have a national rather than a local focus. While it is true that new groups such as these have formed, there is no evidence that locally based groups have declined. More important, as discussed in Chapter 3, local party organizations have not declined, as so many have assumed. In fact, the power of national and local party organizations appears to be consonant—both have grown stronger, not zero-sum, meaning that the national organizations have not become stronger at the expense of local party strength. What, then, about the increase in activism outside of the party system? We will discuss the civil rights, women's, and gay rights movements below. In each case, we find that while these movements are formally "outside" the parties, their activities are clearly directed toward working within the party system. This is particularly true of their initial efforts at reforming the Democratic Party.

If it is indeed the socially atomized—those inadvertent television watchers—who participate in mass movements, then the toughest test of the adequacy of mass society theory would be an analysis of riot participants. A riot, by definition, is unorganized, and one would expect the most socially disengaged to participate. One of the most persuasive studies on this point is David Sears and John McConahay's study (1973) of participants in the Watts riot of August 1965 in Los Angeles. The Watts riot lasted 6 days, covered 47 square miles, and resulted in an estimated property damage of $40 million. More than 1,000 people were injured, and 34 persons were killed, virtually all of whom were black. Nearly 4,000 people were arrested in the riot, 60% of whom were convicted. Sears and McConahay found that riot participants were not the socially atomized regardless of how this was measured: as the "criminal element," an economic ghetto underclass (i.e., the least educated, lowest income, or welfare recipients), southern newcomers to Los Angeles, or products of broken families. Those most likely to participate tended to be those most integrated and active in the local community: native, long-time residents and regular churchgoers. This evidence clearly contradicts many of the basic tenets of mass society theory.

Resource Mobilization Theory and Political Movements

John McCarthy and Mayer Zald (1973) argue that contemporary mass movements are best explained by *resource mobilization theory*. While classic social movement theory finds that resources such as money, contributions of time and effort, and leadership come from the group's own membership, McCarthy and Zald (1973) point to the recent development of professional reformers who selectively choose to provide resources for disadvantaged groups. The creation of a large pool of college students and middle-class professionals with enough discretionary time to devote to causes and political activities and the changed funding patterns of charitable trusts and foundations, government grants, and churches have created a "massive social movement industry" (p. 27).

The resource mobilization theory assumes that movements are primarily organized by elites and resources from outside the group. McCarthy and Zald point to the civil rights movement as an example: "Early civil rights organizations, for instance, were heavily peopled by whites, while the primary beneficiaries of any successful civil rights actions were black" (pp. 17–18). We will discuss the civil rights model below and point out—contrary to McCarthy and Zald—that the key to the civil rights movement was the resources and participation of black groups.

There are, however, several organizations—known as "public interest groups"—that appear to fit this model of movement organization. David Vogel (1980) defines a "public interest movement" as encompassing a "wide variety of law firms, research centers, lobbying groups, membership associations, and community organizations committed to public policies that attempted to reduce the power and privileges of business" (p. 607). These groups do not have a true grass-roots or mass membership—in fact, in most cases they do not represent a concrete social group, but rather an abstract economic or political category (e.g., consumers). One study found that about one-third of citizens lobbies had no membership at all (Berry, 1984). Instead, they tend to be "staff" or "checkbook" organizations lacking even the mechanisms of grass-roots control—membership only meant a contribution, not participation through an elected board of directors. One recent study found that nearly 90% of citizens groups had received financial start-up assistance from government agencies and private foundations (Walker, 1983). And a small number of middle-class "public contributors" regularly contribute to diverse citizen's groups:

> There seem to be about 100,000 households in the country that contribute at least $75 a year to three or more of the following: Common Cause, Nader's Public Citizen, LWV [League of Women Voters], ACLU [American Civil Liberties Union], public television/radio, and environmentalist lobbies. (McFarland, 1984, p. 45)

There is a strong overlap between contributors to these groups. About one-half of those contributing to Ralph Nader's Public Citizen foundation also give to Common Cause. Members of Common Cause are also typically members of the LWV and the ACLU (McFarland, 1984).

These organizations tend to reflect middle-class politics of the haves. It is noteworthy that while public interest and other political movement groups may indeed reflect the values or worldview of a particular social class identifiable by social science analysts, they differ from social movements in fundamental ways.

Political movements do not advocate a philosophy or way of life demanding change in the private sphere—of nonparticipants. To the extent that they have a philosophy, their philosophies tend to be reassertions of widely accepted socially desirable goals and behaviors. For example, the environmental movement stresses living with nature and recycling. The widespread social desirability of these tenets among elites is evident in the extent to which environmental perspectives are widely taught in the elementary schools. Schoolchildren, for example, are taught that disposable diapers damage the environment and should not be used, a message that they bring home to their families. By contrast, one would have difficulty imagining intermarriage among blacks and whites being advocated in the schools.

Political movements have a truncated political organization. Among political movements, one commonly finds groups organized by an entrepreneur—a single self-selected leader who has undertaken the personal costs of organization, often assisted by foundation grants (Salisbury, 1969). This is true, for example, of Common Cause (John Gardner), of Mothers Against Drunk Driving (MADD) (Candy Lightner), and the former Moral Majority/Liberty Federation (Jerry Falwell). Another organizational form is a small number of groups focused on a narrow, single issue such as abortion.

Political movements do not demand a personal transformation among their participants. One would be, of course, surprised to learn that a committed environmentalist did not recycle or used disposable diapers. However, we are talking here about individual behaviors in discrete areas—very distinct from the holistic nature of the transformation occurring among social movement participants. Consider a thought experiment: Could you imagine a black active in the civil rights movement marrying a white racist? On the other hand, could you imagine an active environmentalist marrying someone who was an unregenerate user of disposable diapers? The point is that environmentalism does not reflect such a fundamental world view that it would bar relationships between individuals of divergent recycling habits.

Political movements do not socialize conflict. Groups such as those urging a nuclear freeze or penalties against drunk drivers do not wish to expand the scope of government action to restrict the influence of private interests—the socialization of conflict (Schattschneider, 1960). What these groups seek to do is to merely alter the direction of an already existing public policy. Were the law to be changed in the direction preferred by the group organizers, it would lose its raison d'être. Groups that seek to socialize conflict will always be on the left ideologically. But political movements may be either liberal (e.g., environmental, public interest, and nuclear freeze movements) or conservative (e.g., new right and prolife, antiabortion movements).

We conclude that the resource mobilization theory is useful, but that it applies only to one type of mass movement—political movements. Political movements are important avenues of activism and work toward many laudable goals. For example, the Children's Defense Fund, a public interest group, is one of the few effective voices for children, a group outside of traditional politics. But political movements do not broaden the political system because they represent the interests of groups already having representation at elite levels. It is only through social movements, to which we now turn, that new groups are brought into politics.

Social Movements: A Distinctive Formation of the Have Nots

Social movements, while directed toward political change like political movements, are broader in that they also seek change in social spheres.[5] Social movements are strongly linked to social classes, although they are not limited to the "proletarian movement." "If political, economic, and ethnic cleavages coincide, it is difficult to prevent specific grievances and interests from generalizing, thus giving protest a more diffuse character (Smelser, 1963, p. 279). As sociologist Rudolf Heberle noted some years ago, social movements result in a group conflict of the distribution of resources. "A genuine social movement is an attempt of certain groups to bring about fundamental changes in the social order, especially in the basic institutions of property and labor relationships" (pp. 348–49).

Social movements are distinguished by "group consciousness." Certainly, some individuals may participate in a group out of support for a group, even if they are not members of that group. It is critical to distinguish between those who participate out of a sense of "class" responsibilities—noblesse oblige,

---

[5]This discussion is adapted from Baer and Bositis (1988).

TABLE 5-1
Social and Political Movements Compared

Social Movements	Political Movements
Ideology	Lifestyle
Multiple Leaders	Single Leader Entrepreneur
Social and Political Spheres	Political Spheres Only
Have-Nots	Haves
Social Group Identity	Diverse Social Groups
Group Consciousness	Issue Positions

or a sense of social consciousness (e.g., white college students and mothers in the civil rights movement [Blumberg, 1980]), or through the voluntary tradition among middle- and upper-class housewives (Gold, 1971)—from those who participate because they had *personally* suffered the discrimination. Group consciousness is important because it increases political participation. Sidney Verba and Norman Nie (1972) demonstrated that group consciousness among blacks can overcome the deficit of their generally lower socioeconomic status, and Claire Knoche Fulenwider (1980) found feminist consciousness to increase political activity among women.

A social movement is unique in that the participants are linked by a common social identity that generates a group consciousness so strong it overrides competing sources of differences (e.g., class, region of resident, age, gender, etc.) among potential group members. Often the basis of social discrimination, this social identity is crucial because it cannot easily be changed: blacks cannot become white, women cannot become men, gays and lesbians cannot become "straight" simply through a change of mind or conversion. Moreover, this social identity is usually socially detectable through visible social characteristics such as physical appearance, dress, speech patterns, and behavior. Group identity is based in part upon this social identity and in part on the group subculture that develops among group members who interact on a face-to-face basis.

Social movements are episodic, spontaneous, and autonomous (Wilkinson, 1971). Because protest is personally costly, social movements usually only arise under specific circumstances where success is likely. Characteristic of social movements is an organizational structure of multiple groups, with leaders recruited *and* deposed from within (Gerlach and Hine, 1970). First, there must be some sort of economic or social dislocation or change. This may arise from economic modernization or changes in the economic or social roles of different social groups. Second, potential leaders of the movement who are most aware of the group-level implications of these changes discuss these issues among themselves. It is these leaders who articulate justification for group action and how government may redress their grievances. Third, these individuals, drawing upon their leadership positions in local community groups or institutions controlled by the outgroup, lay the groundwork for movement organizations. Fourth, group consciousness based upon a social identity links together nonelite group members. Fifth, the social movement develops when a catalyst galvanizes outgroup members at the mass level. It is this critical mobilizing event that signals to nonelite group members that success for their collective goals is likely. And sixth, an active social movement is characterized by the spontaneous independent development of multiple, diverse social movement organizations which organize at all levels of government—local, state, and national—and within private organizations, such as professional associations.

As explained in Chapter 2, collective goals, such as a change in public policy, are available to all whether or not they join a movement group. For this reason, even active social movements are considered partially organized. Unless success is imminent, social group members have little incentive to actively participate. Thus, a social movement may lose its mass following, most notably after achieving major successes or having been severely repressed. Following this last and active phase, the social movement organizations may either disappear or else evolve into traditional interest groups offering selective incentives (e.g., friendship, subscription to group publications, low-cost life insurance, discounts on travel, etc.) available only to those who actually join the organization.

Because of social discrimination, social movements are usually drawn from the have-nots in society. This disadvantaged status and group consciousness results in broad ideological or collective goals. Recall that E. E. Schattschneider pointed out that advantaged groups prefer to keep conflict in the private sphere, while recourse to the public sphere—the only recourse of the socially and economically disadvantaged—requires an ideological justification. The early labor movement of the late 1800s and early 1900s was continually repressed by the use of the police, paid strikebreakers, and private security agents. Success for the labor movement quickly followed passage of the National Labor Relations Act (the Wagner Act) in 1935, which recognized strikes and legitimated union organizing by prohibiting the firing of workers engaging in union organizing.

Social movements are easy to recognize because they are organized for action in both private and public spheres. Any group that demands a personal change but makes no effort to promote social acceptance of the group by making political demands remains a cult, not a social movement (Turner and Killian, 1972, p. 247). Women, for example, separately organized in professional groups (e.g., women physicians, women economists, women political scientists), in public office (Congressional Caucus for Women's Issues), and for political change (National Organization for Women, National Women's Political Caucus).

Like political parties, social movements are based in a "social formation"; unlike parties, social movements are only partially organized. Social movements are based in social and personal transformation, hence, there is a focus on consciousness-raising and voluntary commitment (Freeman, 1975). All social movements have their own terminology for those who possess the social characteristics but lack the requisite group consciousness. Blacks, for example, refer to "oreos"—those who are black on the outside, but white on the inside. Feminists characterize professionally successful women who deny any need or interest in a women's movement as "Queen Bees," while gays and lesbians raise concerns about those who remain "in the closet."

Social movement recruitment is intensely personal, primarily occurring through personal friendships at the grass-roots level. Political and religious movements may recruit through personal networks, but more commonly such recruitment occurs via the activities of noted or charismatic leaders or through media appeals. Indeed, many political movements thrive solvely on "checkbook" members, whose only contact with the group is through the mail. By contrast, the personal nature of recruitment in social movements results in the formation of diverse, locally based organizations, not a unitary hierarchical or bureaucratic organization. Social movements are characterized by a multiplicity of autonomous, independent groups, with no designated leader with the delegated authority to speak for the whole group. In fact, it is impossible to isolate a single leader for any social movement, as we shall illustrate for the civil rights movement.

THE CIVIL RIGHTS MODEL

With the adoption of the Reverend Martin Luther King's birthday as a national holiday in 1986, the widespread celebration of February as black history month in the public schools, and the popularity of the widely acclaimed PBS series, *Eyes on the Prize*, very few people remain unconvinced that blacks in the United States suffered tremendous privations solely on the basis of their skin color. Until recently, African-Americans had no effective civil or political rights, and racial discrimination shut them out of the pressure group system, out of party politics, and prevented them from registering and voting.

In 1944, Gunnar Myrdal, a Swedish sociologist, and his associates published *An American Dilemma* in which blacks were described as a separate caste in American society. American intellectuals increasingly found racial discrimination intolerable, yet elite attitude change was insufficient for racial integration. Like the working class in the earlier labor movement, protest for blacks was structurally precluded. Because white had control of the police and the courts, and they controlled many of the jobs available to blacks, racial protests exacted a high personal cost. After the withdrawal of federal troops from the states of the old Confederacy ended Reconstruction in 1877, there were at least 5,000 acknowledged lynchings of southern black citizens. To thinking people at the start of the civil rights movement, racial equality seemed like an idea whose time had come. Yet if one considers the few economic, social, and political resources available to blacks at that time, it is surprising that the civil rights movement occurred at all.

The civil rights movement was characterized by a diverse set of grass-roots–based organizations. Many unfamiliar with the history of the civil rights movement assume that black protest was the brainchild of the best-known civil rights leader, the Reverend Martin Luther King, Jr. King was noted for leading the year-long (1955–56) boycott against segregated bus lines in Montgomery, Alabama. Along with other black church leaders, King organized the Southern Christian Leadership Conference (SCLC) in 1957. The SCLC served as the base for many well-known nonviolent marches, protests, and demonstrations for black rights such as the 1963 march on Washington and the 1965 voter-registration drive in Selma, Alabama. King, who received the Nobel Peace Prize in 1964, was assassinated in 1968 at the age of 39. King was certainly a very charismatic leader and gifted orator, but he in no way originated the civil rights movement, nor was he the only leader of consequence.

An important precursor to the SCLC and King's emphasis on nonviolent action was the Brotherhood of Sleeping Car Porters, the largest black trade union, and its president A. Phillip Randolph. In 1941, Randolph threatened to lead 100,000 blacks on a march to Washington to protest racial discrimination in defense employment. President Roosevelt averted the march by issuing an executive order prohibiting discrimination and establishing the Fair Employment Practices Commission. Randolph repeated his success in 1948, once again threatening a massive march and obtaining an executive order from President Truman integrating the armed forces.

The "Big Four" of the civil rights movement included the SCLC and three other groups: The National Association for the Advancement of Colored People (NAACP), the Congress of Racial Equality (CORE), and the Student Nonviolent Coordinating Committee (SNCC). The NAACP has been credited with the major legal successes in its Supreme Court strategy (i.e., attempting to achieve its objectives by bringing its legal arguments to the Supreme Court). CORE, a biracial group organized by James Farmer in 1942, used nonviolent direct action such as sit-ins to integrate restaurants in Chicago, Baltimore, and Los Angeles, sent "freedom riders" to test a court ruling integrating interstate bus travel in 1947, and was responsible for coordinating the 1961 Freedom Rides. SNCC, led by Stokely Carmichael, H. Rap Brown, and Fanny Lou Hamer, initiated the Greensboro, North Carolina, lunch counter sit-ins and focused on black voter registration and Democratic Party reform.

Even these groups did not control the civil rights movement. While the

Big Four did initiate about 85% of the movement events in the early years, between 1968 and 1970 other organizations accounted for nearly half (47%) of all events initiated by formal movement groups (McAdam, 1983, p. 304). Another important group was the Leadership Conference on Civil Rights (LCCR), a coalition of 58 black, labor, and religious groups (now 185 organizations) founded by A. Phillip Randolph, along with Arnold Aronson, then program director of what is now the National Jewish Community Relations Advisory Council, and the late Roy Wilkins, then acting executive secretary of the NAACP. The LCCR formed out of a January 1950 protest rally against racial injustice staged in Washington and a conference held in 1952.

The civil rights model of social movements consists of four basic elements:[6]

1. Leaders: social networks, communication and personal ties
2. Organizational base and structure
3. A sense of collective oppression and a need for a common solution
4. The critical mobilizing event

Group consciousness among blacks is extremely important—it is the solidarity that binds together blacks of all social classes. Dr. Raymond A. Winbush, Cleveland State University's vice president for minority affairs and human relations, makes this point when he discusses feeling out of place as a black man in a white society with black students at Cleveland State:

> "I know I find that when I go into a building and I see only white people and I need directions to get somewhere, if I see a brother over there mopping up, I'll go ask him for directions," Winbush said. The students laugh and share their own experiences. (Holthaus, 1990, p. B3)

A sense of oppression among the black community was a cumulative effect of three important pre-existing movements among blacks:

The Niagra Movement (1905–1920s): Organized by W. E. B. Du Bois, Monroe Trotter, and other black leaders, the Niagra movement organized a number of black political conferences, pressing for equal rights and black solidarity. The Niagra movement resulted in the formation of the National Association for the Advancement of Colored People (NAACP) in 1909.

The Garvey Movement (1914–1925): Marcus Garvey founded the Universal Negro Improvement Association in Jamaica and transported it to the United States. He stressed principles of black pride and racial separatism and a back-to-Africa movement in local associations and in his newspaper, *Negro World*. Garvey's career as the most influential black leader of the 1920s was

---

[6]This framework for analyzing social movements was originally proposed by Nancy McGlen and Karen O'Connor (1983). Our development of the civil rights and the women's rights movement within this framework differs in some areas from theirs.

cut short when he was jailed in 1925 and deported to his native Jamaica in 1927.

The Black Muslim Movement (1930–present): Arising first in Detroit, the Black Muslim movement attained national prominence with leaders Elijah Muhammad and Malcolm X, whose famous autobiography was published in 1964 (the year he was assassinated). Black Muslims seek a self-sufficient black nation within the United States and emphasize self-discipline, thrift, industriousness, pooled resources, and self-defense, along with Muslim religious beliefs. W. Deen Muhammad, son and successor to Elijah Muhammad, dissolved the sect in 1985, leaving the some 200 mosques and worship centers to operate independently. The best known Muslim leader is Louis Farrakhan, whose Nation of Islam has been active in the black inner city, providing protection unforthcoming from the police for beleaguered residents of public housing. Young Black Muslims, dressed in suits and bow ties, with their erect posture and proud demeanor are a welcome sight in the inner city. Farrakhan endorsed Jesse Jackson's candidacy for the Democratic nomination in 1984 and 1988. His apparently anti-Semitic statements have given Black Muslims an unpopular public image at variance with their strong support in the black community.

The critical mobilizing event for the civil rights movement was the 1954 Supreme Court decision *Brown* v. *Board of Education of Topeka*, which integrated public schools. This decision shot through the black community like a proverbial bolt of lightning, but it did not come "out of the blue." The *Brown* decision was the culmination of 40 years of litigation by the NAACP Legal Defense and Education Fund. The NAACP was formed in 1910 as a merger of the Niagra movement of black leaders who opposed the politics of accommodation advocated by Booker T. Washington of the Tuskegee Institute (most notably W. E. B. Du Bois) and a group of whites concerned about the widespread repression of blacks in the South. Lynchings became common-place in the South following the Reconstruction and the removal of federal troops by President Rutherford B. Hayes. This was exacerbated by the subsequent legitimation of comprehensive southern segregation laws by the 1896 Supreme Court decision *Plessy* v. *Ferguson*. The NAACP had earlier achieved minor victories in the abolition of the white primary and the integration of graduate and professional schools. Key to the NAACP's success was the regular exchange of ideas among black lawyers, who, not coincidentally, shared a common law school experience at Howard University Law School (Vose, 1972). Located in Washington, D.C., Howard is the most prestigious of the network of southern black colleges and universities.

In addition to Howard University, two groups were central to the recruitment of black civil rights leaders and the development of the civil rights movement: the Brotherhood of Sleeping Car Porters and the network of black women's sororities. These groups provided experience in public speaking and organizing, helped to develop the self-confidence of their members, and provided a large interpersonal network of influential friends and acquaintances. However, these groups lacked resources for sustained organized protest. While Howard University was a beacon for black intellectual leadership, it was publicly chartered and funded by the federal government.

The black churches and the southern black colleges and universities were critical to the civil rights movement by providing an organizational base and a leadership group not controlled by whites. The recruitment of outgroup elites from institutions controlled by the outgroup itself is central to an understanding of social movements. Individual outgroup members recruited through traditional elite institutions and organizations are socialized to dominant (in this case white) elite values. This co-optation of an outgroup's potential leaders weakens its potential for successful future protest. Prior to the 1950s, African-Americans did vote in some southern municipalities (e.g., Virginia, Tennessee, and North Carolina), but only by working with the Democratic political machine. After World War II, a number of dramatic changes took place in the South: the return of black soldiers who had experienced the wider world, the development of agricultural planting and harvesting machinery, and the decline of the old southern agriculture based in hired labor, increasing industrialization, and the increasing population of southern cities. In 1910, 80% of blacks were employed in agriculture or domestic services; by 1960 only 10% were so employed. And in 1900, 90% of blacks lived in the South, with about three-quarters living in rural areas. By 1960, about half of blacks lived in the North, with about three-quarters living in cities.

Only those cities with a large black population could support a black professional class independent from white patronage. It is not surprising that the District of Columbia, which developed a black middle class earlier than most other southern cities, boasted a concerted local campaign to desegregate housing, employment, recreation facilities, schools, and restaurants a decade prior to the famous 1955–56 Montgomery bus boycott. Opponents of segregation such as the NAACP, CORE, black civic associations, and the Urban League worked with white groups (e.g., American Friends Service Committee, American Veterans Committee, Jewish Community Council) used letters, petitions, sit-ins, and peaceful picketing to achieve racial integration in public (government employment, transportation, education) and private areas (restaurants and bathrooms) (Green, 1967).

The Montgomery bus boycott may have been led by Martin Luther King, but it was not his idea. In fact, King himself did not even ride the buses. King, the new pastor of the Dexter Avenue Baptist Church in Montgomery, came from a privileged background. King was the son of the pastor of the Ebenezer Baptist Church in Atlanta, Georgia—the most elite church of the black community. Despite his privileged background and elite credentials (he had just received a doctorate from Boston University), King had earned his undergraduate degree from Morehouse College, an Atlanta-based black college. The daily insult of riding the segregated buses was usually the lot of black women (like Rosa Parks, the black seamstress whose refusal to give up her seat on a segregated bus initiated the boycott) who shopped or traveled to white sections of the community to work in white homes or businesses. Not surprisingly, the plan to target the municipally chartered bus company came from Jo Ann Robinson, an English professor at Alabama State College and president of the black Women's Political Council (WPC), founded in 1949. Black women and the WPC "had been the driving force behind all of the black community efforts of the last few years," yet the proposed boycott could not succeed without the support of the black ministers who were influential with the more conservative elements of the black community (Garrow, 1986, p. 17). The WPC leaders themselves could not take a public role without loss of their jobs at the publicly controlled university.

A diverse set of secular and religious leaders drawn from local community groups organized the boycott: the WPC, the local NAACP chapter, the Citizens Steering Committee, and the Baptist Ministers Alliance. Longtime black leaders such as E. D. Nixon, a member of the Brotherhood of Sleeping Car Porters and a past president of the Montgomery NAACP, Rufus Lewis, a businessman and former Alabama State football coach, and the Reverend Ralph D. Abernathy, the secretary of the Baptist Minister's Alliance, worked with Robinson to forge a consensus on the proposed bus boycott. The boycott, ultimately lasting more than a year, required the establishment of a complex system of reduced cab fares by black taxicab firms and free rides provided by those with automobiles. Only the black clergy had the economic independence to publicly lead the boycott, and the black churches had the resources (e.g., meeting rooms, mimeograph machines, paper, telephones) for organizing mass protests and collective action. Yet no established organization had commanded a broad enough membership to lead the boycott. King, a 26-year-old pastor new to Montgomery and acceptable to all of the various factions, was the compromise choice as the public leader of the newly created Montgomery Improvement Association.

King himself was not terribly interested in partisan politics. In fact, the SCLC was sharply criticized by the younger generation of civil rights activists in SNCC for being politically naive. King's efforts to integrate Chicago were extremely disappointing when he faced the famous Daley machine, led by Mayor Richard J. Daley. SNCC, much more active in partisan politics, organized the Mississippi Freedom Democratic Party (MFDP) that challenged the all white Mississippi delegation to the 1964 Democratic convention, laying the groundwork for reform of the Democratic Party in 1972. In fact, many people are still surprised to learn that the Reverend Martin Luther King, Sr., had voted Republican all his life, only voting Democratic in 1960 after John Kennedy phoned Martin Luther King, Jr., during his imprisonment in the Selma jails when his family feared for his life.

The civil rights movement was significant in recruiting an entire generation of African-American leaders. Of particular importance was the growth

---

BOX 5-3
Major Civil Rights Legislation

1957 Civil Rights Act. Established the Civil Rights Division of the Justice Department, authorized it to bring suit on behalf of qualified blacks prevented from registering to vote.

1963 Equal Pay Act. Requires equal pay for equal work.

1964 Civil Rights Act. Banned discrimination in places of public accommodation, established the Equal Employment Opportunity Commission, with power to investigate complaints against employers, and provided for the withholding of funds from federally assisted programs operated in a discriminatory manner.

1965 Voting Rights Act. Targeted six states and part of a seventh where black registration and turnout was below 50% and authorized the attorney general to send out federal registrars to register blacks and to overrule changes in their electoral system.

1967 Age Discrimination Act. Bans discrimination based on age.

1968 Fair Housing Act. Banned discrimination in the rental or sale of most houses.

1972 Higher Education Act. Bans discrimination based on sex by universities and colleges receiving federal aid.

1974 Equal Credit Opportunity Act. Bans discrimination in obtaining credit based on sex, marital status, race, age, or recipient of public assistance.

1982 Voting Rights Act. Established that plaintiffs need only show discriminatory impact, even if that was not the intent of the policy. This ensures many new black and minority districts following the 1990 redistricting.

1990 Americans with Disabilities Act. Bans discrimination in employment, transportation, public accommodations, and telecommunications based on physical or mental disability.

---

in the election of black mayors: Kenneth Gibson in Newark, New Jersey; Richard Hatcher in Gary, Indiana; Harold Washington in Chicago; Carl Stokes in Cleveland; Dutch Morial in New Orleans; Wilson Goode in Philadelphia; Maynard Jackson and Andrew Young in Atlanta; Tom Bradley in Los Angeles; and Marion Barry in Washington, D.C. Jesse Jackson, a young SCLC pastor more politically astute than his colleagues, organized the successful 1972 Democratic Convention challenge to the Daley delegation along with white Chicago alderman William Singer. Because of the crucial role that the black church continues to play in the black community, in addition to Jesse

Jackson, many contemporary black leaders (like Andrew Young and former U.S. Representative William Gray [D-PA]) are pastors.

The civil rights movement resulted in a large number of changes in public policy that have reduced the impact of racism: the integration of public schools, buses, motels and hotels, and restaurants, and the banning of discrimination in higher education and in employment. The Voting Rights Act of 1965 and the sending of federal registrars to the South greatly increased the proportion of blacks registered to vote: in 1960, only 29% of eligible blacks were registered; by 1980, 58% of blacks were registered (Asher, 1992, p. 50). Through its success in establishing the case for Democratic Party reform, the civil rights movement has fundamentally transformed southern politics and the basis of party competition (see Box 5-4). The recruitment of a new generation of black political leaders will probably have longlasting effects on the participation of blacks. By 1984, black registration had increased to 66%, in large part due to the electoral campaigns waged by black politicians. In Chicago, only 30% of eligible blacks actually voted in the 1980 presidential election; by contrast, 66% of blacks voted in the 1983 mayoral election of Harold

---

BOX 5-4
Mississippi Governor Fails to Oust Black from Party Post

The effort by Mississippi's young new Gov. Ray Mabus to oust the black chairman of the state's Democratic Party and replace him with a handpicked white person ended in failure yesterday. By a vote of 56 to 41, the state Democratic committee voted to keep Ed Cole, 43, in the party chairmanship for a four-year term.

Cole, an aide to retiring Sen. John C. Stennis (D-Miss.), became state chairman when the previous chairman retired. He had originally supported a rival to Mabus in last year's gubernatorial race. Mabus had backed Billie Thompson, a white businesswoman from Tupelo, for the chairmanship.

After yesterday's vote, all parties involved insisted that Mississippi Democrats would remain harmoniously united. Cole said he hadn't wanted a fight with the governor, but hoped Mabus would now "accept that he belongs to our party and our party does not belong to him."

Some observers had described the fight as a racial split in the party. But at today's meeting all the nominating and seconding speeches were made by blacks. Black votes have kept the Democrats competitive in statewide races in Mississippi.

Washington Post, April 10, 1988, p. A12.

Washington, Chicago's first black mayor. And in the 25 states that held primaries in 1984, voter turnout increased 18% in the 12 states in which presidential candidate Jessee Jackson received at least 15% of the vote. In the remaining 13 states in which Jackson was not a factor, voter turnout declined 9%.

The civil rights movement also introduced new forms of political participation and techniques for "outsider" influence (boycotts, sit-ins, marches, and demonstrations) now available to other social and political movements, as well as traditional interest groups. We now apply the civil rights model to a social movement arising a decade later: the women's rights movement.

THE WOMEN'S RIGHTS MOVEMENT

Women's rights groups and civil rights groups share an intimate, yet often conflicting history. The first women's rights movement (1869–1875) originated when women abolitionists were refused seats at an international conference and realized that their situation was not much different than that of the slaves they sought to free. This early movement sought to obtain broadly defined civil and political rights in the public sphere and equality with men in the private sphere of the family. The second movement—the suffrage movement (1890–1920)—focused only on the narrow goal of the vote for women. The suffrage movement was an alliance of strange bedfellows. First was the Women's Christian Temperance Union (WCTU), which favored female suffrage as early as 1879 as a tool for abolishing the liquor trade. The WCTU's more than 200,000 members were primarily traditional, religious women, and its "impact was particularly important in the South, where its goals were very compatible with religious fundamentalism" (McGlen and O'Connor, 1983, p. 54). Second were the middle-class women active in the settlement house movement, the Women's Trade Union, and National Consumer's Leagues, who sought to improve the working conditions of women and children. Third, the progressives sought to reform political parties. Finally, the nativists sought to dilute the vote of immigrant males with that of white women. The contemporary women's movement (1960–present) developed in part from the participation of white women in the early civil rights movement. Because of the development of group consciousness, the contemporary movement has broad-based social and political goals, unlike the narrow political goal of the suffrage movement.

Because each social identity is unique, each social movement possesses distinctive characteristics and ideologies. Women differ substantially from blacks in their social and economic roles, socialization experiences, and their pursuit of equality. Contemporary sexism takes different forms from racism in that women are neither geographically nor economically segregated. Women live with men, and while women earn less on average than men, they are not restricted to one social class.

By the 1950s, the organizations active in the suffrage era had either ceased to exist or else were disengaged from politics. The National American Women Suffrage Association (NAWSA), which had led the effort to achieve ratification of the Nineteenth Amendment, had transformed itself into the League of Women Voters (LVW) following ratification in 1920. The LVW is a nonpartisan community group stressing voter education and good government. Alice Paul (1885–1977), 1912 Ph.D. in political science and the author of the Equal Rights Amendment (first introduced in 1923), still resided in the Sewell-Belmont House—the Capitol Hill office of the National Women's Party—from which the famous marches for the women's vote were launched. But the Women's Party, which continued to lobby for the ERA, had no active membership to speak of. Other existing women's organizations, like the Business and Professional Women (BPW) and the American Association of University Women (AAUW), and women's colleges were uninterested in leading a women's movement. Thus, unlike blacks, women had no preexisting group similar to the NAACP to lay the groundwork for a grass-roots movement organization or to work for constitutional change (e.g., the *Brown* v. *Board of Education* decision).

One very significant development for the contemporary women's movement has been the major transformation of American family life from 1950 to 1980. Part of this transformation consists of delayed marriages and smaller families. While the overwhelming majority of men (about 85%) and women (90%) do eventually marry (at least once), women married on average nearly 2 years later in 1980 than they did in 1950. Also, in 1980, 45% of women 20 to 24 years old had never married, up from only 25% in 1950. While most women are mothers by the age of 40 (92%), women are starting their families later and having fewer children. In 1950, women had an average of 3.3 children; by 1980, this figure had dropped to 1.8 children, which is below the level necessary for population replacement.

A second part of this transformation lies in women's labor force participation and educational attainment. By 1980, nearly half of the bachelors and masters degrees were granted to women. Employment represents an even more dramatic area of change: while only about one-third of adult women participated in the labor force in 1950, this figure had increased to a majority of women by 1980. The greatest increase in labor force participation has been among women with preschool children. In 1950, only 12% of women with children under the age of six worked; by 1980, 45% of women with preschool children worked, and 62% of women with school-age children were in the labor force.

Despite these increases, women still earned less on average than men. In 1980, a female college graduate earned only 62% of a male college graduate's salary. Census figures show that a man with only 1 to 3 years of high school earned more than a female college graduate. What makes these disparities particularly salient is that the financial responsibilities of women have also increased. Of young single women, 54% headed their own households in 1980, compared to only 12% in 1950. And with rising divorce rates, women more often have sole responsibility for children. In 1950, slightly more than a third of female family heads had dependent children, whereas by 1980 nearly two-thirds had such responsibilities. These structural changes in family life and in the roles of women and mothers created a large potential demand for social change (Di Bianchi and Spaine, 1983).

The contemporary women's movement required the formation of a new group before responding to demands for change. The impetus for organization was provided by President Kennedy. In 1961, Kennedy appointed the President's Commission on the Status of Women at the request of Esther Peterson, who had been active in his campaign and was then Kennedy's director of the Women's Bureau in the Labor Department. Shortly thereafter, all 50 states followed suit in establishing state commissions modeled after the federal commission. The research conducted by these commissions and the establishment of a personal network of experienced political women drawn from traditional women's groups and the ranks of party activists laid the groundwork for the establishment of new organizations. In 1963, Betty Friedan's best-selling book *The Feminine Mystique* identified the problem with "no name." Women were unhappy, but the source of the problem remained unidentified because of the feminine mystique, which sent women back into the home. *The Feminine Mystique* served as the basis of many newly formed discussion groups, such as the one organized in Washington, D.C., by Arvonne Fraser, the wife of then U.S. Representative Don Fraser (D-MN).

On Capitol Hill, the activities of several female representatives were achieving modest success in the drafting of new legislation. While "sex" was included in the text of the 1964 Civil Rights Act in an effort to defeat it (proposed by opponent Howard Smith [D-VA], then chair of the House Rules Committee), the impassioned advocacy of Representative Martha Griffiths (D-MI) was essential to its passage as the first major legislation prohibiting employment discrimination against women. When Griffiths documented cases demonstrating the lack of enforcement by the EEOC of the ban on sex discrimination in employment, copies of her June 1966 speech were distributed to women attending a White House conference on state commissions on women.

Professional women particularly felt the problems of sex discrimination. For example, Dorothy Osler, a Republican state representative in the Connecticut legislature in the early 1970s, was turned down for a loan to purchase a car to drive to the state capitol. "Even though she had just been elected to the state legislature, where she drew a salary of $5,000 a year, the local bank refused her a loan without the co-signature of her husband. This happened despite her personal friendship with the bank president and the fact that she had banked there for the last twenty-five years" (Tolchin and Tolchin, 1974, p. 111).

Several feminist organizations were formed which initially stressed insider—or elite—techniques of influence (lobbying and litigation) similar to those of the NAACP. Not surprisingly, the same individuals were instrumental in forming different organizations. The "Washington community" of elite political women—encompassing female members of Congress, wives of Washington public officials, lobbyists, and political party members. The first of the contemporary women's rights organizations, the National Organization for Women (NOW), was born in 1966 at the third annual meeting of the National Conference of State Commissions after several concerned commissioners discovered that they were not allowed to pass resolutions, take positions, or lobby the government on behalf of women. Betty Friedan was selected as the first president of NOW.

Following the organization of NOW, several similar organizations were formed. The Women's Equity Action League was organized in 1968 by Elizabeth Boyer, along with Bernice Sandler, Arvonne Fraser, and Marguerite Rawalt, as a more conservative alternative to NOW. Carol Burris and Flora Crater organized The Women's Lobby in 1970. U.S. House Representatives Bella Abzug, Shirley Chisholm, and Patsy Mink along with Gloria Steinem, Betty Friedan, and Arvonne Fraser organized The National Women's Political Caucus (NWPC) in 1971 to exert pressure on the Democratic and Republican Parties to include more women as delegates and party officials.

In later years, NOW and the NWPC both developed local chapters. The NWPC remains somewhat small, with a membership of about 35,000, while NOW has greatly increased in size. Between 1967 and 1974, NOW went from 1,000 members in 14 chapters to 40,000 members in over 700 chapters. NOW's membership grew rapidly when it assumed the leadership of the ERA ratification efforts in the late 1970s; by 1982 after the ERA failed, NOW had a membership of 220,000. The national organization's emphasis, however, has been on organizing mass rallies and demonstrations, with a heavy dependence on direct mail to raise money for its activities.

The grass-roots nature of the contemporary women's movement is best seen in the myriad feminist groups that never federated nationally. Organized student activists against the Vietnam war in the late 1960s and early 1970s provided a social network of experienced women who felt excluded from leadership. These locally based feminist groups organized a number of well-publicized early protests, such as the demonstration at the 1968 Miss America pageant, several demonstrations at bridal fairs in 1969, and a sit-in at the *Ladies Home Journal.* Other activities included "whistle-ins" subjecting men to the same humiliation as women, "speak-outs" where women offer public testimonies on experiences of rape, prostitution, and abortion, and "take back the night" marches in which women march to reclaim the freedom to walk safely at night without a male escort. These groups also engaged in consciousness-raising, provided shelter for abused women, teaching self-defense, and other services, such as pregnancy testing and abortion counseling. These groups formed spontaneously and independently. Jo Freeman (1983) reports that in 1967 organizations were formed in five different cities—Chicago, Toronto, Detroit, Seattle, and Gainesville, Florida (p. 20). Many of these groups were organized by women who had been active in recently formed new left, civil rights, anti-war and student protest groups.

Traditional women's groups which have a strong local community organization have embraced the contemporary women's agenda and regularly form coalitions with feminist groups. In 1988, forty-two women's organizations (including occupational, labor union, civic, ethnic and church groups as well newer feminist groups) co-sponsored the Women's Agenda Conference, held in Des Moines, Iowa, January 22–24 to which all declared presidential candidates were invited to speak (see Box 5-5). Even those organizations that

---

BOX 5-5
The Women's Agenda

PUBLIC POLICY PRIORITIES FOR THE
1988 ELECTION

This agenda focuses public policy priorities shared by more than 40 national organizations representing 15,000 grassroots chapters of citizen activists. These issues, which disproportionately affect women and their families, rank high in the concerns of all Americans. In this election year, women's issues are vital to our human future. Whatever their party, candidates for national, state or local office will be expected to address the Women's Agenda in 1988.

- Family policies assuring access to housing, child and elder care, family and medical leave, and equitable education.
- Economic opportunity including occupational preparation, pay equity, raising the minimum wage, and welfare reform.
- Comprehensive health care and safety including longterm care, minimum health coverage, and reproductive health care.
- A federal budget balancing adequate defense with global economic and human development.
- Equality under the law including the Equal Rights Amendment, protection of civil rights and reproductive choice.

Source: Statement adopted at the Women's Agenda Conference, Des Moines, Iowa, January 22–24, 1988.

had been initially reluctant to take the initiative on women's rights in the 1960s now target women's issues. For example, the AAUW supports reproductive choice, passage of the ERA, and has made child care, family leave, pay equity, and education funding priority issues. The BPW, an organization whose membership has been traditionally Republican, has embraced comparable worth and pay equity for women. Two professional associations representing predominantly women professionals—the American Nurses Association (ANA) and the National Association of Social Workers (NASW)—have endorsed positions advocating pay equity, family leave, civil rights, and affirmative action.

While the ERA was not ratified, the women's movement has achieved a number of important successes that for practical purposes have rendered the ERA loss less painful. There were many significant victories during the unsuccessful ERA ratification process. New legislation such as the Civil Rights Act of 1964 and the 1972 Equal Employment Opportunity Act prohibited employment discrimination, the Equal Credit Opportunity Act of 1974 guaranteed credit opportunities for married women, and the 1978 Pregnancy Non-Discrimination Act protected the jobs of pregnant women. Equal education opportunities have been mandated by Title IX of the 1972 Educational Amendments Act, which prohibits sex bias in admissions, treatment of students, and hiring and personnel practices.

The contemporary women's movement has produced a whole new generation of political leaders, of whom Patricia Schroeder (D-CO), a U.S. Representative, is one of the most widely known. Women currently hold 10% of the seats in Congress, and there are currently six women senators, Nancy Kassebaum (R-KS), Barbara Mikulski (D-MD), Diane Feinstein (D-CA), Barbara Boxer (D-CA), Carol Moseley Braun (D-IL), and Patty Murray (D-WA). In 1988, two women served as governors (Madeleine Kunin, a Vermont Democrat, and Kay Orr, a Nebraska Republican) and five as lieutenant governors in Michigan, Minnesota, Missouri, Massachusetts, and Iowa. This number will probably double, and may even triple, following the 1992 general election. In 1991, three women served as governors (Democrats Joan Finney of Kansas, Ann Richards of Texas, and Barbara Roberts of Oregon) and six as lieutenant governors in Connecticut, Iowa, Michigan, Minnesota, Nebraska, and Nevada. Possibly the most dramatic changes have been in the proportion of women serving in state legislatures and as elected mayors of cities. From 1974 to 1993, the proportion of women state legislators increased from 8 to 20%.

The gender gap favors the Democratic Party: in 1988, it was estimated that 10 million more women would vote than men, and since 1976, women under the age of 44 have outvoted their male counterparts. The women's movement (notably the NWPC) has also played an important role in party reform. The social issues introduced into the political agenda have altered the basis of party competition to the extent that major women's groups such as NOW and the NWPC are regarded by many Republicans as Democratic interest groups. In 1980, the Republican Party dropped its endorsement of the ERA from its platform, after nearly doing so in 1976. In return, many women and women's groups have subsequently endorsed and supported the candidates of the Democratic Party. The Democratic Party also appears to be increasing its support among women. In the three states that keep registration figures by gender and party (Iowa, Pennsylvania, and Delaware), women comprised 60% of new registered voters. In Iowa, for example, Democratic women comprised 59% of all new registrants (*Women and Politics Election '88*, a publication of Business and Professional Women).

THE GAY RIGHTS MOVEMENT

Another major social movement of the 1970s and 1980s is the gay rights movement. Both gay men and lesbian women seek redress from discrimination and recognition of their civil and political rights. What they have in common is a sexual preference that is regarded as abnormal—even diseased or an abomination—by many segments of mainstream society. While gays and lesbians are both homosexual groups, they do not share a common identity, lifestyle, or sense of community despite their collaboration on political goals and joint participation in political organizations such as the Gay and Lesbian Caucus, organized following the 1987 Gay Pride March in Washington, D.C.

A key factor defining the different meanings of gay and lesbian identities is the meaning of being homosexual in an essentially male-dominated society. As Dennis Altman (1982) explains, "for a man to be homosexual has always been seen as a relinquishing of his privileges as a member of the dominant sex, . . . [while] for women . . . homosexuality is often a way of affirming their position as women and rejecting the need to be defined solely in relationship to men" (p. 10).

Gay men and lesbian women (many of whom have children) also have different needs. Rising divorce rates and the slightly lower proportion of men (85%) compared to women (90%) who marry at least once has affected the male role, just as women's entry into the labor force has affected the female role. The persistence of the "family wage" system (higher salaries paid to male breadwinners) depended on the "breadwinner ethic." But as feminist Barbara Ehrenreich (1984) notes,

> In the 1950s, there was an expectation for men that they would grow up, marry and support their wives. The man who deviated was judged "less than a man" by both expert opinion and public bias. But at the beginning of the 1980s, the man who remains single even into middle age, who avoids women who might become financial dependents or who declines the burdens of fatherhood entirely is not likely to be considered odd or unmanly. Men still have the incentives to

work, but not necessarily to share their wages with a family. . . . Feminists were not the first to flee the family. Men have been on the run for years. (p. 25)

Estimates of the incidence of homosexuality range as high as 1 in 10 Americans. Historians verify that homosexual and bisexual behavior has appeared throughout history. The development of a gay or lesbian identity, however, is a new phenomenon. This is reflected in the establishment of the first Gay and Lesbian Studies Center in 1987 at Yale University.

Among educated or professional women in the late nineteenth or early twentieth century, it was perfectly acceptable for two unmarried women to develop a lifelong partnership—these were known as "Boston" or "Wellesley marriages." Lesbianism was not acknowledged during this era. It was not until the popularization of Freudian theory in the 1920s that homosexual behavior was identified and labeled as a developmental maladjustment and illness. From the 1920s until 1973 when the American Psychiatric Association removed homosexuality from its official classification of psychiatric disorders, homosexuality was regarded as an aberration of normal heterosexual development. Young boys and girls were both viewed as initially bisexual, with the "normal" development of attachment to the same-sex parent resulting in a heterosexual sexual preference. Homosexuality was viewed as a latent tendency that all adults could develop. Yet because our culture has traditionally viewed women as less sexual than men, lesbian relationships have been less systematically recognized or punished by society.

There were homosexual communities in Weimar Berlin and a legendary community of lesbians in Paris between the World Wars (most notably the author Gertrude Stein and her partner Alice B. Toklas, who presided over a cultural salon frequented by artists and intellectuals such as Picasso, Matisse, Hemingway, Sherwood Anderson, and F. Scott Fitzgerald). However, these remained singular displays of gay identity. The development of gay and lesbian identities in the United States did not start until the 1950s. The Mattachine Society, an organization of gay men, was organized in the early 1950s in San Diego, San Francisco, Oakland, Berkeley, New York, and Chicago. The Daughters of Bilitis (DOB), a lesbian organization, was formed in 1955.

Gays and lesbians organized separately, since each was responding to different needs. Lesbian women, who sought to live independently from men, suffered economic discrimination in the labor force. Job discrimination was especially difficult, because a lesbian identity "often means to surrender the possibility of social mobility through marriage" (Altman, 1982, p. 157). For gay men, the rejection of heterosexual marriage, the breadwinner role, and family ties made social mobility easier. However, gay men faced discrimination in the military, in immigration, and through police harassment of gay bars and gay couples in other public areas. Today, some 24 states still have laws banning sodomy and other homosexual practices.

The organization of the gay rights movement is local rather than national in focus. Gay bars, saunas/discos, bookstores, newspapers (e.g., *Gay Community News, The Advocate*), radio stations, publishing houses, and service centers can be found in all large urban areas. Large gay communities exist in San Francisco, New York, Washington, D.C., Boston, Chicago, Miami, and Houston.

The culture and ideology of the gay movement is that of gay men. The redefinition of sexuality, "an affirmation of sexuality that is sanctified by neither religion nor the state," has also affected straight culture and language as the development of singles bars (which parallel gay bathhouses) and the term "cruising" (meaning the search for sexual partners) originally drawn from gay culture exemplify (Altman, 1982, p. 176). Discos initially developed in gay communities. Fashion has also been affected, both in the "macho" style of dress and in the high technology style of decor. Because the family is not the basic unit of the gay community, gays have placed greater emphasis on communal living and adult friendships. One of the more fundamental changes in contemporary cities is the rebirth of decaying inner cities as middle-class singles are moving back to the city, and the development of gay communities as places of residence, work, and social life have played a major role in this gentrification of previously blighted urban areas.

Lesbians experienced discrimination as women rather than as lesbians. Because the vast majority of feminists and women are straight, the key question was whether the feminist organizations forming in the 1960s would accept self-identified lesbians. The growing presence of lesbians in feminist organizations provoked controversy in the period 1969–1971 during which some feminists warned of the "lavender crisis." The national director of NOW, who supported lesbian demands for recognition, was forced out of office; the NOW executive committee was divided on the issue. Author Rita Mae Brown's open lesbianism provoked a schism in the New York NOW organization, resulting in the formation of a new group, Radicalesbians. Feminist theorist and author Kate Millett's admission of her bisexuality in one meeting resulted in her appearance on the front cover of *Time* magazine, accompanied by a scathing article on the women's movement. The potential split between straight and lesbian feminists was averted when the 1971 national NOW convention adopted a statement acknowledging "the oppression of lesbians as a legitimate concern of feminism" (Deckard, 1975, p. 361). With this issue resolved, lesbians have been much more active as feminists seeking rights for women as women rather than as lesbians active in gay rights organizations. Reflecting this linkage, the current president of NOW, Patricia Ireland, elected in 1991, recently admitted to having a longtime female "companion."

Feminists have the same goals as lesbians, and some radical feminists have argued that women should choose lesbianism as a political alliance of women (as opposed to a permanent sexual preference that one either has or does not have). Thus, lesbian thought, which stresses the community of women, is contained within the accepted range of feminist thought. Lesbian communities[7] are linked with straight feminists in the urban network of women's and rape crisis centers, coffee houses, consciousness-raising groups, dances and concerts, newspapers and bookstores described above. Thus, we view lesbians as participating in a social movement with women and as co-participants in a political movement with gay men.

Gay men, however, do constitute a social movement. The gay movement is identifiable through its community, culture, and identity, and political activism. While the 1950s had its own rebels against marriage—the Playboy attack on married domesticity and the "beat movement" (Jack Kerouac, Allen Ginsberg, Neal Cassady)—men who chose not to be married were regarded as, at best, immature or, worse, possibly homosexual. It was not until the 1970s, after cardiologists attacked the stressfulness of the corporate breadwinner role as risky Type A behavior, after Abraham Maslow initiated the "human potential movement" with his stress on self-actualization, and after the "men's liberation movement" developed as a companion to the feminist critique of the traditional nuclear family, that single men were accepted as normal. This created the potential for a "gay identity" to become culturally accepted.

The gay identity has its origins in World War II. The sex-segregated nature of the armed services provided

> the first opportunity for thousands of homosexuals to meet other gay people; contacts were made, relationships developed, and spontaneous gay communities developed on bases and ships. Gays learned both on and off the battlefield to be proud of who they were and of their contribution to the war effort. (Smith, 1991, p. 6)

While discretion and secrecy were characteristic of gays in the military, a major exception were the all-soldier entertainment shows, which featured female impersonation. Straight soldiers were largely unaware of the significance of the double entendres; while "the shows opened up a social space where gay men expanded their secret culture within the military." With demobilization, "large numbers of gay men and lesbians returning from the war settled in cities where there was a gay subculture" (Smith, 1991, pp. 7–8). With the spread of the gay bar, the basis existed for the development of group consciousness. Key to this were the gay performers—the drag queens. "Reigning over the bar culture were the queens; they not only provided entertainment, some of them actively promoted a gay political consciousness" (Smith, 1991, p. 8). One of the more important performers was Jose Sarria, who performed in the 1950s in San Francisco. Sarria's act was to appear as "Car-

[7]A major exception is what is probably the only community in the United States in which lesbians are openly accepted in Northhampton, Massachusetts.

men," drawing both on the grand opera character and the movie star Carmen Miranda. According to one member of the audience,

> Jose would make these political comments about our rights as homosexuals, and at the end of them, he would have everyone stand and we would put our arms around each other and sing, "God Save Us Nellie Queens." I get very emotional about this and it sounds silly, but if you lived at that time with the oppression coming down from the police department and from society, there was nowhere to turn—and to be able to put your arms around other gay men and stand up and sing "God Save Us Nellie Queens." We were saying, "We have our rights too." (Smith, 1991, p. 9)

Sarria became the first openly gay candidate for political office, running for the San Francisco Board of Supervisors in 1961.

The modern gay movement began with the Stonewall riots in 1969. About midnight on June 27, 1969, seven New York City plainclothesmen of the Public Morals Section raided the Stonewall Inn, a bar with a known homosexual clientele, for illegal liquor sales. Bar patrons resisted and 13 were arrested, including folk singer Dave Von Ronk. It was the "street queens" who led the rebellion, as patrons, checked at the door for identification, were arrested if they failed to produce identification or were suspected of crossdressing. As described by a reporter from the *Village Voice*, whose offices were 50 yards away,

> cheers would go up as favorites would emerge from the door, strike a pose, and swish by the detective with a "Hello there fella." The stars were in their element. Wrists were limp, hair was primped, and reactions to the applause were classic. "I gave them the gay power bit, and they loved it girls." (Smith, 1991, p. 4)

Crowds angered by the raid and the arrests rioted for four successive nights. Two years later, on June 28, 1971, 5,000 gay rights activists marched from Greenwich Village to Central Park in commemoration of the Stonewall riots. Today, the anniversary of the Stonewall riots is celebrated internationally as Gay Pride Day. The Stonewall Riots had a catalytic effect on gay organizing. It was estimated that 3 months after the Stonewall resistance, only about 50 gay organizations existed in the United States; by the mid-1970s, more than 1,000 were in existence; about 4,000 were counted in 1980 (Smith, 1991). Another critical (although secondary) mobilizing event was the discovery of the acquired immune deficiency syndrome (AIDS) among gay men in the early 1980s. Now no longer viewed as a gay disease, AIDS in the early years encouraged many in the gay community to come out of the closet to fight the stigmatization. The early response of gay men to AIDS really reflects their considerable organization *prior* to the onset of the AIDS epidemic.

Following nationally well-publicized antigay campaigns, like Anita Bryant's effort in 1977 to repeal an antidiscrimination ordinance in Dade County, Florida (Miami) and the 1978 Briggs initiative proposed in California to limit the employment of homosexuals, the political activities of gays increased. The Briggs initiative was defeated, primarily due to the activity of Harvey Milk, then a gay activist and San Francisco City supervisor. Milk, a charismatic leader, who had put together a coalition of gays, feminists, union members, and Asian activists, was assassinated in 1978 along with the San Francisco mayor George Moscone by Dan White, a disgruntled former city supervisor. The gay organizational base is urban and centered in local businesses and neighborhoods. Milk, for example, was a businessman in the Castro area of San Francisco. The group's members communicate through gay newspapers and magazines and through professional associations. Gays and lesbians are, of course, found in all professions—a Gay and Lesbian Caucus of political scientists was formed, for example, in 1988; a more open gay presence is found in other professions such as in fashion, photography, advertising, the creative arts, and library science. The pioneer gay civil rights organization is the National Gay Lesbian Task Force (NGLTF, originally the National Gay Task Force).

Just as feminists are found in both parties, gays are found in both parties as well. However, the gay lifestyle has found acceptance only in the Democratic Party. Democratic party platforms since 1980 have endorsed civil rights for gays and lesbians. From 1982 to 1983, gays and lesbians were recognized as an official caucus of the Democratic National Committee. Official recognition of the DNC Gay and Lesbian Caucus was revoked along with that of six other official caucuses (women, blacks, Hispanics, Asians, liberals, and business/professionals) in an attempt to reduce the role of special interests in the party. The Gay and Lesbian Caucus still exists, albeit without official sanction, recognition, or resources. Gays have not made significant public policy gains, with gays still banned from the military[8] and sodomy still outlawed in many states. However, one major advance was the addition of gays to the Hate Crime Statistics Act in 1988, which requires the federal collection of statistics on violence and others types of bias crimes directed toward gay people.

Gays have been increasingly active in Democratic Party politics. Democrat Kathy Whitworth, the former mayor of Houston, was elected with the support of gays and later endorsed a local gay rights ordinance. Former New York City Mayor and Democrat Ed Koch has solicited gay support by appearing at Gay Pride Marches. Koch also signed into law a New York City ban on discrimination against gays. Current New York City Mayor David Dinkins shocked many when, instead of marching at the head of the nation's oldest and largest St. Patrick's Day Parade in 1991, he marched with the Irish Gay and Lesbian Organization, who were only allowed to march in the parade after Mayor Dinkins intervened. Michael Dukakis received support from gays in his election to the Massachusetts governor's seat and also supported civil rights leg-

---

[8]President Bill Clinton pledged in his 1992 campaign to rescind the ban. While he could do this with a stroke of the pen (via executive order), this is unlikely to happen immediately.

islation for gays, but he later raised the ire of many gays by giving preference to nongay couples in the Massachusetts foster care program.

Several congressional districts have large, politically active gay communities, such as the California 24th, which includes Hollywood, represented by Henry Waxman (D-CA), and the New York 17th, which includes Greenwich Village, represented by Ted Weiss (D-NY). Harvey Milk's seat on the San Francisco City Council was filled by another gay activist, Harry Britt. In 1988 Britt narrowly lost a Democratic primary election for the U.S. Congress to Nancy Pelosi (D-CA) in the Fifth District. Voter registration in the Fifth Congressional District, home to a large gay community, currently has a 64% Democratic registration, the highest of any California district without a black or Hispanic majority.

In addition to Harry Britt, other politicians are acknowledged homosexuals. Many Republican and conservative activists were shocked to learn that Terry Dolan, the Director of the National Conservative Political Action Committee (NCPAC) was gay. Dolan died of AIDS in 1987. In 1980, Robert Bauman, then a Republican U.S. House Representative from Maryland active in the Conservative Opportunity Society, was arrested and charged with soliciting sex from a teenage boy in Washington, D.C. Bauman was defeated in his 1980 reelection attempt. For both, their homosexual behavior was a closely held secret. The same has not been true of Democratic politicians. In 1983, Gerry Studds (D-MA) publicly admitted his homosexuality on the floor of the U.S. House after he was censured by the House of Representatives for having had sex with a 17-year-old male page a decade earlier. Studds admitted an error in judgment, but asserted that "I do not believe that a relationship which was mutual and voluntary; without coercion; [and] without any preferential treatment express or implied . . . constitutes 'improper sexual conduct.' " Barney Franks (D-MA), a longtime U.S. representative, decided to disclose his homosexuality in 1987 in an interview with the Boston *Globe*. It is quite clear that Studds' homosexuality represented no breach with the party; while he was under censure and could not hold a subcommittee chairmanship, his committee chairman (the late Walter B. Jones [D-NC]) personally chaired Studds' subcommittee (on Coast Guard and Navigation) until Studds could resume his position after his period of censure. Both representatives were easily reelected to their seats.

SOCIAL MOVEMENTS AND SOCIAL CHANGE

Social movements are distinctive forms of political action. Social movements are characterized by a common social identity that transcends other possible bases of social diversity. Social movement organizations arise spontaneously and independently of one another because of commonly felt problems and discrimination. Yet their leaders and members are linked via a personal network of associations. Finally, the active phase of social movements begins with a critical mobilizing event of salience to all social group members, which signals likely success for the movement. Social movements not only arise out of social change, but they assist disadvantaged groups in responding and adapting to social change. These characteristics of social movements are essential in their totality in distinguishing social from political movements. This requires analysis of the history and organization of a movement before it can be classified—a process that can only be conducted retrospectively. Retrospective analysis obscures the dynamic relationship between social movements and social change. We will explore this further by briefly considering two potential social movements—Latinos (or Hispanics) and the disabled.

Latinos as a Potential Social Movement

The term "Hispanic" implies a common ethnic cultural identity which has yet to develop.

> "Hispanic" ignores and obscures the reality of Mayan or other native American ancestry, and it obscures also the political identities expressed in such terms as La Raza and Latino. . . . However, usage varies among Latino (Hispanic) groups in ways that reveal their diverse identities. . . . Cubans in Miami use the terms "Latin" or "Hispanic"; among them, the name "Latino" is often associated specifically with Mexican Americans. (Browning, Marshall, and Tabb, 1990, p. 3)

The term "Hispanic" actually derives from a Census Bureau classification, but literally means "pertaining to Spain or Spanish culture," when "very few 'Hispanics' in the United States have anything to do with Spain other than a shared language" (Browning, Marshall, and Tabb, 1990, p. 3). "Hispanics" may be black, white, or of mixed racial heritage—and thus, the Hispanic refers to a diverse set of ethnic heritages whose common link is the Spanish language. Yet, Hispanics are the nation's second largest and fastest growing minority, increasing from 4.5% of the population in 1970 to 6.4% in 1980 and 9% in 1990. The three major Hispanic groups in the United States are Chicanos (61%) of Mexican heritage who live primarily in the Southwest, Puerto Ricans (15%) found mostly in the Northeast (primarily in New York, New Jersey, and Illinois), and Cuban-Americans (6%) located mostly in Dade County, Florida. In addition to their distinct geographic residence, each of these groups has a separate cultural identity and a distinctive set of political concerns that has delayed the development of a common Latino identity.

Consider first those of Mexican heritage. Many Mexican-Americans are impoverished and suffer economic discrimination. The best-known Chicano leader is Cesar Chavez, who organized the National Farm Workers Association in 1962 (later, the United Farm Workers). Chavez used nationwide produce boycotts as a tool to force the growers to accept unionization of the migrant workers. Most issues of current concern to Chicanos are local—schools, police,

TABLE 5-2
Three Social Movements Compared

	Civil Rights Movement	Women's Rights Movement	Gay Rights Movement
Economic and social transformation	World War II veterans Migration north and west Increasingly urban and non-domestic employment	World War II employment Delayed marriage, smaller families Increase in college attendance; labor force participation	World War II military experience Increasing divorce rate Acceptance of single lifestyle
Leader's personal network preexisting movement organization	Howard University law grads, Brotherhood of Sleeping Car Porters, network of black women's sororities, District of Columbia with large black middle class	Washington community of women (including members of Congress, spouses, women lobbyists, and party and organizational leaders) Civil rights/antiwar protest marches, rallies	Social network developed through gay bars and bathhouses Leftist political activity
Organizational base and resources essential for movement organization	Black churches, Black colleges and universities	Women's colleges ("7 Sisters") Women's organizations (BPW, AAUW, LWV, NASW, ANA) Women's party organizations and clubs National Student Association Student Mobilization Com-	Urban economic base Mattachine Society Daughters of Bilitis Select professional organizations

	(Civil Rights)	(Women's Movement)	(Gay Movement)
Sense of oppression/need for common solution	Developed through three prior movements developing black pride: •Niagra movement (1905–1916) •Garvey movement (1914–1925) •Black Muslim movement (1930–????)	mittee to End the War in Vietnam SNCC Developed through two prior movements developing feminism: •Women's rights (1869–1875) •Suffrage movement (1890–1920) Problem with no name identified by Betty Friedan in *Feminine Mystique* (1963)	Developed in all-soldier entertainment shows (WW II) Drag queen theater stressing gay political consciousness (1950s–????) Flaming faggots stress on promoting gay culture (1970s–????) Radical fairie movement (1979–????)
Critical mobilizing events	1954: Supreme Court decision, *Brown v. Board of Education* 1957: Pres. Eisenhower sends federal troops to ensure integration of Little Rock, Arkansas, Central High School	President's Commission on the Status of Women (1961) Betty Friedan, *Feminine Mystique* (1963) Lack of enforcement of sex provision by the EEOC (1966) Formation of National Organization for Women (NOW) in 1966 Antiwar protests/Exclusion of women from protest leadership	1969 Stonewall riot 1980s AIDS crisis

and municipal services—economic issues of a more national focus have yet to emerge as organizing forces. While Chicanos are increasing in numbers, about half of Chicanos are below legal voting age. While the largest population of Mexican descent resides in Los Angeles, Mexican-Americans constitute a majority in San Antonio, Texas. In 1981, Henry Cisneros became the first mayor of San Antonio of Mexican descent in 140 years.

Puerto Ricans are torn between the island of Puerto Rico (a colony of the United States since 1898) and mainland United States. Statehood and self-rule for Puerto Rico is an overriding issue. Puerto Rico became a commonwealth in 1948, a status that allows them to elect their own governor. Puerto Ricans have been American citizens since 1917 and may vote in American elections upon establishing mainland residency. The 18th District of New York (the Bronx) has a 51% Hispanic majority and has consistently elected a Puerto Rican to the U.S. House of Representatives, first Herman Badillo and currently Robert Garcia (D-NY). However, Puerto Rico has no electoral college vote and has no representation in Congress. Puerto Ricans also suffer economic discrimination; by 1984, the median family income of Puerto Rican families had dropped to less than half that of white families.

The third largest group, those who immigrated from Cuba, present yet another set of distinctive concerns. Many Cuban immigrants settled in Miami, Florida, which now has a majority Latino city. Most, in particular the earliest immigrants who were well educated and shared a managerial and professional background, fled Cuba after Fidal Castro assumed power in the Cuban Revolution of 1959. Cubans are vehement anticommunists and are registered to vote as Republicans by a two-to-one margin. In addition, in part because of the assistance they received as refugees and the resources that the early immigrants were able to bring with them upon immigration, Cuban family income is increasing faster than the national rate. Thus, the economic issues that may potentially unite Chicanos and Puerto Ricans would have little appeal to Cubans.

At this point, the issues that divide Chicanos, Puerto Ricans, and Cubans are at least as great as the bilingualism that unites them. There is no national Hispanic or Latino identity. Mexican-Americans and Puerto Ricans tend to support Democratic candidates, while Cuban-Americans are overwhelmingly Republican.[9] One institution shared by Hispanics is the Catholic church. Unlike the black churches in the civil rights movement, the Catholic church is hierarchical, externally controlled, and assimilationist. The Vatican ban on priests and nuns holding political office has also been a problem.

Finally, Latino communities are less concentrated geographically and "appear to assimilate more rapidly than blacks" (Browning, Marshall, and Tabb, 1990, p. 220). Latino leaders have not yet developed a strong sense of

---

[9]Of Latinos registered to vote in Dade County, Florida, about 75% are Republicans (Warren, Stack, and Corbett, 1990).

mobilization, nor have they commonly formed coalitions with other minorities, particularly in cities such as New York and Miami, where blacks and Latinos are deeply divided. The League of United Latin American Citizens (LULAC) is committed to total assimilation, while the more activist La Raza (formerly NO MAS—National Organization for Mexican American Services) became the first Latino lobbying presence in Washington, D.C., in 1963, a latecomer to civil rights advocacy. NO MAS joined the Leadership Council on Civil Rights (LCCR) in its push for the 1964 Civil Rights Act. One study of minority incorporation concludes that Mayor Henry Cisneros[10] "does not promote either his Mexican-American identity or the specific interests of that community" (Muñoz and Henry, 1990, p. 183), while another Mexican-American mayor, Federico Peña of Denver, "was not the product of minority electoral mobilization or demand-protest and was not endorsed by established Mexican American politicians" (Browning, Marshall, and Tabb, 1990, p. 220). An exception was black Chicago[11] Mayor Harold Washington, whose reform coalition included blacks and Latinos.

There are, however, several factors that suggest that there is reason to classify Latinos as a potential social force. First, there are several elite-level Hispanic organizations—the Hispanic Caucus in the U.S. Congress and voter registration groups (the Southwest and Midwest Voter Registration Education Projects and the National Puerto Rican Hispanic Voter Participation Project)—and groups like La Raza are becoming more assertive in the civil rights community. Latino efforts to gain LCCR opposition to employer sanctions for those who hire illegal immigrants contained in the 1986 Immigration and Reform Control Act were unsuccessful because both the AFL-CIO and the NAACP supported the controversial provision. As a consequence, Latino leaders threatened to resign from LCCR and boycotted the 1990 LCRR leadership banquet. Second, there is the beginning of a legal strategy to advance Hispanic rights. In 1988, U.S. District Court Judge Lucius D. Bunton ruled that the FBI had discriminated against its Hispanic agents (who comprise about 5% of the Bureau's nearly 10,000 agents) in promotions and job assigments. And third, bilingualism remains a salient common link. The retaining of their language means being able to keep their heritage and identity.

Probably the issue most likely to mobilize Hispanics is the recent backlash against bilingualism in both voting and education. In 1965, the Elementary and Secondary Education Act provided for bilingual education. However, it was not until 1970 that the Supreme Court ruled in *Cisneros v. Corpus Christi Independent School District* that de jure segregation of Chicanos in "Mexican

---

[10]Cisneros, who was interviewed by 1984 Democratic presidential nominee Walter Mondale for the vice presidential nomination, surprised his supporters by leaving office at the end of his third term in 1988, acknowledging rumors of a marital affair. Cisneros is currently head of the National Civic League.

[11]Chicago has the largest proportion of Latinos in the country, about 14% of the total population in 1980.

schools" was ruled unconstitutional. Amendments in 1975 to the Voting Rights Act required bilingual (and multilingual) ballots where census data show a substantial number of non–English-speaking people. A number of local initiatives and referenda intended to either limit bilingualism or to formally express support for establishing English as the official language have been placed on ballots in Dade County, Florida, and in other localities in at least 15 states. Eight states already have such laws. There is also a proposed constitutional amendment designed to designate English as the "official language of the nation," sponsored by Quentin N. Burdick (D-ND).

Disabled Persons as a Potential Social Movement

The disabled comprise another potential movement. Two classes of disabled individuals have increased greatly in the past 20 years. Because of the advances in battlefield medicine, the Vietnam war produced more disabled veterans than any previous war. Many of these veterans attended college on the G.I. bill and have been welcomed by such schools as the University of Illinois, which redesigned their campuses for wheelchair access. Disabled veterans have viewed themselves as a distinctive group and have been most active as veterans, rather than part of a larger group of disabled citizens. In 1988, veterans achieved a longstanding goal in achieving cabinet status for the Veterans Administration.

Another group are the deaf, which includes a large group who became deaf in utero during the 1964–65 rubella epidemic. Many deaf people, like those who lost their hearing due to the rubella epidemic, are born to hearing families and would not be expected to identify primarily with the deaf community. However, until recently with public school efforts at mainstreaming the disabled, many deaf children attended schools for the deaf from as early an age as 2 or 3. These were perforce boarding schools, which engendered an identity among the deaf community that became politically significant in 1988.

In March 1988, Gallaudet University, the only American university for the deaf, was closed down for 4 days due to a vehement student protest over the selection of a hearing president, Elizabeth Zinser, by the Board of Trustees. The student leaders of the protest were most emphatic that the selection of a hearing president signified a continued erroneous belief in the incompetency of deaf individuals. The issue for Gallaudet (a federally chartered university) was resolved when Zinser resigned, and the first deaf president, I. King Jordan, was subsequently appointed. With widespread immunization against rubella, the number of young deaf Americans is declining, but the solidarity shown at Gallaudet in 1988 suggests an increasingly politically active deaf community.

Clearly, there are important potential issues that differentiate the dis-

BOX 5-6
On Mainstreaming and Deaf Culture:
Excerpts from a Computer Dialogue

Here are seven different views of mainstreaming:

That depends, if we are talking about culture, yeah, I am Deaf, but on an employment application I will put down "Hearing Impaired."

Looks like if I don't call myself a Deaf person, then I am not politically correct about it. Gallaudet is divided into two camps: Deafies and those who prefer to call themselves "hearing-impaired."

Hearing-impaired means to me is that I have to compromise with hearing world to satisfy their standard. History has showed that we, Deaf people, have been sold our souls to hearing in order to win their respects. It is time for us to stand and tell the world that we no longer accept your so-called hearing image as normal function. Let's educate them that Deaf is a beautiful label that we love to wear it.

Frankly, y'll, I prefer to be called deaf because I am culturally Deaf and I feel a certain amount of pride in having a unique culture.

Very rarely, if ever, mainstreaming works for deaf students. More likely, those with very minor hearing loss may be able to hack it there. Half my life, my parents were bombarded with advices from well-meaning professionals. They were very strong supporters of oralist programs. As you may have guessed, I grew up in oral and or hearing schools. To tell you the truth, it was pure hell. I was constantly made to defend myself in such way some people ended up in hospital due to my deafness.

But never, never, never take their culture from deaf students. I would have called that a real murder and sickness and no respect!!!!!!

I am a supporter of DEAF SCHOOLS. I am devoted to Deaf Culture and I thank my parents for their great sacrifice to send me to Idaho School for the Deaf when I was only 3 years old. My parents finally learned sign language because of me. I had no communication before I came to school and it was first time when parents saw me smile . . . which is a great milestone for me when I came home from school.

Source: DEAF-L, an international computer network for the deaf, begun by Dr. Roy Miller, Southern Illinois University–Carbondale.

abled from the able-bodied—most important, education and employment discrimination and access to public transportation, buildings, and events. Until recently, these issues have been fought primarily by the able-bodied—those professionals who derive their livelihood from working with the disabled and parents of disabled and retarded individuals. One issue attracted national interest in 1988, which has the potential to mobilize the disabled community— parental rights. A disabled California couple had two natural infants taken away from them (the second at birth) because the state of California felt that they were unable to care for their children. The mother, Tiffany Callo, finally agreed to an open adoption (with the possibility of occasional visitation) rather than suffer an expected court-ordered termination of her parental rights (which would have resulted in a closed adoption with no contact with her sons). Like gays, the family cannot comprise the basic social unit (the sources of disabilities are diverse, multiple, and usually not hereditary). Locally based organizations are an important prerequisite for a social movement of the disabled. Veterans groups who have been successful in obtaining benefits via their veteran status and the small number of universities that enroll disabled students provide an insufficient basis for group mobilization. In 1990, the Americans with Disabilities Act was passed, which banned discrimination in employment, transportation, public accommodations, and telecommunications against persons with physical or mental disabilities. This act, which requires substantial changes among commercial establishments and employers, became effective only in 1992. It does have the potential to become a "critical mobilizing event" for the disabled as the *Brown* v. *Board of Education* Supreme Court decision did for blacks.

SOCIAL MOVEMENTS AND DEMOCRACY

Social movements exhibit several characteristics that distinguish them as mass movements from political and religious movements. Unlike intellectual movements, mass movements, whether social, political, or religious in character, must involve grass-roots activism. Religious movements differ from social movements in that they focus only on private religious institutions and practices. Certainly, a religious movement could have an impact on politics or the public sphere. In that case, the movement would be transformed into a political or a social movement. Political movements are organized by the haves in society and focus on fairly narrow class interests or political issues. Participants in a political movement do not share a common identity or community, and their collaboration is based upon shared political goals. Political movements do not produce new leaders, they are begun by leaders of existing groups. Their origins are usually best explained by the resource mobilization theory of mass movements, i.e., by the provision of resources by preexisting groups and the existence of "checkbook" members and "staff" organizations.

Social movements are distinctive: they are organized by the members of the outgroup itself and are based on a common identity. They focus on social as well as political goals. Using the civil rights movement as a model, we have explained the development of two other social movements: the women's movement and the gay rights movement. A question to consider at this juncture is, Do other social groups have the potential to become full-fledged social movements? Two groups considered here that appear to have this potential are Hispanics and the disabled.

In the past, social movements were linked with the formation of third parties. In the contemporary era, social movements act *within* the existing party system. This is critical because the contemporary alignment was frozen in the progressive era—frozen to exclude blacks, women, and others. Walter McFarland (1983) has pointed to social movements as a countervailing influence to interest groups and minority factions. We think this is misleading: social movements do have organizations that function just like other interest groups, *and* they are not free-standing—their major influence is within the party system. Social movements are successful when their group members are recruited into the ranks of elites. Their goal is not to remain a permanent alternative organization, but to gain admittance to the leadership ranks. *Social movements are thus an antidote to elite oligarchy.* Of course, like any chronic disease, the antidote, however permanent for that group, will not preclude future oligarchic tendencies.

chapter 6

The Party Elite Theory
of Democracy

Democracy is a treasure which no one will ever discover by deliberate search.

Roberto Michels, 1962, p. 368

We now conclude with our own theory of mass-elite interdependence, which builds on previous elite theory and incorporates modern social movement theory. We term our position a *party elite* theory of democracy. The pressure system, as Schattschneider reminded us, "sings with a strong upper-class accent." In other terms, organized interests are biased toward ingroups, and the more heterogenous and promiscuous political parties offer more opportunity to members of outgroups. The reforms of the past 20 years—in political parties, in the U.S. Congress, and in the statehouse—have made the parties more permeable to outgroup elites. The breadth of change is obvious when these reforms are compared to the 1950 assessment of American politics offered by the American Political Science Association Committee on Political Parties (see Appendix). Now parties are ruled by coalitions of elites from both ingroup elites and various outgroup elites. Any useful theory of contemporary American politics must take account of the following facets of American politics:

1. Elite tendencies in organizational behavior
2. The decline of third parties in the twentieth century
3. The democratization of the political system expressed through the development of social movements and the challenges they present to elite oligarchy

As we saw in Chapter 4, understanding the role and limitations of elites as democratic leaders is central. We define elites as those who exercise power, compared to nonelites who do not. In line with Michels' observation about the psychological transformation of elites in the recruitment process, we assume that "the mentality of leaders is never identical with that of the masses even if the leaders are of the same social composition as the masses" (Michels, 1962, p. 189). *Elites will always differ from nonelites.* Incorporated in this assumption is the fundamental sociological truism that organized elites tend toward oligarchy (Michels, 1962). This is true even among those elites, like contemporary feminists, who consciously try to be inclusive. As seen in Chapter 4, all elites will also act to protect their position even to the extent of restricting suffrage and excluding some groups from participation. This pervasive group-level discrimination only ended with the organized pressure of new social and political movements, which resulted in the reform of the party system and the political system. We argue that mass-level movements constitute a necessary, albeit episodic challenge to elite oligarchy. Both political and social movements provide grass-roots support for new policy directions. But it is social movements that broaden and democratize the political system by representing outgroups.

Parties—distinct from bureaucratic organizations—are promiscuous and permeable. While party leadership is usually restricted to those recruited from within the party, this does not mean that parties are institutionalized in the same ways as bureaucracies. As we learned in Chapter 3, parties *must* compete for electoral support, and thus remain open to political competition. Organized interests and active social and political movements can indeed bid for party power, and thus for the same say over the major prize in American politics—the presidency. Further, parties are not based on expertise or organized hierarchically in the classic bureaucratic fashion. Competition between group-based subcoalitions in the party may result in upward recruitment for some (promotion) and in a loss of position for others (demotion) (Eldersveld, 1964, p. 144).

In contrast to many contemporary elite theorists, we do not define elites as those who receive "the most of what there is to get" (Lasswell, 1958, p. 13), but rather those who determine "who gets what, when, [and] how." Our definition of elites is as a *leadership group*, which is a matter of influence and a matter of degree, not a categorical distinction. This would include those who occupy leadership positions in the parties, in government, and in interest groups, as well as those who do so in major economic, educational, and social institutions.

Critically, we diverge from Duverger and Lasswell in our conceptualization of the *basis* of elite influence. Duverger articulated the concept of the cadre party as based "in the groupings of notabilities" (1954, p. 64). For Duverger, cadre parties are "decentralized and weakly knit" because they are organized around (occasional) elections and the conduct of time-bound campaigns (1954, p. 67). Our use of the term "cadre" refers to the membership of the decentralized federal structure of the American party system. However, we argue that these cadres are no longer comprised of occasional elites drawn from the ranks of economic notables, but are increasingly comprised of full-time party leaders whose organization persists from one election to the next. This organizational coherence is evident at all levels of the party. State and national parties are increasingly interdependent—a marked change from the stratarchical characteristics of independence and "reciprocal deference" (Eldersveld, 1964).

We also diverge from the power structure and other contemporary elite theorists who stress property and wealth as the basis for elite influence. There are many persons with substantial property rights, yet who have little or no political influence. Most important, *property (or economic notability) is no longer a prerequisite for elite influence.* In our view, contemporary elites in the United States obtain their positions and their influence primarily through a mastery of information. We intend the term "information" to refer to a marshalling of the facts so as to produce a better, i.e., managerial, understanding of the true state of public affairs and politics. This is a different use than those who base their theory in mass society. For example, Harold Lasswell refers to information as the use of the "symbols of the common destiny," which are "the 'ideology' of the established order and the 'utopia' of counter-elites" (1958, p. 31). Lasswell was concerned primarily with the promulgation of propaganda. Information facilitates communication and enables interests to place their demands before political elites in a credible way. This is quite different from the hypothesized use of propaganda (or symbols) used to beguile the uninformed (mass) voting public to prevent them from recognizing their true grievances.

Information when viewed as the marshalling of facts is essential to effective political action. Voting is only one form of participation and, by itself, communicates very little information to political elites. Once an election is over, elites are free to claim whatever meaning they wish to their victory, whether or not a mandate truly was registered in the electoral results. Those who only vote are engaging in *symbolic participation*—an act that has meaning to the participant—not in an instrumental act that exerts ongoing influence on political leaders. In our view, the essential indicators for democratic participation are the degree of participation by groups in parties, pressure groups, and political and social movements. The act of voting is only weakly related to these more demanding forms of participation. Electoral mandates are not created by an election, but through group subcoalitions within the winning party coalition. In an electorally based democracy, all elites are potentially susceptible to pressure. While it is true that property-based elites may buy "experts" to provide the needed information, it is not their exclusive province. Information is potentially available to all those with the requisite level of education and wit. It is not restricted to those who control the organs of mass communication. *An elite based on information is fundamentally more permeable than one based on property.*

An elite or leadership stratum is an inevitable part of any political system. The critical *democratic* question is whether or not the elite social stratum is *permeable*. While we personally favor a high level of political participation, any polity of large size—like the United States—must depend on some delegation of decision making. Carole Pateman (1970) has argued most persuasively that a high level of participation is unlikely without a fully developed sense of efficacy derived through true participation in other and more immediate spheres of social life—the family, the schools, the workplace, and other primary groups. Even if society provided such avenues of widespread participation, this is highly impractical. Group decision making, as any one who has tried it knows, is a very time-consuming and personally demanding process. We think it unlikely that someone who is active on their condominium board of directors will also be active in the school PTA as well as in their local county party functions. In modern society, we are all so enmeshed in so many different spheres of activity that some delegation of decision making to others— the leaders or elites—is inevitable and practical.

Unlike many, we do *not* regard the category of mass or nonelite as a negative classification. Someone is not an elite in politics (or in any other sphere of life) may have other pursuits and interests that are meaningful to them. However, this distinction between elite and nonelite does have significant and negative implications *if certain individuals are systematically excluded from elite leadership positions in all spheres of society*—i.e., a group or caste disadvantage. This is important for our definition of democracy: the masses, per se, are not excluded from power, but different groups may be. Following Duverger, *we define true democracy as liberty for all groups in society*: "not only liberty for those privileged by birth, fortune, position or education, but real liberty for all, and this implies a certain standard of living, a certain basic education, some kind of social equality, some kind of political equilibrium" (1954, p. 242). We agree with Duverger when he stresses that "liberty and the party system coincide" when it is no longer the case that "economic and financial powers alone disposed of the Press, of techniques of information and propaganda, and of a means of organizing the electorate" (1954, pp. 424–25). Parties are unique in that they promote democracy by encouraging the development of new elites.

Like the preeminent party theorists, V. O. Key and E. E. Schattschneider, we believe in party responsibility. Both Key and Schattschneider stressed the role of party competition in a two-party system as critical in ensuring responsibility. We agree, but party competition has changed fundamentally with the close of the Progressive era. The myriad changes in the electoral system have resulted in the decline of third parties in the twentieth century. While organized competition is important in promoting the permeability of parties, defining democracy to be the product of competition *alone* ignores the issue of whether groups are included or excluded. For example, there may be a temporary one-party state (Kemal's Turkey) (Duverger, 1954) that promotes liberty, or a two-party system (the realignment of 1896 in the South) (Schattschneider, 1960) that undermines liberty. While it is certainly true that "a regime without parties is of necessity a conservative one" (Duverger, 1954, p. 426), the critical issue for democracy is *not* whether parties exist—they may indeed be present in a fascist or a totalitarian form. Nor is it whether there are only one or two or more parties.

The key issue is whether the party system functions to incorporate new elites recruited through their *own* groups (i.e., groups that they control themselves). This, of course, has been the major thrust of the successful reforms implemented since 1950 (see Appendix). As Duverger noted, when "a man of the people" is recruited through the institutions of the governing oligarchy, "he must also work his way up the ladder of middle-class education and lose contact with the class in which he was born" (1954, p. 426). Essentially, our definition of democracy demands that all social groups—and not merely the dominant social class—engage in the "honor of participating in government recruiting" (Michels, 1962, p. 355). As we learned in Chapter 2, interest groups alone cannot accomplish this. The party elite theory of democracy emphasizes the party system as the crucial agency for promoting democracy by promoting more active forms of participation and, in doing so, developing new political elites.

We prefer to consider each party system on its merits. This avoids defining parties mechanistically (i.e., by the number of parties). Instead, we define a party system as democratic depending on whether it produces liberty for all groups and whether elites are recruited from all groups—a substantive result. Unfortunately, both Key and Schattschneider wrote well before the development of the civil rights movement and the development of scholarly literature on social movements. The failure of the APSA Committee on Political Parties report, a comprehensive *model* of party reform, to predict how reform was to be initiated, reflects this theoretical gap in party theory.

With the economic and social changes engendered by World War II, new groups advanced to press their claims for representation in American politics. As discussed in Chapter 5, the development of the civil rights movement in the 1950s, the women's rights movement in the 1960s, and the gay rights movement in the 1970s meant that new groups began to engage in the "honor of government recruiting." The introduction of new elites and the expansion of participation has also expanded the scope of conflict—new issues have been framed and introduced for public resolution. Most critics of party reform have expressed concerns about the new social and political movements of the past 30 years, saying that we now have too much democracy and the preferences of the people have been given too much weight in the selection of leaders. We disagree. None of these new groups reflect mass society—instead, they reflect what can only be termed a resurgence of pluralism. All of the social movements considered here are based on local and face-to-face groups—intermediary groups. Further, parties are strengthened and are more responsible and accountable (see Appendix).

Because third parties have virtually disappeared as threats to two-party dominance, our position differs from Schattschneider's and contemporary critics of party reform in that we do not agree that "democracy is not to be found in the parties, but between the parties" (1960, p. 60). We do not equate democracy with simple (individual) mass-level participation. Our conception of a democratic system requires that no one be excluded from elite ranks based upon social category. We do not argue for an elitist theory of democracy, that is, we do not argue that elites should rule because of superior knowledge, talents, information, or values.

It is our position (Baer and Bositis, 1988) that the most important typology for American party politics—at least at this particular historical juncture—is one of *outgroup* versus *ingroup* elites. This is consistent with traditional elite theory because it does not require us to ascribe motives to these elites that are inconsistent with traditional elite theory. This is also consistent with pluralist theory because we stress the critical importance of group-based behaviors and attitudes. Outgroup elites are important because they are recruited and socialized in outgroup organizations. They seek power, like all elites, and, most important, in order to achieve status and power for themselves, they must also work to achieve status and power for the members of their own outgroups. For example, black elites can only achieve power and regularize their own status, that is, transform their status from outgroup member to ingroup member, by working to do the same for those blacks who are not part of any elite. New social movements may arise, but they depend upon group consciousness, mobilization, and organization.

Elites do possess superior political information, but that is because they are in elite positions, which reduces the information cost of being informed about politics. Our theory emphasizes instead the crucial significance of the recruitment and socialization of elites formed within social groups, especially the recruitment of elites formed within social outgroups. This not only democratizes the system at the elite level, but also offers more meaningful opportunities for participation at the mass level because these outgroup elites are an essential link between the members of their group (or social category) and the larger polity. Elite formation is critical—and permeable. Participation is not only key in developing citizen (mass) character, but also in this process of elite formation. The formation of new elites through social movements has had significant effects on the party system. For the first time, we find the development of a true coalition at the elite level as well as at the mass level precisely *because* of the increase in grass roots participation in the parties. Elites and nonelites differ—each with their own independent spheres of action—yet they are interdependently linked through groups. We conclude that a fundamental shift has taken place: the parties are resurgent, and politicized groups have increasingly made their presence known with political parties as the preeminent representative agencies.

Toward a More Responsible Two-Party System: A Tally and Assessment

The Committee on Political Parties of the American Political Science Association issued its famous report, *Toward a More Responsible Two-Party System*, over 40 years ago. This report was immediately attacked as inapplicable to American culture and politics. Given the immense changes in the American political landscape since, one would expect this report to be as outdated as so many others. Yet, as John S. Jackson III notes in his recent review of the report, "no other report of an academic association in the United States has ever created more sustained intellectual foment and so dominated a discipline's research agenda" (1992, p. 63).

The report divides its recommendations into three major areas: party organizations, congressional parties, and the party-in-the-electorate. The president is not included because the committee focused on congressional parties as the heart and soul of parties as policy-making bodies. A tension exists in the report between advocacy of a more disciplined national party system that would draw its discipline from centralized control through a national "party council," and a grassroots system featuring broadbased participation in party affairs at the mass level. These are two opposing models, which Jackson emphasizes.

Parties can be responsible *for* something, a program or ideology advocated by elites. Parties can be responsible *to* someone, the grassroots members. They have a difficult time creating the organizational structures and behavior patterns to do both (1992, p. 80).

Thus, parties cannot be both a centralized organization dominated by a network of party leaders who set the party agenda for others to follow, and an organization whose leaders serve the policy preferences of the masses. While the report provides a model of what a responsible party system *might* be like, it does not resolve the essential paradox of how party cohesion is to be developed. One method involves top-down enforced discipline despite a divergence of views at the base, while another employs a bottom-up consensus through which all are voluntarily persuaded to accept the common view.

Reflecting this paradox, many of the recommendations have in fact been implemented, while in other areas opposite movement is evident, along with trends and political movements not specifically anticipated or advocated by the Committee on Political Parties (CPP). For this reason, David Price concludes that the report was both "less visionary" than might be supposed because the parties *have* become more issue oriented, yet "more important" because fragmentation of the political system makes the central role of parties—the mobilization of governmental majorities—even more pressing (1984, pp. 263–64). The CPP recommended changes focused on formal, legal, and structural changes that promote fragmentation, while the most important changes have occurred first among elites who have set the agenda, as well as responded to changes in the electorate. Jackson argues that "the parties' organizations, their elites, have responded to political pressures and opportunities in their external environments"—changes that have resulted in a palpable increase in "ideological and issue-oriented coherence" (1992, p. 79). The salutary changes in party cohesion and accountability have occurred in the absence of *increased* party discipline enforced from above. Similarly, Price concludes that "what the parties do in the policy realm . . . depends less on the laws and rules under which they operate than on how they define their role and how skillfully and energetically they pursue it" (1984, p. 264).

AREAS WHERE THE REPORT WAS SILENT. Because the report was so comprehensive and detailed, little attention has been paid to those areas where the report was silent. One of the most glaring omissions concerns how an increased partisanship among Democrats and Republicans might not also involve dramatic cultural differences in addition to philosophical or ideological differences. In some areas of change advocated by the report, we see divergence rather than convergence in the type of response in the two parties. From the perspective of the arguments about how social movements affect reform and partisan change, there are several key areas not covered in the report: the importance of participation beyond voting, race and gender discrimination (poll taxes and literacy tests are mentioned without any reference to their intended target), and the issue of the vote for 18 year olds (granted in 1970). While the report stresses the role of a party council and leadership by elites, the thrust of the 1960s and 1970s congressional and party reforms were to break down party oligarchies. Another interesting omission concerns the problem of independent presidential candidates in lieu of a genuine third party. Since the report was written, three independent candidates—George Wallace in 1968, John Anderson in 1980, and H. Ross Perot in 1992—have been influential factors. In contrast to the report's opposition to the electoral college as weakening party responsibility, it is the electoral college that has limited the effect of nonparty candidates.

While the changes in American politics and party organizations were not initiated in response to the report itself or because of the controversy it generated among academics, and they were not generated via the mechanisms suggested by its authors, the report serves as an important model and benchmark against which to measure the progress of democratic party politics in America. Changes first appeared in party organizations in the 1960s, in large part in response to popular demands, followed by major changes in congressional parties and in the electoral system that regulates popular participation. In the chart that follows, specific recommendations are listed, followed by the extent to which each has been implemented by the major party organizations. For each recommendation, one of the following assessments is made:

FULL IMPLEMENTATION: Structural change that fully implements the proposed recommendation.

PARTIAL IMPLEMENTATION: Structural change that partially implements the proposed recommendation.

SOME DEFACTO MOVEMENT: Actual or proposed changes that only partially implement the recommendation as originally proposed.

NEGATIVE MOVEMENT: Any structural change or movement in the *opposite* direction of the proposed change.

NO ACTION TAKEN: No detectable movement or change in this area.

RECOMMENDATIONS OF THE 1950 APSA COMMITTEE ON POLITICAL PARTIES: TOWARD A MORE RESPONSIBLE TWO-PARTY SYSTEM

EVOLUTION OF CHANGES EFFECTIVE 1992

Party Organizations

Reforms in party organizations are primarily associated with the McGovern-Fraser Commission reforms in effect for the 1972 presidential election. There are a wide range of areas in which the Democratic and Republican Parties have been strengthened, occurring in a number of cases prior to the assumption of rule-making authority in the national Democratic Party.

Recommendations	Democratic Party Changes	Republican Party Changes
National conventions should meet at least biennially (p. 38).	**PARTIAL IMPLEMENTATION** 1974: Democratic Charter authorized mid-term conferences; mid-term conferences held in 1974, 1978, and 1982; discontinued for 1986 and 1990. Future status is uncertain, although framework remains in place.	**NO ACTION TAKEN**
National conventions should include substantial portion of ex-officio delegates (including national committee members, state chairs, congressional leaders and prominent leaders outside the party organization) (p. 38).	**FULL IMPLEMENTATION** 1980: Winograd Commission rules create at-large pledged delegate slots equal to 10% of each state delegation to encourage selection of top party and elected officials (although no specific allocations were provided for these groups). 1984: Hunt Commission rules create a special category of 568 *unpledged* delegates—called "Superdelegates"—(about 14% of the 3,933 convention delegate votes). There were 400 unpledged slots allocated among the state parties (with additional allocations available, if needed) to include all Democratic officials in the state holding positions of state and vice chairs, governor, U.S. Senate and House of Representative members (House and Senate Democratic caucuses were authorized to select 60% of their membership), and big-city may-	**SOME DEFACTO MOVEMENT** 1988: Republican congressional members granted floor privileges at the convention to enable them to sit with their state delegations. **Comment:** Despite this change, to be a voting delegate requires congressional members (and any other prospective delegates) to run for the slot against local campaign workers (an effort few avail themselves of). Guest credentials in recent years have been liberally available through state delegations.

(continued)

Recommendations	Democratic Party Changes	Republican Party Changes
	ors (cities with populations of 250,000 or more). **1988:** Fowler (Fairness) Commission rules created four special types of unpledged Superdelegates (about 15.5% of the delegates): (1) All DNC members; (2) 80% of House and Senate Democrats; (3) all Democratic governors; and (4) all distinguished former Democratic leaders (includes former presidents, vice presidents, Speakers of the House and senate majority leaders). **1992:** DNC rules added a fifth category to include other elected and party officials, equal to one delegate slot for every four DNC member delegate votes in a state's DNC membership. In 1992, 18% of the delegates were Superdelegates (including 408 DNC members, 7 distinguished former leaders, and 80 other elected and party officials).	
National conventions should be smaller in size (limited to approximately 500 to 600 delegates) (p. 38).	**NEGATIVE MOVEMENT** **Comment:** Democratic convention size has more than tripled (from 1,234 delegates in 1948 to 4,319 delegates in 1992).	**NEGATIVE MOVEMENT** **Comment:** Republican convention size, while about one-half of Democratic conventions, has more than doubled (from 1,094 delegates in 1948 to 2,210 delegates in 1992).
National committees should reflect proportional party strength (p. 39).	**FULL IMPLEMENTATION** **Comment:** Prior to 1974, the DNC had a confederal structure: 1920 to 1974, DNC composed of 1 man and 1 woman	**NEGATIVE MOVEMENT** **Comment:** Prior to 1952, the RNC was confederally structured: 1924 to 1952, RNC composed of 1 man and 1 woman

National conventions should participate in selection of national committee members (p. 39).

from each state; 1848 to 1920, DNC composed of 1 man from each state. **1974:** Democratic Charter redesigned DNC to reflect population and constituency groups, expanding the DNC to about 350 members. **1988:** DNC further expanded to a maximum of 410 members.

SOME DEFACTO MOVEMENT
1988–90: Rule adopted at 1988 convention granted a bonus national committee member to states whose convention delegations selected DNC members: this was reversed by DNC in 1990. National convention still ratifies the results of various state selection procedures (some states authorize the convention delegation to select DNC members; others use the state central committees, state conventions, or primaries).
Comment: Ex-officio status of DNC members as convention Superdelegates

from each state; 1856 to 1924, RNC composed of 1 man from each state. **1952–68:** State chairs added as members of the RNC based on a formula, thereby resulting in 2–3 members per state. **1968:** State chairs were added to RNC representation as automatic members, reinforcing the confederal structure. **1992:** A New York state organization, the Freedom Republicans, filed in federal court against the Federal Election Commission charging that the FEC should withhold funds for the 1992 Republican Convention on grounds that party rules governing RNC membership and delegate selection process is racially biased and violated Title VI of the U.S. Civil Rights Act.

NO ACTION TAKEN
Comment: National convention still ratifies the results of various state selection procedures (some states authorize the convention delegation to select RNC members; others use the state central committees, state conventions, or primaries).

(continued)

Recommendations	Democratic Party Changes	Republican Party Changes
	beginning in 1988 makes this less critical a provision.	
A national party council of 50 members should govern party in-between conventions (pp. 39–44). The national party council was assigned a number of specific responsibilities: platform writing, holding public platform hearings, interpreting the party platform, screening potential federal candidates, coordinating different party organizations, and governing party in-between-conventions.	**SOME DEFACTO MOVEMENT**	**SOME DEFACTO MOVEMENT**
	1956–61: Democratic Advisory Council (DAC) created as result of APSA Report by DNC Chair Paul Butler. Shunned by congressional leaders, it never attained intended role.	**1919:** RNC created a party council, but this was never ratified, as required by the 1920 Republican Convention.
	1974: Democratic Charter reaffirms historic supremacy of the national convention: the convention may revise the charter with a simple majority vote, while the DNC must muster a 2/3 supermajority to revise the charter. However, the charter results in a *de facto* expanded role for the chairman's 40 member executive council (primarily based on DNC members) as DNC is enlarged with adoption of the charter [early draft of the charter did provide for a party council: this was omitted from the final draft adopted in 1974].	**1961:** Former President Eisenhower created Republican Citizen's Committee to help formulate Republican policy.
		1965: RNC Chair Ray Bliss organized Republican Coordinating Committee to advise Republican Party and advise on policy.
		1975: Rejection of Rule 29 Committee report by RNC signals national preeminence of RNC, but rejects required compliance of state party implementation of "positive action" on affirmative action.
	1980s: Democratic Campaign Committees (DCCC and DSCC) become more active and engage in candidate recruitment (Herrnson 1988, 1990).	**1977:** Five advisory councils formed with participation by members of Congress and former Republican administration officials.
	1990: DNC adoption of new rule asserting its right to ratify any rule changes adopted by the convention prior to their implementation—it has enhanced its role as the supreme body of the party.	**1970s:** Somewhat expanded role for chairman's 28 member executive council (based on RNC members), which governs party in-between meetings of full RNC with increasing activity of RNC in providing services to state and local parties under RNC Chair Bill Brock (1976–81).

National party and party council should force compliance with national party among state and local parties (pp. 46–48).

PARTIAL IMPLEMENTATION

COMPLIANCE WITH NATIONAL PARTY POLICY AND ORGANIZATION
Some DeFacto Movement

1971: House Democratic Caucus considers but defeats a resolution to strip 5 Mississippi members (William Colmer, Thomas Abernathy, Jamie Whitten, Sonny Montgomery, and Charles Griffin) of Democratic committee seniority for refusing to support and register with the state Democratic Party recognized as official by the 1968 Democratic National Convention.
1980: DNC adopts new party rule requiring 50/50 gender balance at all levels of party; Committee on State Participation seeks to implement through 1984 under direction of Chair Robert Washington, a DC attorney. Committee drops effort in 1984 under new Committee Chair, Ron Brown [later DNC Chair in 1989]. Framework remains in place, although there is no effort to enforce provision.

1980s: Republican Campaign Committees (NRCC and NRSC) become more active and engage in candidate recruitment (Herrnson 1988, 1990).

NEGATIVE MOVEMENT

COMPLIANCE WITH NATIONAL PARTY POLICY AND ORGANIZATION
Negative Movement

1977–: Beginning with RNC Chair Bill Brock (1977–81) and continued by subsequent RNC Chairs, RNC provides substantial financial, professional, and technical services to state parties.
1980: Rule adopted at 1980 national convention prohibits RNC from contributing to any candidates except the Republican Party nominee or an unopposed Republican in a primary *without* the prior permission of that state's 3 RNC members (this in response to active unprecedented role of RNC's Local Elections Campaign Division in 1978, which included 20 staffers and a budget of $1.7 million).
Comment: National, state, and local parties are now *interdependent*, not hierarchical; Republican development is to emphasize national provision of services, not rule-making authority (Cotter *et al.* 1984).

(continued)

211

Recommendations	Democratic Party Changes	Republican Party Changes
	1985–89: Under DNC Chair Paul Kirk, national party provides Democratic Party Election Force funding trained professionals in 16 states. State parties receiving the service are required to sign agreements cooperating with the national party. **Comment:** National, state, and local parties are now *interdependent*, not hierarchical; Democratic development is to emphasize rule-making authority (Cotter *et al.* 1984).	
	NATIONAL COMMITTEE CONTROL OVER MEMBERSHIP **Full Implementation** 1952: DNC refused to accept Wright Morrow (TX) as DNC member. 1958: DNC refused to accept a replacement for Camille Gravel, Jr. (LA).	*NATIONAL COMMITTEE CONTROL OVER MEMBERSHIP* **No Action Taken** **Comment:** RNC structure is based on membership selected entirely by the states (state chairs and two national committee members).
	CONVENTION CONTROL OF ACCREDITING DELEGATES **Full Implementation** 1956: Convention passed new rule to limit tactics of Dixiecrat revolt of 1948—requires party nominees to be listed on the ballot. 1964: Hughes Guidelines adopted to ban discrimination. 1968: Mississippi delegation refused seating; replaced. 1972: Illinois delegation refused seating;	*CONVENTION CONTROL OF ACCREDITING DELEGATES* **No Action Taken** **Comment:** Republican Party tradition is to defer to state practices in selection of delegates. Reform effort in 1970s was rejected in favor of deference to state practices. Apportionment among state delegations remains a decision of the preceding convention, and advantages traditionally Republican states. 1975: *Ripon Society* challenge to Republi-

	Democratic	Republican
(continued from previous page)	replaced by alternate delegation according to national McGovern-Fraser rules; upheld in *Cousins v. Wigoda* (1975). **1984:** Wisconsin state party forced to select convention delegates via a party caucus when the state's traditional use of open primary is banned by the party.	can Party delegate apportionment formula as favoring conservative states is rejected by Supreme Court in *Ripon Society v. National Republican Party.*
Local party meetings should be held frequently, even monthly (p. 47).	**SOME DEFACTO MOVEMENT** **1970s–:** By late 1970s, most Democratic county party committees (usually comprised of precinct leaders) were meeting bimonthly or more often (Cotter, Gibson, Bibby, and Huckshorn 1984, p. 43).	**SOME DEFACTO MOVEMENT** **1970s–:** By late 1970s, most Republican county party committees (usually comprised of precinct leaders) were meeting bimonthly or more often (Cotter *et al.* 1984, p. 43).
Local party leagues and groups separate from existing local party committees should help shape national party policy (pp. 47, 67–70).	**PARTIAL IMPLEMENTATION** **1970s:** Local parties have little policy role in national politics apart from participation in presidential campaigns. Policy development is usually dominated by the White House when controlled by the Democrats, and by the congressional leaders and national think tanks when out of power (Price 1984, p. 290). However, increasing local-state-national party integration increases policy involvement at the local level, as well as an enhanced role for extra-party groups with local organizations (Cotter *et al.* 1984). **1974–:** The institutionalized Democratic Party now formally and informally incorporates the party [e.g., Women's Caucus, Federation of Democratic	**SOME DEFACTO MOVEMENT** **1970s:** Local parties have little policy role in national politics apart from participation in presidential campaigns. Policy development is usually dominated by the White House when controlled by the Republicans, and by the national committee's establishment of policy councils and national think tanks when out of power (Price 1984, pp. 270–73). However, increasing local-state-national party integration promotes policy involvement at the local level, and offers an enhanced role for extra-party groups with local organizations (Cotter *et al.* 1984). **1974–:** The institutionalized Republican Party now formally and informally incorporates the party [e.g., Federation of *(continued)*

Recommendations	Democratic Party Changes	Republican Party Changes
	Women, Black Caucus, Young Democrats, Rainbow Coalition (1984), Democratic Leadership Council (1985), Coalition for Democratic Values (1990)] and interest groups (e.g., labor, education, feminist, and gay groups) (Baer 1992).	Republican Women, Young Republicans, Young Americans for Freedom (1960), Ripon Society (1962), Republican Mainstream Committee (1988)], and interest groups (e.g., business, evangelical and right to life, farm) (Baer 1992).
Regional party conferences should be held (pp. 46–47).	**SOME DEFACTO MOVEMENT** **1974:** DNC members are organized on a regional basis as provided in the Democratic Charter; chairs of these 4 regional DNC caucuses serve on the DNC Executive Committee. **Comment:** Regional organizations and conferences conducted occasionally, although they have played little role in the national party (Huckshorn 1976, p. 192). The South has traditionally been the strongest region in the party; formation of the extra-party Democratic Leadership Council in 1985 with its southern base has compensated for lack of official regional organization.	**SOME DEFACTO MOVEMENT** **1976:** Regional associations in the Republican Party have been formally recognized as an official party of party leadership. As recommended by the 1974 Rule 29 Committee Report and adopted by the 1976 Republican Convention, RNC members elect 8 RNC vice chairs on a regional basis who also serve on the governing 28 member RNC Chairman's Executive Council as provided in Rule 23 of Republican Party Rules. **Comment:** Regional associations of Republican state chairs organized in 1950s and 1960s. They were somewhat more active than in the Democratic Party, and more influential in the national party as state chairs comprise 1/3 of RNC. Regional meetings were usually conducted in tandem with meetings of the national committee (Huckshorn 1976, pp. 171–79, 193–96).
Permanent headquarters with staff should be maintained (pp. 48–50).	**FULL IMPLEMENTATION** **1984:** Permanent building in Washing-	**FULL IMPLEMENTATION** **1970:** Permanent building in Washing-

	Democratic Party	Republican Party
	ton, DC owned by the Democratic Party on corner of S. Capitol and Ivy Streets, S.E., within a few blocks of the Capitol.	ton, D.C. (Eisenhower Center) owned by RNC, housing 3 party committees, at 310 S. 1st Street, S.E., adjacent to the Capitol.
Parties should hire full-time research staff (pp. 50, 81–82).	**FULL IMPLEMENTATION** 1970s–: DNC staff grew from 30 in 1972 to 160 by 1988 (Herrnson 1988, p. 39; 1990, p. 51). Combined staff of all three national Democratic Party Committees grew from 39 in 1972 to 290 in 1988 (Longley 1992, p. 7).	**FULL IMPLEMENTATION** 1970s–: RNC staff increased from 30 in 1972 to 600 by 1984 (Herrnson 1988, p. 39; 1990, p. 51). Combined staff of all three national Republican Party committees grew from 40 in 1972 to 593 in 1988 (Longley 1992, p. 7).
Party platform as interpreted by national party council should be binding (pp. 51–53).	**SOME DEFACTO MOVEMENT** Comment: While no Democratic Party Council has been created, and platforms are not binding, party platforms have been found to reflect genuine party positions and tend to be adopted into law (Pomper 1967; Pomper and Lederman 1980).	**SOME DEFACTO MOVEMENT** Comment: While no Republican Party Council has been created and platforms are not binding, party platforms have been found to reflect genuine party positions and tend to be adopted into law (Pomper 1967; Pomper and Lederman 1980).
National party council should use public hearings for platform (pp. 54–56).	**FULL IMPLEMENTATION** Comment: Public hearings held during primary season before platform committee (which includes nondelegates) writes the final draft. In 1992, one public hearing was held; in previous years multiple hearings have been held.	**FULL IMPLEMENTATION** Comment: Public hearings held during primary season before platform committee (comprised only of delegates) writes the final draft in the week prior to the convention. Some of these have been televised.
Platform draft should be written before convention by party council (pp. 55–56).	**NEGATIVE MOVEMENT** Comment: Candidates have been given proportional representation on all convention committees, including the plat-	**SOME DEFACTO MOVEMENT** 1984: First drafts of platform written under close supervision of staffs of presumptive nominee.

(continued)

Recommendations	Democratic Party Changes	Republican Party Changes
	form committee. This means that the platform represents the views of the apparent nominee, not the party generally.	**Comment:** Confederal structure of all convention committees (1 man and 1 woman delegate from each state or territory), including the platform committee, means that the platform is dominated by the views of the state parties, not the national party or the apparent nominee.
Parties should publish information on party activities (p. 80).	**PARTIAL IMPLEMENTATION** Newsletter provided to contributors, and to the state parties. Available to public on request.	**PARTIAL IMPLEMENTATION** Numerous publications provided by subscription and to local parties.
Party regulations should be compiled and made available (p. 80).	**FULL IMPLEMENTATION** **1974:** Democratic Charter that permanently authorizes the DNC to require written national party by-laws as well as state party by-laws (which regulate local parties). The charter also mandates that the by-laws should be made publicly available as well as kept on file (and continuously updated) at the national headquarters.	**FULL IMPLEMENTATION** There is no rule requiring this, but Republican national and state party rules are readily available (some state parties charge a nominal fee). State party by-laws are usually kept on file in the office of the RNC Counsel.

Congressional Parties

Congressional parties have been transformed markedly since the report was initially written, although in ways quite different from what the report envisioned. David Rohde argues that what we have in Congress is "conditional party government," where party responsibility is evident "*only if* there were widespread policy agreement" (1991, p. 31). Such a model depends on cohesion, not discipline.

> [Party] leaders do not command or control the mass of the membership (although they may seek to do so to marginal individuals who can make the difference between winning and losing). Instead the leaders use powers granted to them by the members to accomplish goals they hold in common. (Rohde 1991, p. 35)

Reforms in Congress were initiated primarily by a caucus of liberal minded House members energized by the presidential victory of Richard Nixon in 1968. Originally formed in 1958, The Democratic Study Group (DSG) now acts as an arm of the party leadership even though it is not an official party organ. Two major types of reforms were implemented primarily in the 1970s: reforms in congressional party organization (governed by rules of the majority and minority party caucuses), and reforms in committee structures, jurisdictions, and procedures (governed by Senate and House rules as well as by law).[1]

One area of congressional reform clearly unanticipated by the Report was the devolution of power *within* committees to subcommittees in the House. The House "Subcommittee Bill of Rights," passed in 1973, mandated that legislation be referred to subcommittees; that each subcommittee have adequate staff and budget; and that they be able to meet, hold hearings, and report legislation. In 1974, committees were required to have at least 4 subcommittees. By 1975, House Democrats established a "bidding" procedure within committees for subcommittee assignments, which only partially reflects seniority. In 1976, each committee caucus was empowered to determine both the number and jurisdictions of their subcommittees. Subcommittee chairs were mandated elected by secret ballot in 1977 in each committee caucus. With the increasing decentralization of power *within* committees, an increasing

[1]Changes in this section are not individually footnoted. There is no single published source that comprehensively discusses congressional reforms in both parties. Published sources that discuss these changes include: Baumer, 1991; Dodd, 1989; Patterson and Little, 1992; Pitney, 1990; Rieselbach, 1977, 1986; Rohde, 1991; Sinclair, 1992; and Smith, 1990. Additional information was also obtained by consulting: *Comparative Data on the U.S. House of Representatives* (compiled by the Republican Staff of the House Rules Committee), *The Rules of the Republican Conference of the United States House of Representatives, 102nd Congress, Rules of the United States Senate Republican Conference*, and the *Preamble and Rules of the Democratic Caucus* (the Senate Democratic Caucus has no written rules). Many thanks to several scholars who shared some of their own work in progress and provided additional information not otherwise available in published sources: Paul Rundquist (Congressional Research Service), Chris Deering (George Washington University), Paul Herrnson (University of Maryland), John Jackson (Southern Illinois University), and John Pitney (Claremont College).

tension has developed over whether the allegiance of the subcommittees was to the committee chair (still a rather feudal relationship) *or* to the party and the Caucus. In 1975, Appropriations subcommittee chairs were elected by the full Caucus rather than the committee. The major thrust of 1992 Caucus rule changes was to more tightly bind subcommittee chairs to the Caucus and party leadership as well as to curb the independence of committees in determining the congressional policy agenda.

The House and the Senate differ markedly in traditions. As one scholar concludes, "Party positions usually are not articulated in the Senate, even for major legislation" (Smith 1992, p. 179). A major reason is that unlike the House, where rule changes granting more influence to the rank-and-file were accompanied by a strengthening of leadership prerogatives, no additional powers were given to Senate party leaders to assist in coping with "the more active, assertive, and hence less predictable membership" (Sinclair 1990, p. 243). Senate rules provide only one major resource to the Majority Leader— the right to be recognized first before other senators on the floor. The House of Representatives, by contrast, grants considerable powers to the majority party to act. The Democratic House Caucus, in the majority since 1955, has strengthened the role of the party caucus. The recommendations and changes discussed below are divided into two types: (1) those under the jurisdiction of party caucuses, and (2) those under the jurisdiction of chamber rules and statutes or legislation.

Rules Changes Under the Jurisdiction of Party Caucuses

Recommendations	Democratic Party Changes	Republican Party Changes
Party leadership in Congress should be broader, include all leaders (pp. 57–59).	*U.S. HOUSE OF REPRESENTATIVES* **PARTIAL IMPLEMENTATION** **1973:** Speaker, Majority Leader, and Whip are made members of Committee on Committees. **1973:** House Democrats create 24 member Steering and Policy Committee composed of party's elected leaders (Speaker, floor leader, caucus chair), 12 members elected by Democratic Caucus to represent geographic regions, and 9 others to be appointed by the Speaker (including the party whips and representatives of the Congressional Black Caucus, women members, and freshmen Democrats). **1989–90:** Whip system expanded to 102 members (Whip, Chief Deputy Whip, 15 Deputy Whips, 3 task force chairs, 64 at-large whips, and 18 zone whips). **1991:** Whip system expanded to include 3 Chief Deputy Whips, each given a seat on steering and policy, now includes nearly 2/5 of members. **1992:** Whip system expanded to include 4 Chief Deputy Whips. All 4 whips included in Steering and Policy Committee.	*U.S. HOUSE OF REPRESENTATIVES* **PARTIAL IMPLEMENTATION** **1949:** Steering Committee, chaired by Minority Leader, is enlarged and renamed as Policy Committee. **1959:** Policy Committee reconstituted with a separate chair. **1965:** Research Committee established to formulate policy positions (from a Republican Party Committee subcommittee). The Policy Committee now has 31 members: Republican Party leaders; ranking members of 4 major committees; 8 regional members; 7 at-large members appointed by Republican leader; and 2 members each from the freshman and sophomore classes. **1965:** Members of the leadership prohibited from serving as ranking members of standing committees. **1989:** Whip apparatus reduced and streamlined, after growth from mid-1970s through 1980s. New Chief Deputy Whip (for a total of two) appointed by newly elected Whip Newt Gingrich (R-GA) for strategy and special projects (the other chief deputy whip handles traditional legislative work on the floor).

(continued)

Recommendations	Democratic Party Changes	Republican Party Changes
	Comment: Recent Democratic Chairs of the DCCC, Tony Cohelo (D-CA) [DCCC Chair 1981–86], and Vic Fazio (D-CA) [DCCC Chair 1991–present] have been involved in legislative strategy.	**1992:** Effective in 103rd Congress, Ranking Committee members are limited to 3 terms and on only one committee (beginning in the 104th Congress), thus ensuring more rapid rotation. The president of the freshman class was made a member of the leadership. **Comment:** There are currently 8 elected Republican Party leaders: Republican leader, Whip, conference chair, vice chair and secretary; Policy and Research Committee chairs, and chair of the National Republican Congressional Committee (NRCC) (ranking members on Rules, Appropriations, Ways and Means, and Budget are "designated" members of the House Republican leadership). Longtime NRCC Chair Guy Vander Jagt (R-MI) has chosen not to play a strategic role.
	U.S. SENATE **SOME DEFACTO MOVEMENT** **1988:** Senate Steering Committee is appointed a Chair other than Majority Leader by Majority Leader Mitchell. **Comment:** Chief Deputy Whip position is now an elective post, while the DSCC Chair remains an appointment by the Majority Leader. Over 30% of Demo-	*U.S. SENATE* **SOME DEFACTO MOVEMENT** **1979–80:** Conference and Policy Committee staffs separated, enhancing staff expertise available to separate Conference and Policy Committee chairs. **1980:** Chair of NRCC made an elected post (previous practice regularized). **1981:** Republican leadership dropped

cratic senators serve in leadership positions in the 102nd Congress (Patterson and Little 1992, p. 20).

practice of appointing assistant whips upon assumption of majority status (1981–86).
Comment: Approximately 35% of Republican Senators served in leadership positions in 102nd Congress (Patterson and Little 1992, p. 20).

Party leadership should be consolidated to increase accountability for each party in House and Senate (policy proposals, committee structure, and legislative schedule) (pp. 59–61).

U.S. HOUSE OF REPRESENTATIVES
FULL IMPLEMENTATION
1965–: Liberal Democratic Study Group (DSG), first organized in 1958, spearheads reform movement in the House and begins evolution into unofficial policy arm of House Democrats with its research arsenal, informational briefings, and whip system (Davidson 1992).
1973: House Democratic leaders (Speaker, Majority Leader, and Whip) made members of party Committee on Committees and Steering and Policy Committee established with Speaker as chair.
1974: Caucus Committee on Organization, Study and Review (OSR) used to rework recommendations on committee reorganization made by Select Committee on Committees.
1974: House Speaker given authority to make multiple referral of bills to committees.
1975: Steering and Policy Committee given party's committee on committee powers. Speaker-appointees (1/3) and

U.S. HOUSE OF REPRESENTATIVES
SOME DEFACTO MOVEMENT
1986: Republican Party leader authorized to designate "leadership issues" for "early and ongoing cooperation between the relevant committees and the Leadership."
1988: Republican Party leader is authorized to appoint minority membership on Rules Committee.
1988: Republican Party leader granted a weighted vote on Committee on Committees [the leader has 12 votes, and the Whip 6; all state delegations with 5 or more Republican members elects its own representative with votes equal to the delegation size; smaller states are grouped according to delegation size (1 member, 2 members, and so forth) and elect a member based on the total size of their group-based members; the two most recent classes each elect a member with one vote].
1992: Republican Conference forms a committee to study the reduction and streamlining of elective leadership posts.

(continued)

221

Recommendations	Democratic Party Changes	Republican Party Changes
	party leaders now comprise a majority of the Steering and Policy Committee, which the Speaker chairs. **1975:** Speaker empowered to nominate Democratic members of Rules Committee. **1977:** Speaker authorized to set time limits on multiple committee consideration of bills. **1979:** Working majority established on 4 major committees. **1990s:** Under direction of Majority Leader Dick Gephardt (D-MO), Democratic Party and committee leaders establish a "Message Board" to define and propound common Democratic themes and media messages. **1992:** Size and number of subcommittees are limited, thereby reducing decentralization. Subcommittees are limited to 60% of the whole committee membership. Except for Appropriations (which is allowed 13 subcommittees) all major and exclusive committees are limited to 6 subcommittees, nonmajor committees are limited to 5 subcommittees. Seniority of new committee members of same class determined by the order chosen in Steering and Policy Committee. Caucus must also be notified of the creation of any committee subunits within **7 days** by the committee chair.	**Comment:** In the longtime minority, Republican House Conference Rules are largely irrelevant to House governance and agenda setting. House Republicans are increasingly active in policy area in development of alternative policy proposals, although this has been used primarily to frustrate the majority's ability to enact core legislation (excessive quorum calls, requests for roll call votes on routine matters, etc.). House Republicans have proposed increasing the powers available to the Republican leader beginning in the 103rd Congress.

Comment: The major effect of these changes was to increase the potential power of the Speaker. Speaker Tom Foley (D-WA) (1989–present) has not used these tools as aggressively as Speaker Jim Wright (D-TX) (1986–89).

U.S. SENATE
NO ACTION TAKEN
Comment: Senate Democratic leadership is more formally centralized than is true for Senate Republicans: the party leader chairs the caucus, policy, and steering committees (modified by current Sen. Majority Leader George Mitchell in 1988, with creation of a new position of co-chairman of the Policy Committee and appointing a colleague as chair of the Steering Committee). Mitchell has utilized Rule 22 providing for cloture and bans nongermane amendments to enhance his control over scheduling. This does not represent any permanent changes in Senate or the Democratic Caucus (which has not written rules), but a strategic exploitation of parliamentary procedure and deference by Democratic Senators to their Majority Leader.

U.S. SENATE
NO ACTION TAKEN
Comment: Few formal powers are available to the Republican Party leader, as the caucus, policy, and committee on committee positions are chaired by separate individuals. (In contrast to the Democratic Senate tradition, the Republican Conference chairman and Floor leader were reconstituted as separate posts in 1945).

(continued)

Recommendations	Democratic Party Changes	Republican Party Changes
Party leadership should be elected every two years (a "vote of confidence") (p. 59).	*U.S. HOUSE OF REPRESENTATIVES* **FULL IMPLEMENTATION** **1977:** Democratic Caucus, not the committee itself, empowered to elect the chair of the Democratic Congressional Campaign Committee. *U.S. SENATE* **FULL IMPLEMENTATION**	*U.S. HOUSE OF REPRESENTATIVES* **FULL IMPLEMENTATION** *U.S. SENATE* **FULL IMPLEMENTATION**
Party caucuses should make policy decisions in House and Senate (p. 61).	*U.S. HOUSE OF REPRESENTATIVES* **FULL IMPLEMENTATION** **1969:** House Democratic Caucus will meet if requested by 50 members. **1971:** House Democratic Caucus required to meet at least once a month; all members could place items on agenda. **1970s:** Caucus begins to employ power to make policy decisions on an *ad hoc* basis, passing 3 resolutions intended to end military involvement in Southeast Asia and one concerning the oil depletion allowance. **1980s:** Expansion of use of Speaker's task force system is used to develop long-range policy positions within Democratic Caucus task forces; includes nearly half of Democratic members (Patterson and Little 1992, p. 17). Party Effectiveness Committee (1981–82) inaugurates series of policy luncheons (Price 1992, p. 84).	*U.S. HOUSE OF REPRESENTATIVES* **PARTIAL IMPLEMENTATION** **1980s:** Development of task force system; Republican Research Committee task forces in 102nd Congress included more than 1/3 of Republican Conference members. **1992:** Ranking committee members required to work with the Republican party leadership to draft written plans for dealing with key issues.

1990: Caucus Task Forces coordinated by Rep. David Price (D-NC) produce issues handbook, *Investing in America's Future.*

1992: Democratic Caucus directs that all committee assignments be completed during the December organizing caucus, and that all committees should organize within 4 days after the full House formally elects committee members (proposed by each party caucus) in January, thus enhancing the House's capacity to organize early and focus on legislative proposals more quickly each Congress. **Comment:** Democratic Caucus currently meets, on average, biweekly to discuss committee assignments, organization, rule changes, pending legislation, and long-range strategy (Price 1992, p. 83).

U.S. SENATE
SOME DEFACTO MOVEMENT
1950s–60s: Few conference meetings called under the majority leadership of Lyndon Johnson (D-TX) (1955–61) and the early leadership of Mike Mansfield (D-MT) (1961–77). The Policy Committee, closed to nonmembers, issued a few policy statements.

1968–75: Increasingly, Mansfield used the Policy Committee to approve resolutions for the Democratic Senate conference to approve as party recommendations.

U.S. SENATE
NO ACTION TAKEN
Comment: Earlier position adopted in 1925 stating that Republican Senators are not "bound in any way" by Conference actions remains in effect. Republican Senate Conference usually meets at beginning of each Congress to organize; other meetings are irregular. Weekly Policy Committee luncheons (used since the 1950s) rather than conference meetings provide a regular forum to discuss policy matters.

(continued)

Recommendations	Democratic Party Changes	Republican Party Changes
	1976–80: Majority Leader Robert Byrd (D-WV) called few conferences or Policy Committee meetings. **1980–86:** Upon loss of the majority status, Byrd increased use of the conference and utilized task forces to develop policy alternatives. **1986–88:** On regaining the majority, Byrd instituted regular weekly conference meetings. **1989–92:** New Senate Majority Leader George Mitchell (D-ME) continued to hold weekly conference meetings, and rejuvenated the Policy Committee, which held weekly luncheons open to all Democrats and approved an agenda. **Comment:** The Senate Democratic Caucus has no written rules.	*U.S. HOUSE OF REPRESENTATIVES* **PARTIAL IMPLEMENTATION** **1971:** Republican Conference granted a vote on Committee on Committee nominations for ranking minority members, empowered to use other criteria than seniority. **1986:** Republican ranking minority members now have "an obligation" to manage floor consideration of Republican Conference positions "in accordance with such position." **1992:** Ranking member on House Administration Committee [Bill Thomas
Committee chairs who oppose party positions should be removed despite seniority (pp. 61–62). This proposal affects more senior members of the party—those who have attained leadership positions—and ensure that they follow party policy.	*U.S. HOUSE OF REPRESENTATIVES* **FULL IMPLEMENTATION** **1965:** Two Democratic members [Albert Watson (D-SC) and John Bell Williams (D-MS)] stripped of seniority on Commerce Committee for supporting 1964 Republican presidential nominee Barry Goldwater. **1967:** One Committee Chair deposed [Adam Clayton Powell (D-NY)]. **1969:** One Democratic member [John Rarick (D-LA)] stripped of seniority on Agriculture Committee for supporting 1968 American Independent presiden-	

tial candidate George Wallace.

1971: Committee on Committees empowered to use other criteria than seniority to nominate committee chairs; 10 members may force a vote in the Democratic Caucus on their chairperson.

1973: One-fifth of those present and voting in Democratic Caucus may force a vote on each nominee for committee chair.

1975: Three chairs deposed [Agriculture Chair W.R. Poage (D-TX); Armed Services Chair F. Edward Hebert (D-LA); Banking and Currency Chair Wright Patman (D-TX)]; 4th challenged [Wayne Hays (D-OH), retained on second ballot].

1975: Appropriations subcommittee chairs may be selected without regard to seniority.

1979: One chair challenged [Appropriations Chair Jamie Whitten (D-MS)].

1985: One chair deposed [Armed Services Chair Melvin Price (D-IL)].

1987: One chair challenged [Armed Services Chair Les Aspin (D-WI), retained only on third ballot].

1992: One chair [ailing Appropriations Chair Jamie Whitten (D-MS)] denied renomination by the Steering and Policy Committee; Caucus affirmed Committee nomination of William Natcher (D-KY) as new Appropriations Chair. Another chair [Veterans Affairs Chair Sonny (R-CA)] denied renomination by the Committee on Committees, the first time a sitting ranking member was ousted by the Committee. The Republican Conference narrowly rejected the Committee's recommendation of Paul Gillmor (R-OH) as ranking member 83 to 72. Thomas was later nominated and reinstated by the Conference.

(continued)

Recommendations	Democratic Party Changes	Republican Party Changes
	Montgomery (D-MS)] challenged, retained in close vote of 127 to 123. New rule changes further bind committee leadership to caucus instruction: Upon recommendation by the Steering and Policy Committee, the caucus may declare a committee or subcommittee post vacant at any time, not just at the start of a new Congress. Debate time for consideration of chair nominations is increased from 30 to 60 minutes, and nominations for committee chairs are now permitted in caucus by a vote of 14 members of Steering and Policy, or by request of 50 caucus members. And, on request of 50 members, or the Steering and Policy Committee, *all* subcommittee chairs (normally elected by their respective committee party caucus) are subject to a full caucus vote. *U.S. SENATE* **PARTIAL IMPLEMENTATION** **1975:** Democratic Caucus members adopt plan to vote in full caucus by secret ballot for chairs on request of 1/5 of the caucus; empowered to use other criteria than seniority to select committee chairs.	*U.S. SENATE* **PARTIAL IMPLEMENTATION/** **Some Negative Movement** **1973:** Senate Republican members on each committee may vote to select their ranking member without regard to seniority. **1975:** Ranking committee members are selected by each committee's minority members, subject to conference approval.

Committee assignment should be subject to regular reevaluation by the party caucus (pp. 62–63). This proposal affects newly elected members and those with less seniority to ensure that they follow party policy.

U.S. *HOUSE OF REPRESENTATIVES*
PARTIAL IMPLEMENTATION

1971: One-half of a state delegation may nominate candidates for committee assignments in opposition to Committee on Committees.

1973: Speaker, Floor Leader, and Whip added to Committee on Committees, formerly comprised of Ways and Means Democrats.

1975: Steering and Policy Committee given committee-on-committee function formerly exercised by Ways and Means Committee; caucus retains right to vote on states recommended for committee assignment.

1983: Rep. Phil Gramm (then D-TX) denied reappointment to Budget Committee as sanction against "collaboration" with Republicans, and other less "Boll Weevils" who voted against party policy were denied new and more desirable committee assignments (Rohde 1991, pp. 78–81).

1987: Nomination of Sen. Richard Lugar (R-IN) as ranking minority member of Foreign Relations Committee by Republican members of that committee rejected by conference members "with instructions [to the committee] to select ranking member on the basis of seniority"—in this case, Sen. Jesse Helms (R-NC).

U.S. *HOUSE OF REPRESENTATIVES*
NO ACTION TAKEN

Comment: Committee on Committees, created in 1917, makes recommendations not subject to approval by House Republican Conference. It is chaired by the Republican Party leader who has extra votes, with each state delegation choosing one member with votes weighted by the delegation size. Initial recommendations are made by an executive committee of 21 members.

(continued)

Recommendations	Democratic Party Changes	Republican Party Changes
	1992: Upon recommendation of the Steering and Policy Committee, the Caucus may remove a member's committee assignment at any time, not just at the start of a new Congress.	
	U.S. SENATE **NO ACTION TAKEN** **Comment:** Democratic leader appoints all members of the Steering Committee. Ability of any individual senator to influence action on the floor makes this provision irrelevant to the Senate.	*U.S. SENATE* **NO ACTION TAKEN** **Comment:** Republican Committee Senate Conference chair appoints Republican Committee on Committees and its Chair (effective in 1973). Ability of any individual Senator to influence action on the floor makes this provision irrelevant to the Senate.
Majority party should have a comfortable margin of control on each committee regardless of overall party ratio (p. 63).	*U.S. HOUSE OF REPRESENTATIVES* **FULL IMPLEMENTATION** **1979:** House Democratic Caucus rules require "firm working majorities on each committee" providing for "a minimum of three Democrats for each two Republicans" regardless of the party ratio. **Comment:** The Democratic Party rules provide for each committee to be 60% Democratic. In the 102nd Congress, this ratio did not result in overrepresentation of Democrats, as the U.S. House was 61% Democratic at the beginning of the congress when committee sizes and assignments were determined. The Rules Committee, however, had 9 Dem-	*U.S. HOUSE OF REPRESENTATIVES* **NO ACTION TAKEN** **Comment:** Republicans have been in the minority in the House since the 83rd Congress (1953–55). No current Republican member of the House has ever served in the majority.

ocrats to 4 Republicans (69% to 31%, or a 2 to 1 plus 1 ratio). Other House committees ranged from 60% to 64% Democratic [the Standards Committee, which deals with ethics, was maintained at a 50-50 balance].

Party leadership and open party control, not a single committee or individual committee chairmen, should control policy (called steering), bill assignment, and scheduling of legislation for floor consideration (pp. 64–65).

U.S. SENATE	*U.S. HOUSE OF REPRESENTATIVES*
NO ACTION TAKEN	**PARTIAL IMPLEMENTATION**
	1961: Rules Committee brought under control of caucus. Caucus considers resolution to instruct Democratic members of Rules Committee to report out legislation expanding the Rules Committee from 12 to 15 members to allow appointment of more responsive committee members. Resolution withdrawn when Rules Chair Howard Smith (D-VA) capitulates and withdraws opposition to expanded size.
	1970: Majority of committee membership empowered to call committee meeting, with ranking majority member presiding over opposition of Chair; and to move floor consideration of a bill if Chair fails to do so within 7 days after a rule is granted.
	1974: House Speaker empowered to make multiple referrals of a bill and to create *ad hoc* committees to expedite consideration.

U.S. SENATE	*U.S. HOUSE OF REPRESENTATIVES*
NO ACTION TAKEN	**NO ACTION TAKEN**
	1988: The Minority Leader was authorized to appoint GOP members of the Rules Committee to ensure aggressive challenges to the Democratic-dominated panel. In the longtime minority, Republican House Conference rules are largely irrelevant to House governance. Democratic Caucus rules maintain a **2-1** majority on the Rules Committee regardless of the party distribution in the House.

(continued)

Recommendations	Democratic Party Changes	Republican Party Changes
	1975: Speaker empowered to nominate Chair and Democratic members of Rules Committee. **1985:** Party whip now an elective position rather than appointed by Speaker. **1992:** A new policy forum to develop an institutional viewpoint, the Speaker's Working Group on Policy Development is established. Under the aegis of the Steering and Policy Committee, the Working Group consists of 20 members (or larger as needed to ensure representativeness) appointed by the Speaker, with at least half selected from the membership of the Steering and Policy Committee. While designed to assist the leadership, individual committees, and the caucus in developing a consensus policy agenda, no committee chairs are required to be appointed. The Steering and Policy Committee will review Working Group recommendations and present them to the full caucus discussion and debate. *U.S. SENATE* **SOME DEFACTO MOVEMENT** Sen. Majority Leader George Mitchell activates Democratic Policy Council to seek to involve greater participation of Senators.	*U.S. SENATE* **NO ACTION TAKEN** **Comment:** In the majority (1981–86), Republican Senators do not view themselves as members of a "permanent" minority.

Rules Changes Under Jurisdiction
of Statute and Chamber Rules

Recommendations	House and Senate Changes
Committee staff should be available to both minority and majority parties to maximize sound party operations and to minimize disruptions when there is a transfer of power between parties (pp. 63–64).	*U.S. HOUSE OF REPRESENTATIVES* **FULL IMPLEMENTATION** **1970:** Minority party is guaranteed a minimum of 10 minutes of debate on amendments. **1970:** Minority party may call its own witnesses on at least one day of committee hearings. **1970:** Minority party in the House may hire one-third of full committee staff under statutory authorization [supplemental staff employed under Annual Funding Resolutions not covered and are hired by the majority; in the 102nd Congress, committee party staff ratios ranged from a low of 66% Democratic (Small Business) to a high of 81% Democratic (Energy and Commerce)]. **1971:** Subcommittee chairs and the ranking minority member granted authority to hire a staff member for the committee. **1975:** Floor debate on conference reports must be divided equally between minority and majority members. *U.S. SENATE* **PARTIAL IMPLEMENTATION** **1975:** Each Senator granted a personal staff member allowance for each committee assignment (maximum of three), thereby greatly decentralizing staff expertise among all committee members. However, this additional staff allowance is now merged in general staff allowances for each Senator and personal staff are not now given automatic access to private committee deliberations. **1977:** Minority party is also guaranteed one-third of committee staff.
Cloture Rule should be amended, which required two-thirds of those present and voting to be able to end a filibuster (as many as 67 votes if all 100 senators are present)—a majority cloture is recommended (p. 65).	*U.S. HOUSE OF REPRESENTATIVES* **Not Relevant** *U.S. SENATE* **PARTIAL IMPLEMENTATION** **1975:** Cloture Rule revised: Sixty senators may cut off debate.

(continued)

Recommendations	House and Senate Changes
	1979: Senate is required to vote on a bill within 100 hours after cloture is invoked to limit post-cloture "filibuster by amendment." **1986:** Post-cloture debate time reduced to 30 hours.

Election System

The report contained a number of recommendations to make the party system more responsive by increasing grass-roots participation, in particular voting and easing access to exercise of the franchise. Some of these recommendations are under the jurisdiction of state and federal law, others would require a constitutional amendment (e.g., abolishing the Electoral College and lengthening the term of U.S. Representatives), yet others (e.g., political activity of professors) are in the private sphere of activity. Of the changes actually implemented, some of the more significant changes have occurred through court decisions, and through the role of social movements.[2]

Recommendations	Electoral Changes
Blanket and open primaries should be abolished (pp. 70–72). (This provision is intended to limit "raiding" in which voters in one party may vote in the opposition party's primary to effect the nomination of a weaker opponent, thereby helping their own party nominee win in the general election.)	**SOME DEFACTO MOVEMENT** **1978:** Louisiana adopts a "unitary" primary in which no party labels appear on the ballot, and any candidate winning majority support is automatically elected (a run-off election is held on the day of the general election between the top two vote getters if no candidate wins a majority). **1980:** Democratic Party bans use of open primaries in presidential selection, a decision upheld by the Supreme Court in *Democratic Party of U.S. v. Wisconsin* (1981); Wisconsin required to use a caucus system in 1984. **1986:** Democratic National Committee agreed to permit states with open primary traditions (Wisconsin) to use their traditional system (beginning in 1988). **Comment:** Blanket primaries (in which voters may choose to vote in the primary of a different party for each of-

[2]Helpful information for this section was provided by Hillary Weinstein (Rainbow Coalition) and Curtis Gans (Committee for the Study of the American Electorate).

Recommendations	Electoral Changes
	fice) are used only in 3 states (Washington, Wisconsin, and Louisiana). About 10 states use some form of open primaries (in which voters may select the primary of either party in the voting booth). The Republican Party continues to defer to local state traditions. The Democratic Party, while affirming its legal supremacy on this question, has reverted back to its deference to state traditions.
Pre-primary endorsements are encouraged (pp. 72–73).	**SOME DEFACTO MOVEMENT** **1989:** Ban on primary endorsements by political parties in California was overturned by the Supreme Court in 1989 in *Eu v. San Francisco Democrats.* **Comment:** A study of governors from 1946 through 1982 found that endorsed candidates win 77% of the time (Jewell 1984). In the mid-1980s, Price (1984) finds that party organizations in 16 states do not regulate endorsements, and whether or not state parties do this depends on their "own discretion and custom" (p. 127).
Presidential nominating convention delegates should be chosen by rank-and-file party (primaries) (p. 73).	**PARTIAL IMPLEMENTATION** **1968–:** Large increase in number of primaries used to select delegates, from 15 states in 1968 to 35 in 1988 and 40 in 1992.
Electoral College should be abolished (p. 74).	**NO ACTION TAKEN** **Comment:** The electoral college does not work as the founders intended, nor does it weaken party responsibility as implied by the report. Electors currently are selected by "teams": The plurality winner of the statewide popular vote is given the right to have his or her electors "vote" (except for Maine and Nebraska, it is a winner-take-all system). The major effect of the electoral college on the party system is now much like the election of a city council using district rather than at-large selection. It is an advantage for those groups which have strength geographically concen-

(continued)

Recommendations	Electoral Changes
	trated and are active in the two-party system. Independent candidates who do not have strength concentrated geographically are disadvantaged. The effect of the electoral college is now to strengthen the Democratic and Republican Parties.
Lengthen the term for Representatives to four years (p. 75).	**SOME NEGATIVE MOVEMENT** **1980s–:** While no action has been taken in terms of lengthening the terms of the U.S. House, the increasing success of the term limitation movement using ballot referendums may prove to be an opposite trend. Colorado was the first state to adopt congressional term limits in 1990 (two 6-year terms for Senate, six 2-year terms for House). **1992:** Fourteen states adopted congressional term limits: Arizona, Arkansas, California, Florida, Michigan, Missouri, Montana, Nebraska, North Dakota, Ohio, Oregon, South Dakota, Washington, and Wyoming. Each limits Senate terms to 12 years, while House terms are limited from a total of 6 to 12 years. **Comment:** It is unclear whether term limits are constitutional (i.e., whether the states can impose limits on members of Congress). Most constitutional scholars believe that the Supreme Court will eventually overturn congressional term limits, unless a constitutional amendment is ratified (as is the case for the president).
National party should control the collection and distribution of campaign funds (p. 75).	**SOME DEFACTO MOVEMENT** **1980s–:** Significant 1970s changes in federal and state laws have immediate effect to limit party role in campaign finance; parties respond in 1980s to reassert role. Federal Election Campaign Act (FECA) passed in 1971 and amended in 1974, 1976, and 1979 is the major legislation regulating federal races, while many states have passed similar regulations of state elections. Party control was significantly revised by Supreme Court *Buckley v. Valeo* decision. Parties are limited in their donations to

Recommendations	Electoral Changes
	candidates; donations go directly to candidates bypassing the party; interest groups [Political Action Committees (PACs)] are not. The 1979 amendments exempt "party-building" expenses (campaign materials, registration, and get-out-the-vote activities) from reporting and limitation requirements. Parties respond by increasing their role in directing PAC contributions to their favored candidates, and in increasing their own federal and nonfederal donations, as well as assisting candidates in the techniques of fundraising.
Redistricting should be done on the basis of one-man-one-vote principle (pp. 75–76).	**FULL IMPLEMENTATION** **1970s–:** Reapportionment revolution effective in 1972 following the 1970 Census. The revolution was initiated by the Supreme Court decisions *Baker v. Carr* (1962) and *Reynolds v. Sims* (1965), which required the "one-man-one-vote" principle. Major effect was to end the significant underrepresentation of urban areas in state legislatures and in the U.S. Congress.
System of permanent registration should be implemented (p. 76).	**SOME DEFACTO MOVEMENT** **1988–:** Twenty-three states enacted motor-voter registration (joining 7 states already providing such a system), easing voter registration in 30 states. An active system whereby registration is encouraged or provided on the same form as the drivers' license application is available in: Arizona, Colorado, District of Columbia, Hawaii, Iowa, Maine, Michigan, Montana, Minnesota, Mississippi, Nevada, New Jersey, New York, North Carolina, Ohio, Oregon, Texas, Washington, West Virginia, and Vermont. Passive systems whereby materials are available are provided in: Alaska, Idaho, Illinois, Louisiana, Maryland (*de facto*), New Mexico, Pennsylvania (*de facto*), Rhode Island, Tennessee (*de facto*), and Utah.[3] No national action taken,

(continued)

[3]Information provided by the Committee for the Study of the American Electorate, October 29, 1992.

Recommendations	Electoral Changes
	although bills have been introduced in Congress to implement nationwide voter registration; such action is likely in the 103rd Congress. **Comment:** Purging from electoral rolls for nonvoting still remains a potential problem in some states, as well as through legal challenges by candidates, party organizations, and other groups. If a voter is challenged close enough to an election, he or she might be unable to reregister by the deadline. In 1986, a purging effort conducted by the RNC in Louisiana was banned by the federal court because it illegally targeted black voters under the Voting Rights Act, but without such racial bias, targeted challenges remain legal.
Residency requirements for registration should be shortened (p. 76).	**PARTIAL IMPLEMENTATION** **1970s–:** In 1970, Congress established 30-day maximum residency requirement for voting in presidential elections. Supreme Court extended this to state and local elections, accepting a maximum of 50-day residency requirements [*Dunn v. Blumstein*, 1972; *Burns v. Fortson*, 1973].
Elections should be on a holiday, or else, on a Saturday or Sunday (p. 77).	**NO ACTION TAKEN** Elections remain on working days.
Poll tax requirements should be "overcome" (p. 77).	**FULL IMPLEMENTATION** **1964:** Twenty-fourth Amendment bans use of poll taxes in federal elections. **1986:** Supreme Court case *Harper v. Virginia State Board of Elections* bans poll taxes in *all* elections (Virginia sought to circumvent prohibition of 24th Amendment by requiring the filing of a certificate of residency 6 months before the federal election to avoid paying a poll tax).
White primaries should be "overcome" (p. 77).	**FULL IMPLEMENTATION** **1944:** White primaries banned in Supreme Court decision *Smith v. Allwright* as a violation of the Fifteenth Amendment.
Educational barriers to voting and literacy tests as precondition to registration should be "overcome" (p. 77).	**FULL IMPLEMENTATION** **1957–60:** Civil Rights Act passed to authorize the Justice Department on be-

Recommendations	Electoral Changes
	half of blacks qualified to register, but denied due to discriminatory application of existing laws (including poll taxes and literacy, and character tests). U.S. Civil Rights Commission established in 1957. **1965:** Voting Rights Act suspended literacy tests in those states and counties where less than 50% of the voting age population had been registered in 1964 (covered six states and part of a seventh). Due to expire in 1970, this law has since been extended through 2007. **1970:** Amendments to Voting Rights Act also included some districts in northern states. **1975:** Amendments broadened protection to include language minorities (e.g., Hispanics, Native Americans). **1982:** Amendments to Voting Rights Act strengthened antidiscrimination measures by requiring proof of the *effect* of discrimination, not the more rigorous requirement of the *intent* of discrimination.
Suffrage should be granted to the District of Columbia (p. 77).	**PARTIAL IMPLEMENTATION** **1960s–:** The Twenty-third Amendment adopted March 29, 1961, grants the District of Columbia presidential electors equal to number of Senators and Representatives to which it would be entitled if it were a state. This permits D.C. to participate in the Electoral College election of the president, and by extension in the selection of delegates to the Republican and Democratic conventions. **1971:** D.C. was granted a single elected, nonvoting delegate to the U.S. House of Representatives (the D.C. delegate can vote in committee on bill mark-ups, but not on the floor for bill amendment or final passage). **1973:** The Home Rule Act of 1973 grants limited self-rule, permitting D.C. residents to elect a mayor and a city council. However, all resolutions, administrative decisions, and budgetary expenditures must come before the U.S. Congress, which has 30 days to disapprove.

(continued)

Recommendations	Electoral Changes
	1978: Constitutional amendment providing for voting representation for D.C. passed by Congress on August 22nd and sent to the states for ratification. Only 16 states ratified by the imposed deadline of 1985 and the proposed amendment failed. It provided that D.C. would be *treated* as a state only for purposes of voting representation in Congress, but did not provide for statehood so that D.C. would remain under congressional jurisdiction.
	1990: Active statehood movement in D.C. elects statehood senators (Jesse L. Jackson, Sr. and Florence Pendleton) and a state representative (Charles Morehead) to lobby for statehood. These elected officials serve as "shadow" representatives along with D.C. delegate Norton.
	1993: D.C. delegate granted right to vote in the "committee of the whole." D.C. delegate can now vote in all circumstances, except final floor passage. **Comment:** Legislation has been introduced in Congress admitting D.C. to the Union as New Columbia, the 51st state. This was reported out of committee, but never brought to a floor vote in the 102nd Congress. Progress in the 103rd Congress is uncertain; President-elect Clinton has said he would sign such legislation if passed by Congress. There is significant opposition in Virginia and Maryland, and among Republicans who fear the increased Democratic Party strength. Reforms proposed in the House Democratic Caucus would permit the D.C. delegate to vote on the floor beginning in the 103rd Congress.
Short ballot should be adopted to increase party cohesion and accountability (p. 77, also pp. 31–33, 35–36). The intent is to concentrate choice on election contests with program implications and reduce limitations on effective voting.	**SOME NEGATIVE MOVEMENT** **Comment:** Party cohesion and accountability are lessened when states make unified government impossible through (1) office bloc ballots (which organize candidate names by the office sought and does not permit straight ticket voting by marking a single box); (2) multiple and independent election of statewide offices

Recommendations	Electoral Changes
	exercising executive power (thereby permitting these officials to be of different parties); and (3) limitation of coattail effects by separating the timing of gubernatorial and presidential elections and governors and their state legislatures. *By the mid-1980s, either no change or negative movement were evident:* • The majority of states used the office bloc ballot (Price 1984, p. 134). • Over half of the states still elected over 7 statewide executive officials (Price 1984, p. 136). • Only 13 states electing less than 14% of the U.S. House of Representatives still elected their governors in the same election year as the president— a drop from 29 states (representing 52% of the U.S. House) in 1956 and 35 states (72% of the U.S. House) in 1936 (Burnham 1988, p. 9).
Election statistics should be compiled by Bureau of the Census (pp. 78–80).	**NO ACTION TAKEN** **Comment:** No national election statistics are collected by the Census Bureau, although the Census Bureau does collect sample survey data on turnout. Registration and turnout figures are maintained by the various states, usually at the local level. National turnout figures are collected by a private organization directed by Curtis Gans: The Committee for the Study of the American Electorate in Washington, D.C.
Professors should be more involved in politics (pp. 82–84).	**SOME DEFACTO MOVEMENT** **1970s–:** Since the 1950s, the American Political Science Association has sponsored some research commissions on topics relevant to parties and elections (e.g., 1964 Commission on Presidential Campaign Debates) following its sponsorship of the Committee on Political Parties, which wrote the report. Some political scientists serve as members or staff assistants to Democratic Party reform commissions of the 1970s (e.g., Austin Ranney, Jeane Kirkpatrick, William Crotty, and others).

Recommendations	Electoral Changes
	1979–: A bipartisan group, the Committee for Party Renewal (CPR), organized in 1979 as a group of political scientists, scholars, political practitioners, and other citizens to conduct research and encourage the revitalization of American parties. State chapters in California and Connecticut organized and were active as a party to Supreme Court cases *Tashjian v. Republican Party* (1986), *Eu v. San Francisco Democrats* (1989) and *Renne v. Geary* (1990), which established the rights of parties under the First Amendment, partially dismantling the underpinnings of state regulation of parties. **1990:** A partisan group, Political Scientists for a Progressive Democratic Party (PDP), organizes to promote a progressive policy agenda for the Democratic Party. PDP members collaborated on a book, *The Democrats Must Lead*, published by Westview Press in 1992. **1992:** A group of 40 Democrats, including many well-known scholars representing 20 prestigious universities, release a "Responsive Communitarian Platform" also published in a scholarly journal, the *Responsive Community* edited by Dr. Amitai Etzioni of the George Washington University. Signatories included Henry Cisneros, Pres. Clinton's nominee as Secretary of Housing and Urban Development, and Clinton's campaign advisor, William Galston.

CONCLUSION

The report is best judged as a work of political science; that is, a scholarly endeavor. As such, it has been extremely influential among political scientists and party scholars, and stands out as one of the most important pieces of scholarship in the history of modern political science. The report provides a model of how a more responsible party system might be fashioned.

The authors of the report recognized that reform required a "political force," but mistakenly thought that established political leaders would provide that "force." Reforms as discussed in this book were fashioned from the demands of outgroup elites—those who were shut out of the system. The report can hardly be faulted for lacking this insight since the theories of social and political change discussed in this volume were not available to the authors at mid-century.

The report is not politics. The report neither caused nor explains how the reforms have taken place. For example, it provides little understanding into the important and critical role of groups, group identities, and social movements in engineering key reforms from the bottom up. Of course, elite agenda setting in most cases presaged and served as critical mobilizing events in catalyzing reforms. However, reforms are rarely realized through elite enlightenment alone—the key factor is mass mobilization. This is an area not envisioned by the authors of the report (although the role of conflict is quite compatible with the larger writings of party government theorist E. E. Schattschneider).

The most important contribution of the report has been to convince thoughtful observers that parties are not simply creatures of their environment and can change and adapt to new circumstances. We base our party elite theory of democracy on the notion that genuine reform must come from interested parties rather than disinterested observers seeking to rationalize politics or make it more "ethical"—the optimism of the report is quite in tune with the energies of the reformers and stands in sharp contradiction to the nostalgia of the restorationists.

Critics of the report have objected to it as a blueprint for reform; in some quarters this has made the report infamous and the subject of opprobrium. Such criticism masks an underlying desire to attack contemporary reforms as illegitimate, with the report serving as a convenient vehicle to do so. Contemporary reforms arose of their own causes, however, and would have done so without the report. The report serves as a useful model to assess the reforms. It is due to the genius of its authors that it has been so prescient in describing most of the reforms which have actually been fashioned in party organizations, in Congress, and in our electoral system.

Bibliography

ADAMANY, DAVID. 1975. "Introduction." In E. E. Schattschneider, *The Semisovereign People*. Hinsdale, IL: The Dryden Press. Pp. ix–xxxi.

ALFORD, ROBERT R. 1963. *Party and Society*. Chicago: Rand McNally.

ALTMAN, DENNIS. 1982. *The Homosexualization of America, The Americanization of the Homosexual*. New York: St. Martin's.

AMERICAN POLITICAL SCIENCE ASSOCIATION COMMITTEE ON POLITICAL PARTIES. 1950. "Toward a More Responsible Two-Party System." *American Political Science Review* 44 (Supplement).

ARENDT, HANNAH. 1954. *The Origins of Totalitarianism*. New York: Harcourt, Brace Jovanovich, Inc.

ASHER, HERBERT B. 1992. Presidential Elections and American Politics, 5th. Ed. Pacific Grove: Brooks/Cole.

BACHRACH, PETER AND MORTON S. BARATZ. 1962. "Two Faces of Power." *American Political Science Review* 56:947–52.

BAER, DENISE L. 1992. "Who Has the Body? Party Institutionalization and Theories of Party Organization." *Midsouth Political Science Journal* 13.

BAER, DENISE L. AND DAVID A. BOSITIS. 1988. *Elite Cadres and Party Coalitions: Representing the Public in Party Politics*. Westport, CT: Greenwood Press.

BANFIELD, EDWARD C. 1961. *Political Influence*. New York: Free Press.

BANFIELD, EDWARD. 1980a. "Party Reform in Retrospect." In *Political Parties in the Eighties*, ed. Robert M. Goldwin. Washington, DC: American Enterprise Institute. Pp. 20–33.

———. [1961] 1980b. "In Defense of the American Party System." In *Political Parties in the Eighties*, ed. Robert M. Goldwin. Washington, DC: American Enterprise Institute. Pp. 133–49.

BANFIELD, EDWARD C. AND JAMES Q. WILSON. 1963. *City Politics*. Cambridge, MA: Harvard University Press.

BARKER, CHARLES A. 1970. *American Convictions: Cycles of Public Thought, 1600–1850*. Philadelphia: J.B. Lippincott.

BAUMER, DONALD C. 1991. "An Update on the Senate Democratic Policy Committee." *P.S. Political Science and Politics* 24:174–79.

BERELSON, BERNARD R., PAUL F. LAZARSFELD, AND WILLIAM M. MCPHEE. 1954. *Voting*. Chicago: University of Chicago Press.

BENTLEY, ARTHUR. [1908] 1980. *The Process of Government*. Chicago: University of Chicago Press.

———. 1949. *The Process of Government*. Evanston, IL: Principia Press. First published in 1908.

BERGER, PETER. 1963. *Invitation to Sociology: A Humanistic Perspective*. Garden City, NY: Doubleday.

BERRY, JEFFREY M. 1977. *Lobbying for the People*. Princeton, NJ: Princeton University Press.

———. 1984. *Interest Group Society*. Boston: Little, Brown & Co., Inc.

———. 1989a. "Subgovernments, Issue Networks, and Political Conflict." In *Remaking American Politics*, ed. Richard A. Harris and Sidney M. Milkis. Boulder, CO: Westview Press. Pp. 239–60.

———. 1989b. *The Interest Group Society*. Glenview, IL: Scott Foresman.

BEST, MICHAEL H., AND WILLIAM E. CONNOLLY. 1987. *The Politicized Economy*. Lexington, MA: DC Health & Co.

BLACK, EARL AND MERLE BLACK. 1988. *Politics and Society in the South*. Cambridge, MA: Harvard University Press.

BLUMBERG, RHODA L. 1980. "White Mothers in the American Civil Rights Movement." In *Research in the Interweave of Social Roles: Women and Men*, ed. Helen Z. Lopata. Greenwich, Conn.: JAI Press, Pp. 33–50.

BODE, KENNETH A. AND CAROL F. CASEY. 1980. "Party Reform: Revisionism Revisited." In *Political Parties in the Eighties*, ed. Robert A. Goldwin. Washington, DC: American Enterprise Institute. Pp. 3–19.

BRAYBROOK, DAVID AND CHARLES E. LINDBLOM. 1963. *A Strategy of Decision*. New York: The Free Press.

BRODER, DAVID. 1979. "Let 100 Single Issue Groups Bloom." *Washington Post*, January 7.

BROOKS, VAN WYCK. 1944. *The World of Washington Irving*. New York: E.P. Dutton.

BROWNING, RUFUS P., DALE ROGERS MARSHALL, AND DAVID H. TABB. 1990. "Has Political Incorporation Been Achieved? Is It Enough?" In *Racial Politics in American Cities*, ed. Rufus P. Browning, Dale Rogers Marshall, and David H. Tabb. New York: Longman. Pp. 212–30.

BURNHAM, WALTER DEAN. 1967. "Party Systems and the Political Process." In *The American Party System: Stages of Political Development*, ed. William N. Chambers and Walter D. Burnham. New York: Oxford University Press. Pp. 277–307.

BURNHAM, WALTER D. 1985. "The 1984 Election and the Future of American Politics." In *Election 84*, ed. Ellis Sandoz and Cicil V. Crabb, Jr. New York: Mentor. Pp. 204–60.

BURNHAM, WALTER DEAN. 1988. "V. O. Key, Jr., and the Study of Political Parties." In *V. O. Key, Jr. and the Study of American Politics*, ed. Milton C. Cummings, Jr. Washington, DC: American Political Science Association. Pp. 3–23.

BUSINESS AND PROFESSIONAL WOMEN. 1988. *Women and Politics—Election '88*. Washington, DC: Business and Professional Women/USA Foundation.

CAMPBELL, ANGUS, PHILLIP E. CONVERSE, WARREN MILLER, AND DONALD E. STOKES. 1960. *The American Voter*. New York: John Wiley & Sons.

CEASAR, JAMES. 1982. *Reforming the Reforms*. Cambridge, MA: Ballinger.

CHAMBERS, WILLIAM NISBET. 1967. "Party Development and the American Mainstream." In *The American Party System: Stages of Political Development*, ed. William N. Chambers and Walter D. Burnham. New York: Oxford University Press. Pp. 3–32.

CHILDS, HARWOOD L. 1930. *Labor and Capital in National Politics*. Columbus, OH: Ohio State University Press.

CONNOLLY, WILLIAM E. 1974. *The Terms of Political Discourse*. Lexington, MA: DC Heath.

CONVERSE, PHILLIP E. 1964. "The Nature of Belief Systems in Mass Publics." In *Ideology and Discontent*, ed. David E. Apter. New York: The Free Press. Pp. 206–61.

COOK, TIMOTHY E. 1986. "The Electoral Connection in the 99th Congress." *P.S.*, 19:16–22.

COTTER, CORNELIUS P., JAMES L. GIBSON, JOHN F. BIBBY, AND ROBERT J. HUCKSHORN. 1984. *Party Organizations in American Politics*. New York: Praeger.

COTTER, CORNELIUS P. AND BERNARD HENNESSY. 1964. *Politics Without Power*. New York: Atherton Press.

CRENSON, MATTHEW A. 1971. *The Un-Politics of Air Pollution: A Study of Non-Decisionmaking in the Cities*. Baltimore: The Johns Hopkins Press.

CROLY, HERBERT. 1909. *The Promise of American Life*. New York: MacMillan.

CROTTY, WILLIAM J. 1980. "The Philosophies of Party Reform." In *Party Renewal in America: Theory and Practice*, ed. Gerald M. Pomper. New York: Praeger. Pp. 31–50.

DAHL, ROBERT. 1956. *Preface to Democratic Theory*. Chicago: University of Chicago Press.

———. [1961] 1963. *Who Governs?* New Haven, CT: Yale University Press.

———. 1985. *A Preface to Economic Democracy. Democratic Theory*. Berkeley, CA: University of California Press.

DAHRENDORF, RALF. 1959. *Class and Class Conflict in Industrial Society*. Stanford, CA: Stanford University Press.

DAVID, PAUL T. 1979. "The APSA Committee on Political Parties: Some Reconsiderations of Its Work and Significance." An unpublished paper.

DAVIDSON, ROGER H. 1992. "The Emergence of the Postreform Congress." In *The Postreform Congress*, ed. Roger H. Davidson. New York: St. Martin's Press. Pp. 3–23.

DECKARD, BARBARA SINCLAIR. 1975. *The Women's Movement: Political, Socioeconomic, and Psychological Issues*. New York: Harper and Row.

DEVRIES, WALTER AND V. LANCE TARRANCE. 1972. *The Ticket-Splitter: A New Force in American Politics*. Grand Rapids, MI: William B. Eerdmans Publishing Co.

DI BIANCHI, SUZANNE M. AND DAPHNE SPAINE. 1983. *American Women: Three Decades of Change*. Special Demographic Analyses, CDS-80-8. Washington, DC-U.S. Bureau of the Census.

DODD, LAWRENCE C. 1989. "The Rise of the Technocratic Congress: Congressional Reform in the 1970s." In *Remaking American Politics*, eds. Richard A. Harris and Sidney M. Milkis. Boulder, CO: Westview. Pp. 89–111.

DOMHOFF, G. WILLIAM. 1967. *Who Rules America?* Englewood Cliffs, NJ: Prentice-Hall.

———. 1978. *Who Really Rules? New Haven and Community Power Revisited*. Santa Monica, CA: Goodyear.

———. 1990. *The Power Elite and the State: How Policy Is Made in America*. New York: Aldine De Gruyter.

DURKHEIM, EMILE. 1950. *Rules of Sociological Method*.

DUVERGER, MAURICE. 1954. *Political Parties*. New York: John Wiley & Sons, Inc.

DYE, THOMAS R. AND L. HARMON ZIEGLER. 1984. *The Irony of Democracy*. 6th Edition. Monterey, CA: Brooks/Cole.

EASTON, DAVID. 1965. *A Framework for Political Analysis*. Englewood Cliffs, NJ: Prentice-Hall.

EASTON, DAVID AND JACK DENNIS. 1969. *Children in the Political System*. New York: McGraw-Hill.

ECKSTEIN, HARRY. 1966. "A Theory of Stable Democracy." In *Division and Cohesion in Democracy*. Princeton, NJ: Princeton University Press.

EHRENREICH, BARBARA. 1984. *The Hearts of Men: American Dreams and the Flight from Commitment*. Garden City: New York: Anchor Books.

ELDERSVELD, SAMUEL. 1964. *Political Parties: A Behavioral Analysis*. Chicago: Rand McNally.

EPSTEIN, LEON. 1967. *Political Parties in Western Democracies*. New York: Praeger.

———. 1983. "The Scholarly Commitment to Parties." In *Political Science: The State of the Discipline*, ed. Ada Finifter. Washington, DC: American Political Science Association. Pp. 127–53.

———. 1986. *Political Parties in the American Mold*. Madison, WI: University of Wisconsin Press.

FAY, BRIAN. 1975. *Social Theory and Political Practice*. Boston: George, Allen and Unwin.

Federalist Papers. 1961. New York: New American Library.

FEIGENBAUM, EDWARD D. AND JAMES A. PALMER. 1988. *Ballot Access*. Washington, DC: Federal Election Commission.

FRANTZICH, STEPHEN. 1986. "Republicanizing the Parties: The Rise of the Service-Vendor Party." Paper presented at the Annual Meeting of the Midwest Political Science Association, Chicago, IL.

FRANTZICH, STEPHEN. 1989. *Political Parties in the Technological Age*. New York: Longman.

FREEMAN, JO. 1975. *The Politics of Women's Liberation*. New York: Longman.

FREEMAN, J. 1983. "On the Origins of Social Movements." In *Social Movements of the Sixties and Seventies*, ed. Jo Freeman. New York: Longman. Pp. 8–32.

———. 1986. "The Political Culture of the Democratic and Republican Parties." *Political Science Quarterly* 101:327–56.

FROMM, ERICH. 1945. *Escape from Freedom*. New York: Rinehart.

FULENWIDER, CLAIRE KNOCHE. 1980. *Feminism in American Politics: A Study of Ideological Influence*. New York: Praeger.

GAMSON, WILLIAM. 1975. *The Strategy of Social Protest*. Homewood, IL: The Dorsey Press.

GARCEAU, OLIVER. 1941. *The Political Life of the American Medical Association*. Cambridge, MA: Harvard University Press.

GARNER, ROBERTA A. 1977. *Social Movements in America*. 2nd Edition. Chicago: Rand, McNally.

GARROW, DAVID J. 1986. *Bearing the Cross*. New York: William Morrow & Co., Inc.

GERLACH, LUTHER P., AND VIRGINIA H. HINE. 1970. *People, Power, Change: Movements of Social Transformation*. Indianapolis, IN: Bobbs-Merrill.

GERTH, H. H. AND C. WRIGHT MILLS. 1946. *From Max Weber*. New York: Oxford University Press.

GIMPEL, JIM. 1991. "Vulnerability to Reform: Why the Eastern Style Machine Could Not Take Hold in the West." A paper presented at the Annual Meeting of the Midwest Political Science Association, Chicago, April 18–20.

GOODMAN, T. WILLIAM. 1951. "How Much Political Party Centralization Do We Want?" *Journal of Politics* 13:536–61.

GOLD, DORIS B. 1971. "Women and Volunteerism." In *Women in Sexist Society*, ed. Vivian Gornick and Barbara K. Moran. New York: Basic Books. Pp. 533–554.

GRABER, DORIS A. 1984. *Mass Media and American Politics*. 2nd Edition. Washington, DC: CQ Press.

GREEN, CONSTANCE MCLAUGHLIN. 1967. *The Secret City: A History of Race Relations in the Nation's Capitol*. Princeton, NJ: Princeton University Press.

GREENSTEIN, FRED I. AND CLEMENT E. VOSE. 1971. "Elmer Eric Schattschneider." *P.S.* 4:503.

GRIFFITH, ERNEST. 1939. *Impasse of Democracy*. New York: Harrison-Hilton Books.

GUNNELL, JOHN G. 1983. "Political Theory: The Evolution of a Sub-Field." In *Political Science: The State of the Discipline*, ed. Ada W. Finifter. Washington, DC: American Political Science Association. Pp. 3–45.

GURR, TED R. 1969. *Why Men Rebel*. Princeton, NJ: Princeton University Press.

GUSFIELD, JOSEPH R. 1962. "Mass Society and Extremist Politics." *American Sociological Review*: 27:19–30.

HARTZ, LOUIS. 1955. *The Liberal Tradition in America*. New York: Harcourt, Brace Jovanovich, Inc.

HEBERLE, RUDOLF. 1949. "Observations on the Sociology of Social Movements." *American Sociological Review* 14:346–57.

HECLO, HUGH. 1978. "Issue Networks and the Executive Establishment." In *The New American Political System*, ed. Anthony King. Washington, DC: American Enterprise Institute.

HERRING, E. PENDLETON. 1929. *Group Representation Before Congress*. Baltimore: The Johns Hopkins Press.

———. 1936. *Public Administration and the Public Interest*. New York: McGraw-Hill.

HERRNSON, PAUL. 1986. National Party Organizations and Congressional Campaigning: National Parties as Brokers." Paper presented at the Annual Meeting of the Midwest Political Science Association, Chicago, IL.

——. 1988. *Party Campaigning in the 1980s*. Cambridge, MA: Harvard University Press.

——. 1990. "Reemergent National Party Organizations." In *The Parties Respond: Changes in the American Party System*, ed. L. Sandy Maisel. Boulder, CO: Westview Press. Pp. 41–66.

HOFSTADTER, RICHARD. 1961. *The Age of Reform: From Bryan to F.D.R*. New York: Alfred Knopf.

HOLTHAUS, TERRY. 1990. "Cleveland State's Very Own Equalizer." *Cleveland Plain Dealer*, March 18, 1990. P. 83.

HUGHES, H. STUART. 1964. *Mussolini*. New York Review of Books.

HUNTER, FLOYD. 1953. *Community Power Structure*. Chapel Hill: University of North Carolina Press.

——. 1959. *Top Leadership USA*. Chapel Hill: University of North Carolina Press.

INGLEHART, RONALD. 1971. "The Silent Revolution in Europe: Intergenerational Change in Post-Industrial Societies." *American Political Science Review* 65:991–1017.

——. 1981. "Post-Materialism in an Environment of Insecurity." *American Political Science Review* 75:880–889.

——. 1986. "The Changing Structure of Political Cleavages in Western Society." In *Electoral Change in Advanced Industrial Democracies: Realignment or Dealignment*, ed. Russell J. Dalton, Scott C. Flanagan, and Paul Allen Beck. Princeton, NJ: Princeton University Press. Pp. 25–69.

JACKSON, JOHN S. III. 1992. "The Party-as-Organization: Party Elites and Party Reforms in Presidential Nominations and Conventions." In *Challenges to Party Government*, eds. John Kenneth White and Jerome M. Mileur. Carbondale, IL: Southern Illinois University Press.

JACKSON, JOHN S. III, BARBARA LEAVITT BROWN, AND DAVID A. BOSITIS. 1982. "Herbert McCloskey and Friends Revisited: 1980 Democratic and Republican Elites Compared to the Mass Public." *American Politics Quarterly* 10:187–212.

JANDA, KENNETH. 1983. "Cross-National Measures of Party Organizations and Party Organizational Theory." *European Journal of Political Research* 11:319–32.

JEWELL, MALCOLM E. 1984. *Parties and Primaries: Nominating State Governors*. New York: Praeger.

JUDD, DENNIS R. 1984. *The Politics of American Cities: Private Power and Public Policy*. 2nd Edition. Boston: Little, Brown & Co., Inc.

KAYDEN, XANDRA AND EDDIE MAHE, JR. 1985. *The Party Goes On: The Persistence of the Two-Party System in the United States*. New York: Basic Books.

KAZANTZAKIS, NIKOS. 1960. *The Last Temptation of Christ*. New York: Simon and Schuster.

——. 1962. *Saint Francis*. New York: Simon and Schuster.

KEY, V. O. 1942. *Politics, Parties and Pressure Groups*. New York: Thomas Y. Crowell.

——. 1949. *Southern Politics in State and Nation*. New York: Alfred A. Knopf.

——. 1955. "A Theory of Critical Elections." *Journal of Politics* 21:5–18.

——. 1956. *American State Politics: An Introduction*. New York: Alfred A. Knopf.

——. 1959. "Secular Realignment and the Party System." *Journal of Politics* 21:198–210.

——. 1964. *Politics, Parties and Pressure Groups*. 5th Edition. New York: Thomas Y. Crowell.

——. 1966. *The Responsible Electorate*. Cambridge, MA: Harvard University Press.

KINDER, DONALD R. 1983. "Diversity and Complexity in American Public Opinion." In *Political Science: The State of the Discipline*, ed. Ada W. Finifter. Washington, DC: American Political Science Association. Pp. 389–425.

KING, ANTHONY. 1969. "Political Parties in Western Democracies." *Polity* 2:112–41.

KIRKPATRICK, EVRON. 1971. "Toward a More Responsible Two-Party System: Political Science, Policy Science or Pseudo-Science?" *American Political Science Review* 65:965–90.

KIRKPATRICK, JEANE JORDAN. 1976. *The New Presidential Elite*. New York: Russell Sage.

————. 1979. *Dismantling the Parties: Reflections on Party Reform and Party Decomposition*. Washington, DC: American Enterprise Institute.

KLEPPNER, PAUL. 1991. "New Historical Views of American Politics: The Ethnocultural Model of Voting Behavior." A paper presented at the Annual Meeting of the Midwest Political Science Association, Chicago, IL.

KORNHAUSER, WILLIAM. 1959. *The Politics of Mass Society*. Glencoe, IL: The Free Press.

KOUSSER, J. MORGAN. 1974. *The Shaping of Southern Politics: Suffrage Restriction and the Establishment of the One-Party South, 1880–1910*. New Haven: Yale University Press.

KRADITOR, AILEEN. 1965. *The Ideas of the Woman Suffrage Movement, 1890–1920*. New York: Columbia University Press.

LADD, EVERETT CARLL, JR. 1977. "'Reform' is Wrecking the U.S. Party System." *Fortune* (November:177–88.

————. 1981. "Party 'Reform' Since 1968: A Case Study in Intellectual Failure." In *The American Constitutional System Under Strong and Weak Parties*, ed. Patricia Bonomi, James MacGregor Burns, and Austin Ranney. New York: Praeger. Pp. 81–95.

LANGLEY, LAWRENCE D. 1992. "Targeting the White House: The DNC and Nomination Reforms." A paper presented at the Annual Meeting of the Midwest Political Science Association. Chicago, IL.

LASSWELL, HAROLD. 1958. *Politics: Who Gets What, When, How*. New York: Meridian Books.

LAWSON, KAY. 1978. "Constitutional Change and Party Development in France, Nigeria and the United States." In *Political Parties: Development and Decay*, ed. Louis Maisel and Joseph Cooper. Beverly Hills, CA: Sage. Pp. 145–78.

————. 1987. "How State Laws Undermine Parties." In *Elections American Style*, ed. A. James Reichley. Washington, DC: Brookings Institute.

LAZARSFELD, PAUL F., BERNARD R. BERELSON, AND HAZEL GAUDET. 1944. *The People's Choice*. New York: Duell, Sloan and Pearce.

LEWINSON, PAUL. 1933. *Race, Class and Party: A History of Negro Suffrage and White Politics in the South*. New York: Russell and Russell.

LINDBLOM, CHARLES E. 1977. *Politics and Markets*. New York: Basic Books.

LINEBERRY, ROBERT L., GEORGE C. EDWARDS III, AND MARTIN P. WATTENBERG. 1991. *Government in America: People, Politics, and Policy*. 5th Edition. New York: Harper Collins.

LINK, ARTHUR S. AND RICHARD L. MCCORMICK. 1983. *Progressivism*. Arlington Heights, IL: Harlan Davidson Inc.

LOWI, THEODORE. 1974. *The End of Liberalism*. New York: Norton.

LOWI, THEODORE M. 1979. *The End of Liberalism*. rev. ed. New York: Norton. Original edition published in 1969.

LUKES, STEVEN. 1974. *Power: A Radical View*. Macmillan: London.

LUTTBEG, NORMAN. 1981. *Public Opinion and Public Policy*. 3rd Edition. Itasca, IL: F.E. Peacock Publishers.

LYND, ROBERT AND HELEN LYND. 1929. *Middletown*. New York: Harcourt, Brace and Co.

————. 1937. *Middletown in Transition*. New York: Harcourt, Brace and Co.

MCADAM, DOUGLAS. 1983. "The Decline of the Civil Rights Movement." In *Social Movements of the Sixties and Seventies*, ed. Jo Freeman. New York: Longman. Pp. 279–319.

MCCARTHY, JOHN D. AND MAYER N. ZALD. 1973. *The Trends of Social Movements in America: Professionalization and Resource Mobilization*. Morristown, NJ: General Learning Press.

MCCLOSKEY, HERBERT, PAUL J. HOFFMAN, AND ROSEMARY O'HARA. 1960. "Issue Conflict and Consensus Among Party Leaders and Followers." *American Political Science Review* 54:406–27.

MCFARLAND, ANDREW S. 1983. "Public Interest Lobbies Versus Minority Faction." In *Interest Group Politics*, ed. Allan J. Cigler and Burdett A. Loomis. Washington, DC: CQ Press. Pp. 324–53.

————. 1984. *Common Cause: Lobbying in the Public Interest*. Chatham, NJ: Chatham House.

McGLEN, NANCY E. AND KAREN O'CONNOR. 1983. *Women's Rights: The Struggle for Equality in the 19th and 20th Century*. New York: Praeger.

McKEAN, DAYTON D. 1938. *Pressures on the Legislature of New Jersey*. New York: Columbia University Press.

McLUHAN, MARSHALL. 1964. *Understanding Media: The Extensions of Man*. New York: New American Library.

McMURTRY, LARRY. 1990. "Blind Criticism." *Washington Post*, July 13. P. A21.

McRAE, DOUGLAS W. 1967. *The Political Consequences of Electoral Laws*. New Haven, CT: Yale University Press.

McWHINEY, GRADY. 1988. *Cracker Culture*. Tuscaloosa: University of Alabama Press.

MAIN, JACKSON TURNER. 1974. *The Anti-federalists*. New York: Norton.

MANNHEIM, KARL. 1940. *Man and Society in an Age of Reconstruction*. London: Routledge and Kegan Paul.

MATTHEWS, DONALD R. AND JAMES W. PROTHRO. 1966. *Negroes and the New Southern Politics*. New York: Harcourt, Brace & World, Inc.

MAYHEW, DAVID. 1988. "Why Did V. O. Key Draw Back from His 'Have-Nots' Claim?" In *V. O. Key, Jr. and The Study of American Politics*, ed. Milton C. Cummings, Jr. Washington, DC: The American Political Science Association. Pp. 24–38.

MEISEL, JAMES H. 1965. "Introduction." In *Pareto & Mosca*, edited by James H. Meisel, pp. 1–44. Englewood Cliffs, NJ: Prentice-Hall.

MERRIAM, CHARLES. 1922. *The American Party System*. New York: Macmillan Publishing Company.

MICHELS, ROBERTO. [1915] 1962. *Political Parties: A Sociological Study of the Oligarchical Tendencies of Modern Democracy*. New York: Crowell-Collier.

MILBRATH, LESTER W. 1953. *The Washington Lobbyists*. Chicago: Rand McNally.

MILEUR, JEROME M. 1980. "Massachusetts: The Democratic Party Charter Movement." In *Party Renewal in America: Theory and Practice*, ed. Gerald M. Pomper. New York: Praeger.

MILLER, WARREN E. AND M. KENT JENNINGS. 1986. *Parties in Transition*. New York: Russell Sage.

MILLS, C. WRIGHT. 1959. *The Power Elite*. New York: Oxford University Press.

MONTJOY, ROBERT S., WILLIAM R. SHAFFER, AND RONALD E. WEBER. 1980. "Policy Preferences of Party Elites and Masses: Conflict or Consensus?" *American Politics Quarterly* 8:319–43.

MOREHOUSE, SARAH McCALLY. 1981. *State Politics, Parties and Policy*. New York: Holt, Rinehart and Winston.

MOSCA, GAETANO. 1939. *The Ruling Class*. New York: McGraw-Hill.

MUÑOZ, JR., CARLOS AND CHARLES P. HENRY. 1990. "Coalition Politics in San Antonio and Denver: The Cisneros and Peña Mayoral Campaigns." In *Racial Politics in American Cities*, ed. by Rufus P. Browning, Dale Rogers Marshall, and David H. Tabb. Pp. 155–78. New York: Longman.

MYRDAHL, GUNNAR, RICHARD STERNER, AND ARNOLD ROSE. 1944. *An American Dilemma: The Negro Problem and American Democracy*. New York: Harper and Row.

NATCHEZ, PETER B. 1984. *Images of Voting/Visions of Democracy*. New York: Basic Books.

NELSON, MICHAEL. 1977. "What's Wrong with Political Science." *Washington Monthly*, September. Pp. 13–20.

NISBET, ROBERT. 1953. *The Quest for Community*. New York: Oxford University Press.

OBERSCHALL, ANTHONY. 1973. *Social Conflict and Social Movements*. Englewood Cliffs, NJ: Prentice-Hall.

ODEGARD, PETER H. 1928. *Pressure Politics: The Story of the Anti-Saloon League*. New York: Columbia University Press.

OLSON, MANCUR. [1965] 1971. *The Logic of Collective Action*. Cambridge, MA: Harvard University Press.

OSTROGORSKI, M. 1902. *Democracy and the Organization of Political Parties*. Volume II. New York: The Macmillan Company.

PARETO, VILFREDO. 1935. *Mind and Society*, trans. Andrew Bongiorno and Arthur Livingston. New York: Harcourt, Brace, Jovanovich.

PATEMAN, CAROLE. 1970. *Political Participation and Democracy.* Cambridge, UK: Cambridge University Press.

PATTERSON, SAMUEL C. AND THOMAS H. LITTLE. 1992. "The Organizational Life of the Congressional Parties." A Paper presented at the Annual Meeting of the Midwest Political Science Association.

PETERSON, BILL. 1985a. "NOW's Time of Choice," The Washington Post, July 4. Pp. A1, A2.

———. 1985b. "NOW Rivals Fight to a Bitter End," The Washington Post, July 21. P. A3.

PETERSON, MARK A. AND JACK L. WALKER. 1986. "Interest Group Responses to Partisan Change." In *Interest Group Politics*, ed. Allan J. Cigler and Burdett A. Loomis. 2nd Edition. Washington, DC: CQ Press.

PHILLIPS, KEVIN. 1978. "The Balkanization of America." *Harper's Magazine*, May. Pp. 37–47.

PIVEN, FRANCES F. AND RICHARD A. CLOWARD. 1977. *Poor People's Movements.* New York: Pantheon Books.

POLSBY, NELSON W. 1959. "The Sociology of Community Power." *Social Forces*, (March), p. 235.

———. 1960. "How to Study Community Power: The Pluralist Alternative." *Journal of Politics* 22:474–84.

———. 1964. *Congress and the Presidency.* Englewood Cliffs, NJ: Prentice Hall.

POLSBY NELSON W. 1980. "The News Media as an Alternative to Party in the Presidential Selection Process." In *Political Parties in the Eighties*, ed. Robert M. Goldwin. Washington, DC: American Enterprise Institute. Pp. 50–66.

———. 1983a. *Consequences of Party Reform.* New York: Oxford University Press.

———. 1983b. "The Reform of Presidential Selection and Democratic Theory." *P.S.* 16: 695–98.

POMPER, GERALD M. 1967. "If Elected, I Promise: American Party Platforms." *Midwest Journal of Political Science* 11:318–52.

POMPER, GERALD M. AND SUSAN S. LEDERMAN. 1980. *Elections in America.* 2nd Edition. New York: Longman.

POPULATION REFERENCE BUREAU. 1990. *America in the 21st Century: Governance and Politics.* Washington, DC: Population Reference Bureau.

PREWITT, KENNETH. 1966. *The Recruitment of Political Leaders.* Indianapolis: Bobbs-Merrill.

———. 1970. *The Recruitment of Political Leaders.* Indianapolis: Bobbs-Merrill.

PREWITT, KENNETH AND ALAN STONE. 1973. *The Ruling Elites.* New York: Harper & Row.

PRICE, DAVID E. 1984. *Bringing Back the Parties.* Washington, DC: Congressional Quarterly Press.

RADCLIFFE, DONNIE. 1990. "Political Hay and the Family Name." *Washington Post*, November 5. Pp. B1, B4.

RAE, DOUGLAS W. 1967. *The Political Consequences of Electoral Law.* New Haven: Yale University Press.

RANNEY, AUSTIN. 1951. "Toward a More Responsible Two-Party System: A Commentary." *American Political Science Review* 45:488–99.

———. 1975. *Curing the Mischiefs of Faction.* Berkeley, CA: University of California Press.

———. 1978. *The Federalization of Presidential Primaries.* Washington, DC: American Enterprise Institute.

———. 1983. *Channels of Power: The Impact of Television on American Politics.* New York: Basic Books.

RAPOPORT, RONALD B., ALAN I. ABRAMOWITZ, AND JOHN MCGLENNON (eds.). 1986. *The Life of the Parties: Activists in American Politics.* Lexington: University of Kentucky Press.

REICHLEY, JAMES. 1985. "The Rise of National Parties." In *The New Direction in American Politics*, ed. John E. Chubb and Paul E. Peterson. Washington, DC: Brookings. Pp. 175–200.

REISELBACH, LEROY N. 1977. *Congressional Reform in the Seventies.* Morristown, NJ: General Learning Press.

REISELBACH, LEROY N. 1986. *Congressional Reform.* Washington, DC: CQ Press.

ROHDE, DAVID W. 1991. *Parties and Leaders in the Postreform House*. Chicago: University of Chicago Press.

SABATO, LARRY. 1978. *Goodbye to Goodtime Charlie: The American Governor Transformed, 1950–1975*. Lexington, MA: Lexington Books.

SALISBURY, ROBERT M. 1969. "An Exchange Theory of Interest Groups." *Midwest Journal of Political Science* 13:1–32.

SALISBURY, ROBERT H., JOHN P. HEINZ, EDWARD O. LAUMANN, AND ROBERT L. NELSON. 1987. "Who Works with Whom?" *American Political Science Review* 81:1217–34.

SALMORE, STEVEN AND BARBARA SALMORE. 1985. *Candidates, Parties and Campaigns*. Washington, DC: CQ Press.

SARTORI, GIOVANNI. 1962. *Democratic Theory*. Detroit: Wayne State University Press.

SCHATTSCHNEIDER, E. E. 1935. *Politics, Pressures and the Tariff*. New York: Prentice-Hall.

———. 1942. *Party Government*. New York: Farrar and Rinehart.

———. 1960. *The Semisovereign People*. New York: Holt, Rinehart and Winston.

———. 1975. *The Semisovereign People*. [Reissue] Hinsdale, IL: The Dryden Press.

SCHLESINGER, JOSEPH A. 1966. *Ambition and Politics: Political Careers in the United States*. Chicago: Rand-McNally.

———. 1984. "On the Theory of Party Organization." *Journal of Politics* 46:369–400.

———. 1985. "The New American Party System." *The American Political Science Review* 79:1152–69.

SCHOLZMAN, KAY LEHMAN AND JOHN T. TIERNEY. 1986. *Organized Interests and American Democracy*. New York: Harper & Row.

SCHUMPETER, JOSEPH A. 1942. *Capitalism, Socialism and Democracy*. New York: Harper.

SEARS, DAVID O. AND JOHN B. MCCONAHAY. 1973. *The Politics of Violence*. Boston: Houghton-Mifflin.

SELZNICK, PHILLIP. 1952. *The Organizational Weapon*. New York: McGraw-Hill.

SHAFER, BYRON. 1983. *Quiet Revolution: The Struggle for the Democratic Party and the Shaping of Post-Reform Politics*. New York: Russell Sage.

SHEFTER, MARTIN. 1983. "Regional Receptivity to Reform: The Legacy of the Progressive Era." *Political Science Quarterly* 98:459–83.

SINCLAIR, BARBARA. 1992. "House Majority Party Leadership in an Era of Legislative Constraint." In *The Postreform Congress*, ed. Roger H. Davidson. New York: St. Martin's Press. Pp. 91–111.

SMELSER, NEIL J. 1963. *Theory of Collective Behavior*. New York: The Free Press of Glencoe.

SMITH, BRADLEY A. 1991. "Note: Judicial Protection of Ballot-Access Rights: Third Parties Need Not Apply." *Harvard Journal on Legislation* 28:167–217.

SMITH, CHUCK. 1991. "Drag Queens, Flaming Faggots and the Rise of Gay Consciousness in the U.S." A paper presented at the 1991 Annual Meeting of the Midwest Political Science Association. Chicago, Illinois, April 18–20.

SMITH, JAMES ALLEN. 1990. *The Idea Brokers: Think Tanks and the Rise of the New Policy Elite*. New York: Free Press.

SMITH, STEVEN S. 1992. "The Senate in the Postreform Era." In *The Postreform Congress*, ed. Roger H. Davidson. New York: St. Martin's Press. Pp. 169–92.

SOMIT, ALBERT AND JOSEPH TANNENHAUS. 1982. *The Development of American Political Science: From Burgess to Behavioralism*. New York: Irvington Publishers.

SONTHOFF, HERBERT. 1951. "Party Responsibility: A Critical Inquiry." *Western Political Quarterly* 4:454–68.

SORAUF, FRANK J. 1963. *Party and Representation*. New York: Atherton.

———. 1967. "Political Parties and Political Analysis." In *The American Party System*, ed. William Nisbet Chambers and Walter Dean Burnham. New York: Oxford University Press, Pp. 33–55.

SOULE, JOHN W. AND JAMES W. CLARKE. 1970. "Amateurs and Profesionals: A Study of Delegates to the 1968 Democratic National Convention." *American Political Science Review* 64:888–98.

STEDMAN, MURRAY S., JR. AND HERBERT SONTHOFF. 1951. "Party Responsibility—A Critical Inquiry." *Western Political Quarterly* 4:454–68.

TICHENOR, PHILLIP J., GEORGE DONOHUE, AND CLARICE N. OLIEN. 1984. "Communication and Community Conflict." In *Media Power in Politics*, ed. Doris A. Graber. Washington, DC: CQ Press.

TILLY, CHARLES. 1983. "Speaking Your Mind Without Elections, Surveys, or Social Movements." *Public Opinion Quarterly* 47:461–78.

TOLCHIN, SUSAN AND MARTIN TOLCHIN. 1974. *Clout: Womanpower and Politics*. New York: Coward, McCann and Geoghegan.

TRUMAN, DAVID. 1951. *Governmental Process: Political Interests and Public Opinion*. New York: Alfred Knopf.

———. 1971. *The Governmental Process*. 2nd Edition. New York: Alfred A. Knopf.

TURNER, RALPH H. AND LEWIS M. KILLIAN. 1972. *Collective Behavior*. 2nd Edition. Englewood Cliffs, NJ: Prentice Hall.

VERBA, SIDNEY AND NORMAN H. NIE. 1972. *Participation in America: Political Democracy and Social Equality*. New York: Harper and Row.

VOGEL, DAVID. 1980. "The Public Interest Movement and the American Reform Tradition." *Political Science Quarterly* 95:607–27.

VOSE, COLEMENT E. 1972. *Constitutional Change*. Lexington, MA: Lexington Books.

WALKER, JACK. L. 1966. "A Critique of the Elitist Theory of Democracy." *American Political Science Review* 60:285–95.

———. 1983. "The Origins and Maintenance of Interest Groups in America." *American Political Science Review* 77:390–406.

WARREN, CHRISTOPHER L., JOHN G. CORBETT, AND JOHN F. STACK, JR. 1990. "Hispanic Ascendency and Tripartite Politics in Miami." In *Racial Politics in American Cities*, eds. Rufus P. Browning, Dale Rogers Marshall, and David H. Tabb. New York: Longman. Pp. 155–78.

WATTENBERG, MARTIN P. 1986. *The Decline of American Political Parties, 1952–1984*. Cambridge, MA: Harvard University Press.

WEBER, MAX. 1947. *The Theory of Social and Economic Organization*, trans. A. Henderson and T. Parsons. Glencoe, IL: The Free Press.

WEISSBERG, ROBERT. 1976. *Public Opinion and Popular Government*. Englewood Cliffs, NJ: Prentice-Hall.

WHITE, JOHN KENNETH AND JEROME M. MILEUR. 1992. *Challenges to Party Government*. Carbondale, IL: Southern Illinois Press.

WHITE, THEODORE H. 1961. *The Making of the President, 1960*. New York: Atheneum.

WILDAVSKY, AARON B. 1964. *The Politics of the Budgetary Process*. Boston: Little, Brown.

WILKINSON, PAUL. 1971. *Social Movements*. New York: Praeger.

WILSON, JAMES Q. 1962. *The Amateur Democrat*. Chicago: University of Chicago Press.

WOODWARD, C. VANN. 1951. *Origins of the New South*. Austin: Louisiana State University Press and the Littlefield Fund for Southern History of the University of Texas.

ZELLER, BELLE. 1937. *Pressure Politics in New York*. New York: Prentice-Hall.

Index